Nirad Chaudhuri
As a Critic of Modern Culture

Basavaraj Naikar

ATLANTIC
PUBLISHERS & DISTRIBUTORS (P) LTD

Published by
ATLANTIC
PUBLISHERS & DISTRIBUTORS (P) LTD

7/22, Ansari Road, Darya Ganj, New Delhi-110002
Phones : +91-11-40775252, 23273880, 23275880, 23280451
Fax : +91-11-23285873
Web : www.atlanticbooks.com
E-mail : orders@atlanticbooks.com

Branch Office
5, Nallathambi Street, Wallajah Road, Chennai-600002
Phones : +91-44-64611085, 32413319
E-mail : chennai@atlanticbooks.com

Printed in India at Nice Printing Press, A-33/3A, Site-IV,
Industrial Area, Sahibabad, Ghaziabad, U.P.

Dedicated to

My father

Late Sri Shivashankarappa

Who instilled moral consciousness in me at an early age

Preface

I was fascinated by Nirad Chaudhuri's high intellectuality right from my student days. Later I had an opportunity of teaching his *The Continent of Circe* to the postgraduate students. Hence I had to make a close study of his other books also. As years went by, I began to study his inspiring and provocative works one by one and was deeply impressed by his vast scholarship and extraordinary clarity, a strong dose of satirical attack on the society, and absence of hypocrisy. In 1985 I put together some five essays of mine on Chaudhuri's works and published it as *Critical Articles on Nirad Chaudhuri* under the banner of Sivaranjani Publications, Dharwad (India). Many of my highly traditional teachers and classmates did not like Nirad Chaudhuri for his attack on the Indian character and satirical approach. But I continued to love and appreciate his frankness and realistic approach to life. On hearing about this publication, Dr. Alastair Niven of England ordered a copy for the library of the University of London.

After nearly twenty years I received a letter, quite unexpectedly, from one Mr. Ashok Patnaik from Delhi, who claimed to be a journalist and who happened to see a copy of my book on Chaudhuri borrowed by his friend from the library of the Sahitya Akademi of New Delhi. Mr. Patnaik had congratulated me for my close reading of and analytical approach to Nirad Chaudhuri's texts. I felt extremely happy to learn that some sensitive and perceptive soul had appreciated what little I had done in my field. Later, on my request he sent me some pages from journals containing valuable information about Chaudhuri's suffering in his office due to Jawaharlal Nehru's prejudice against him and some photographs of Nirad. After a couple of years I wrote twice or thrice to Mr. Ashok Patnaik but never received any reply from him. Alas, I did not know what had happened to him!

On another occasion I came to know that Dr. R.K. Kaul had published his impressive book on Nirad Chaudhuri from (Rawat Publications) Jaipur. Then I sent him a copy of my monograph on Chaudhuri. He replied immediately and appreciated my close reading of the texts and regretted his lack of patience to do the kind of work that I had done in my little monograph. He advised me to bring out a better produced edition of the same work, as I had it printed earlier on newsprint paper.

Once in the All India English Teachers Conference held at Visakhapatnam in 1989, Professor C.D. Narasimhaiah, as the President of the Conference, vehemently attacked V.S. Naipaul and Nirad Chaudhuri for their negative views about India. After half an hour or so, I gave him my monograph on Nirad Chaudhuri and expected him to be very angry with me. But on the contrary he was very graceful in his approach and told me that I had filled a lacuna as there were not many books on Chaudhuri.

In the next All India English Teachers' Conference held at the University of Madras in 1990, I gave a copy of my monograph on Chaudhuri to Dr. K.R. Srinivasa Iyengar, who received it gracefully and thanked me. Afterwards, he wrote to me appreciating my effort in understanding Chaudhuri and advised me to write on his later works also.

When I sent a copy of my monograph on Chaudhuri to Dr. Mohit K. Ray, Professor of English at the University of Burdwan, he read it thoroughly and congratulated me for the close reading of his works. He replied that he admired Nirad Chaudhuri's brilliance although he did not like Chaudhuri's prejudice against the Bengalis.

I must remember to thank my young friend and Commonwealth Fellow, Dr. Shankar Prasad Singha, now Professor of English and Dean, Faculty of Arts, at Vidyasagar University of Midnapore, who obliged me by patiently searching for the latest works of Chaudhuri edited by his son, Dhruva Chaudhuri in the markets of Kolkata and sent me the Xerox copies of these books which are not easily available elsewhere in India.

I have the satisfaction of covering all the major works of Chaudhuri at one place for the convenience of the future scholars. I request the readers to remember that this is not a Ph.D. thesis discussing Chaudhuri's ideas in a systematic and concordant manner, but a collection of my articles written over a period of three decades and recording my own individual response and appreciation for the brilliant author. I am aware of the fact that many scholars may not agree with my views, but I request them to account for why they may not agree with me so that further scholarship and healthy controversy may continue to provoke and inspire the scholars of next generation.

Basavaraj Naikar
bsnaikar@yahoo.com

Contents

Chapter 1

Introduction

Indian English Prose

Indian English Literature has a rich harvest of prose written by a wide range of professional scholars like historians, philosophers, jurists, biographers, autobiographers, religious thinkers, letter-writers, travelogue writers, essayists, educationists, sociologists, anthropologists, and journalists. All the Indian English prose may be described as the prose of thought. Great writers like Raja Rammohun Roy, Bala Gangadhar Tilak, Swami Vivekananda, Sri Aurobindo, Rabindranath Tagore, Mahatma Gandhi, Jawaharlal Nehru, B.R. Ambedkar, Radhakrishnan, Srinivasa Sastri, J. Krishnamurti, Frank Moraes, Khushwant Singh, and Kuldeep Nayar are the prolific prose writers of Indian English. Nirad Chaudhuri belongs to the galaxy of these prose writers.

He has enriched the realm of Indian English prose by writing two autobiographies, a biography, essays of cultural criticism, a history of Hinduism and discursive works. He is comparable to Carlyle, Aldous Huxley and Jonathan Swift in different aspects. His contribution to the prose style is remarkable as it is known for its clarity, pedantry, ironical and satirical tone, caustic humour, encyclopedic range and force of argumentation and persuasion. His prose is neither exhortative like that of Swami Vivekananda, nor romantic like that of Jawaharlal Nehru, nor incantatory like that of Radhakrishnan, but is realistic, analytical, satirical and scholarly at the same time. Although he worked as a military commentator and a journalist for some time, he cannot be equated with other journalists, who look at the contemporary life and write about the trivial details. But what contradistinguishes Chaudhuri is that his analysis of contemporary society and life is backed up by his vast and deep (historical) scholarship and a historical sense. Even when he seems to be commenting on micro-historical events, habits or aspects, he has a remarkable scholarship of relating them to those of macro-history. That is exactly why his argumentation acquires such force. One may not agree with him completely, but one cannot help admiring him for his hard won insights.

LIFE OF NIRAD CHAUDHURI

Nirad Chandra Chaudhuri was born on November 23, 1897 at Kishorgunj, in Mymensingh of British India and now called Bangladesh.

His parents were partly Deists, partly Hindu monotheists, and partly rationalists. His father was a lawyer by profession and had scholarly tastes. As was usual then he had a large family and Nirad had eight brothers and sisters.

He was educated in Kishorgunj and Kolkata (then known as Calcutta). He received his early education in an ordinary Municipal School, but was brilliant as a student. For his FA (school leaving) course he attended the Ripon College in Calcutta along with the famous Bengali writer Bibhuti Bhushan Bandyopadhyaya. Then he attended the prestigious Scottish Church College, Calcutta, where he studied history as his undergraduate major subject. He graduated with honours in history and topped the University of Calcutta merit list. At Scottish Church College, he attended the seminars of renowned historian Professor Kalidas Nag. After graduation, he enrolled for the M.A. level course at the University of Calcutta. However, he did not attend all of his final exams of the M.A. programme because of his nervous temperament and therefore did not earn his M.A. degree.

He began his career as a clerk in the Accounting Department of the Indian Army. At the same time he started contributing articles to popular magazines. His first article on Bharata Chandra (a famous Bangla poet of the 18th century) appeared in the most prestigious English magazine of the time, *Modern Review*. After some time, he left the job in the Accounting Department and started a new career as a journalist and editor.

During this period, he was a boarder in Mirzapur Street near College Square, Kolkata, living together with the writers Bibhuti Bhushan Bannerjee and Dakshinaranjan Mitra Majumdar. He was involved in the editing of the then well-known English and Bangla magazines, *Modern Review, Probasi* and *Sonibarer Chithi*. In addition, he also founded two short-lived but highly esteemed Bangla magazines, *Samasamayik* and *Notun Patrika*. He married a well-known writer, Amiya Dhar in 1932 and the couple had three sons (one of whom is Mr. Dhruva N. Chaudhuri, who has recently compiled and edited three volumes of his father's essays published in different magazines). But he does not reveal much about his wife, children and family in his writings.

In 1938, he obtained a job as secretary to Sarat Chandra Bose, a political leader from the freedom movement in India. As a result he was able to interact with the political leaders of India like Mahatma Gandhi, Jawaharlal Nehru and the more famous brother of Sarat Chandra Bose—Subhas Chandra Bose, the future Netaji. This familiarity with the workings of the inner circle of Indian politics led him to be skeptical about its eventual progress and he became progressively disillusioned about the ability of the Indian political leadership.

Apart from his career as a secretary, he continued to contribute articles in Bangla and English to newspapers and magazines. He was also appointed as a political commentator in the Kolkata branch of the All India Radio. In 1941, he started working for the Delhi branch of the All India Radio.

He was a prolific writer even in the very last years of his life, publishing his last work at the age of 99. His masterpiece, *The Autobiography of an Unknown Indian* published in 1951, put him on the short list of great Indian English writers. He courted controversy in the newly independent India due to his dedication of the book "To the memory of the British Empire in India/ Which conferred subject-hood upon us/ But withheld citizenship." The dedication, which was actually mock-imperial rhetoric, infuriated many Indians, particularly the political and bureaucratic establishment. "The wogs took the bait and having read only dedication sent up howls of protest," commented

Chaudhuri's friend, the editor, historian and novelist, Khushwant Singh. Consequently, Chaudhuri was hounded out of government service, deprived of his pension, blacklisted as a writer in India and forced to live a life of penury. Furthermore, he had to give up his job as a political commentator in All India Radio as the Government of India promulgated a law that prohibited employees from publishing memoirs. Chaudhuri commented later that he had been misunderstood, "The dedication was really a condemnation of the British rulers for not treating us as equals," he wrote in the *Granta* article. Typically, to demonstrate what exactly he had been trying to say, he drew on a parallel with ancient Rome. The book's dedication, he said, "was an imitation of what Cicero said about the conduct of Verres, a Roman proconsul of Sicily who oppressed Sicilian Roman citizens, who in their desperation cried out: *Civis romanus sum*."

For the next two decades—1921 to 1941—he stayed in Calcutta, where he had a chequered career. He never found a stable job and served at various places. But he practiced journalism both in Bangla and in English.

In 1955, the British Council and the BBC jointly made arrangements to take him to England for eight weeks on a travel grant. He was asked to contribute lectures to the BBC. He contributed eight lectures on British life. Later these lectures were collected in the *Passage to England* modified and edited. E.M. Forster reviewed it in *The Times Literary Supplement*. His *The Continent of Circe* (1965) earned him Duff Cooper Memorial Award, becoming the first and only Indian to be selected for the prize. In 1972, he was the subject of a Merchant Ivory documentary, *Adventures of a Brown Man in Search of Civilization*. In 1975, he was awarded the Sahitya Akademi Award for his *Scholar Extraordinary* (1974). He published a sequel to his autobiography entitled *Thy Hand, Great Anarch!* in 1988. In 1990, he was honoured with D.Litt. from the Oxford University of England in recognition of his contribution to literature. In 1992, he was honoured by Queen Elizabeth II of the United Kingdom with the title of Commander of Order of the British Empire (CDE). In 1997, at 100 years of age, he published his last book *Three Horsemen of the New Apocalypse*.

He was a productive and prolific writer till the end of his life. He published his last work at the age of 99. His wife Amiya Chaudhuri died at her 62nd year in 1994 in Oxford. Nirad never got over the feeling of the loss of his wife. He died in Oxford, England two months short of his 102nd birthday in 1999 (aged 101) at Lathbury Road, Oxfordshire (U.K.).

Nirad was physically insignificant in the sense that he was very thin and had already lost a few front teeth at the time of his marriage. He was dark in complexion and later suffered from the racial inferiority due to his dark complexion. He was known for his Western kind of especially Edwardian dress, which was rather incongruous. But he was known for his speed of walking that was common to the Europeans. Likewise he had certain angularities of personality and mental qualities like irritability, stubbornness and inflated ego.

***

As a Writer

He was known by his penname, Balahak Nandi (*Sonibarer Chithi*) and Outsider (Now). He was a Bengali-English writer and cultural commentator.

Although some chauvinistic Indian critics do not like Nirad Chaudhuri's anglophilia and comments on Indian character and culture and his self-opinionatedness, they cannot help admiring his originality, vast knowledge, encyclopedic scholarship, references and quotations from Sanskrit and many European languages and the force of his argument and extraordinary clarity of thinking. The following opinions of some Indian critics will amply testify to his brilliance and his so-called idiosyncrasies. For example, C. Paul Verghese says, "Chaudhuri is a product of the Indian renaissance, which began with the impact of the West on the Indian intellectual early in the nineteenth century and he belongs to a tradition of prose writing in English in India that can be traced back to Raja Rammohan Roy."[1] K. Raghavendra Rao says, "One may detest him, disagree with him at his pedantry and fume over his pretentiousness, but one simply cannot ignore him, for at his worst he is brilliant and original."[2] "His fierce frankness, original intelligence and brilliant expressive power make him a fascinating figure, a 'Grand Solitary,' a writer and a thinker and a universal Momus who stands apart from the muddy mainstream."[3] Tara Sinha says, "Like Shaw he compels our attention by saying the unusual and doing the unexpected. Like Orwell, he discusses the social and cultural problems involved in Imperialism, and throws light on its complex, confusing and ridiculous nature. Like Henry James, he reveals an intense love, and unusual understanding of the subtleties of European culture. Like Swift, he makes a vitriolic attack on the entire social fabric of a people, its men and its morals. And last, but not least, he is as skeptical and critical an intellect as that of Aldous Huxley that cannot accept any faith or belief merely by an appeal to feeling or tradition, instead, it demands its justification on the basis of logical arguments. His style too is ironical and as profusely satirical as Huxley when dealing with the apparent illogicalities of Indian customs, traditions and institutions."[4]

As a writer, Nirad Chaudhuri is highly original and brilliant and does not agree with the common views held by the masses of India. That is because of his wide reading in history and his ability to understand everything against the historical backdrop. In his interview with B. Parvathi, he has confessed: "Why am I alienated in India. Because I do not have one single idea that is common with the upper middle class. I can only talk with them, I am even of them. But not one single idea of theirs I share. I don't believe a single myth generated in India.... On the other hand, I am the greatest admirer of ancient Hindu civilization."[5]

Nirad Chaudhuri, according to K.R. Srinivasa Iyengar, "is the grand solitary among our writers."[6] "I had hardly met an Indian writer," said C.R. Mandy once, "with such coruscating intelligence; his brain dances like fireflies before the monsoon... I would always rate him—cerebrally and stylistically—in the top class of Indo-Anglian writers."[7]

Chaudhuri is known for his wide reading in history, culture and a variety of other branches of knowledge. That is why he had encyclopedic knowledge about many things. Khushwant Singh praises Nirad Chaudhuri whole-heartedly as follows:

"Chaudhuri writes the English language better than any Indian has done before and is much the most erudite writer in the country. His encyclopedic knowledge has made him somewhat of a legend; he is meticulously painstaking about what he writes and is particularly felicitous in expression. He is provocative and at times offensively anglophile at the expense of his countrymen."[8]

R.K. Dhawan quotes Khushwant Singh's opinion to show Niradbabu's encyclopedic knowledge. "Very often Khushwant Singh discussed serious matters with the scholarly genius. He found that Niradbabu was able to 'talk on any subject under the sun.' Singh had heard him 'discuss stars with astronomers'; recite lines from an obscure fifteenth century French poet to a professor of French literature."[9] It is because of his multi-faceted scholarship that Dr. R.K. Kaul compares him to an Elizabethan kind of scholar known for his comprehensive and not merely fragmentary knowledge. "Though he was born in the Victorian era, he wanted to be like a Renaissance scholar. His unacknowledged ambition is to attain the versatility of a Renaissance master. He appears like Bacon or Scaliger to have taken all knowledge as his province."[10]

It is to be noticed that such comprehensive scholars are very rare in modern India. R.K. Dhawan gives him the right compliments when he says, "A brilliant polymath with a phenomenal memory, he was distinguished as much for his robust style as for his provocative ideas. No wonder, he has been considered by some critics as India's greatest prose writer of the second half of the twentieth century."[11]

Mulk Raj Anand rightly says that "Odd genius Nirad C. Chaudhuri was obviously a rebellious child...."[12] Chaudhuri is also a great iconoclast and resembles Bertrand Russell in this respect. In his satirical attitude to India, he may be compared to Jonathan Swift in some respects.

A Critic of Culture

Nirad Chaudhuri happens to be one of the brilliant prose writers of India and the world. His prose may be described as the prose of thought. Though he started his career as a journalist, there is a lot of difference between other journalists and him. He does not write about life from the instant impressions (as other journalists may do) but from a serious and solid historical perspective. It is therefore quite proper to describe him as an angry old man and a critic of culture—both Indian and British (or European). For example, he has observed the details of Indian and British cultures and made his insightful and coruscating observations—like the family life, marriages, class-consciousness, caste conflicts, manners and etiquettes, architecture, empty religiosity, painting music, dances, drama, dress code, British character, Indian (Hindu) character, Hindu-Muslim conflicts, Hindu cowardice and Muslim militancy, Westernization of Indians, social behavior, snobbery, imitativeness, geographical contradictions of India and Indian behaviour, pride and inferiority complex going hand in hand, talkativeness, fanaticism, indulgence in violence in spite of talking about peace, the political life characterized by sheer opportunism, the arrogance of bureaucrats, especially IAS officers, the stagnancy of Indian universities, decadence, slackening of sexual morality, increase of violence and terrorism in the world, etc. Chaudhuri provokes and irritates the smug Indians, who may disagree with him, but cannot easily disprove him. Many Indian historians, sociologists, anthropologists and linguists and such other specialists have to analyze and evaluate his views from their professional perspectives. Mere literary critics are not able and qualified to answer his questions and disprove his theories and views. Since Nirad Chaudhuri is thought-provoking and meant for the serious reader, his views and opinions are taken seriously by the Western scholars, although Indian critics have taken the easier path of dismissing him as a pessimistic writer and classifying him with V.S. Naipaul as India-bashers. His courage of conviction, honesty and integrity of character cannot be questioned at all.

Works

Nirad Chaudhuri was a prolific writer, who wrote many scholarly works, in English as well as in Bangla, which cannot be ignored by any sensitive scholar. He wrote the following works in English. His English books may be listed as follows:

1. *The Autobiography of Unknown Indian,* New Delhi: Jaico Publishing Company, 1972.
2. *A Passage to England*, Delhi: Hind Pocket Books, 1974.
3. *The Continent of Circe*, Bombay: Jaico Publishing House, Fifth Impression, 1974.
4. *The Intellectual in India,* New Delhi: Associated Publishing House, 1967.
5. *To Live or Not to Live,* Delhi: Hind Pocket Books, 1970.
6. *The Scholar Extraordinary,* New Delhi: Orient Paperbacks, 1974.
7. *Culture in the Vanity Bag*, Bombay: Jaico Publishing House, 1976.
8. *Clive of India,* Bombay: Jaico Press Pvt Ltd., 1977.
9. *Hinduism: A Religion to Live By*, Oxford: Oxford University Press, 1979.
10. *Thy Hand, Great Anarch!*, London: Chatto & Windus, 1987.
11. *Three Horsemen of the Apocalypse*, Delhi: Oxford University Press, 1997.
12. *Why I Mourn for England*, Calcutta: Mitra & Ghosh Publishers, Pvt. Ltd., 1998.
13. *From the Archives of a Centenarian,* Calcutta: Mitra & Ghosh Publishers, Pvt. Ltd., 1997.
14. *The East is East and the West is West,* Calcutta: Mitra & Ghosh Publishers, Pvt. Ltd., 1996.

Chaudhuri wrote the following valuable books in Bangla also:

1. *Bangali Jibane Ramani (Role of Woman in Bengali Life)*
2. *Atmaghati Bangali (Suicidal Bengali)*
3. *Atmaghati Rabindranath (Suicidal Rabindranath)*
4. *Amar Debottar Sampatti (My Bequeathed Property)*

5. *Nirbachita Prabandha (Selected Essays)*
6. *Aji Hote Satabarsha Age (A Hundred Years Ago)*

Notes

1. C. Paul Verghese, *Nirad C. Chaudhuri*, New Delhi: Arnold Heinemann, 1973. p. 9.
2. K. Raghavendra Rao, "Indo-British Encounter," in *Critical Essays on Indian Writing in English*, ed. M.K. Naik *et al.*, Dharwad: Karnatak University, 1968, p. 345.
3. K.R. Srinivasa Iyengar, *Indian Writing in English,* Bombay: Asia Publishing House, 1973, p. 590.
4. Tara Sinha, *Nirad C. Chaudhuri*, Patna: Janaki Prakashan, 1981. p. 17.
5. B. Parvathi, "An Interview with Nirad C. Chaudhuri," in *Nirad C. Chaudhuri: The Scholar Extraordinary*, Ed. R.K. Dhawan, New Delhi: Prestige Books, 2000. p. 9.
6. K.R. Srinivasa Iyengar, *Indian Writing in English,* Bombay: Asia Publishing House, 1973. p. 590.
7. C.R. Mandy, quoted by Iyengar, K.R. Srinivasa, *Indian Writing in English,* Bombay: Asia Publishing House, 1973. p. 590.
8. *Ibid.*
9. Khushwant Singh, quoted by R.K. Dhawan. Ed. *Nirad Chaudhuri: The Scholar Extraordinary.* New Delhi: Prestige Books, 2000. p. 9.
10. R.K. Kaul, *Nirad C. Chaudhuri: The Renaissance Man*, Jaipur & New Delhi: Rawat Publications, 1998. pp. 69-70.
11. R.K. Dhawan, Ed. *Nirad Chaudhuri: The Scholar Extraordinary.* New Delhi: Prestige Books, 2000. p. 9.
12. Mulk Raj Anand, Quoted by R.K. Dhawan. Ed. *Nirad Chaudhuri: The Scholar Extraordinary.* New Delhi: Prestige Books, 2000. p. 9.

Chapter 2

Autobiography of an Unknown Indian as Descriptive Ethnology

That an Indian writer in English could be most successful in his first work is something unexpected in India. Though an unknown Indian, Nirad C. Chaudhuri became known to the world only through his maiden work which was, paradoxically enough, written not in the teenage but when he was at the threshold of his fiftieth year. The *Autobiography of an Unknown Indian* has earned for him an important place in the belle-letters of Indian English. Whereas it has earned the critical appreciation of the Western readers, not excluding the famous American psychologist like Erik Erikson, it has incurred the wrath of Indian readers consequent upon its unusual method of presentation. The autobiography of the author, no matter who he is, generally presents a picture of the growth of consciousness of the man including the inevitable crisis and conciliation of conscience. The autobiographer, therefore, tends to be subjective and the objective element comes only as subordinate or as a background. But Chaudhuri's method is different from the conventional one in that he gives us the picture of the objective world shaping the subjective element itself. He wants to show how the subjective element itself is decided, limited and conditioned by the objective world. The modern anthropology and psychology have already established the fact that man is nothing but a product of the hereditary and environmental forces. Nirad Chaudhuri deeply influenced by these sciences wants to interpret human life in the light of this scientific knowledge. That is the reason why his autobiography strikes the reader as something unusual because of his novel technique of writing. That accounts for his unwillingness to call his book by the blanket term called 'autobiography'. Showing the similarity and contrast between himself and the other great autobiographical writers like Askanov, Renan, Anatole France and Tagore, etc., Chaudhuri says that though he resembles them in his recapitulation of childhood memories, he sharply differs from them in shifting the stress from the individual to the environment. "Like these great writers," says Chaudhuri, "I too began to be reminiscent of my childhood when I had long passed my youth. But I am to like them, calling up its memories and recording them either as things interesting in themselves or as a foil to my later life. It is not the aim of this book to create that kind of romantic interest or contrast. There is no room in it, since it is more of an exercise in descriptive ethnology than autobiography, for presenting it as a submerged city of Ys or as the times when the intimations of immortality lay about us. If there is to be any vanished or vanishing Atlantis to speak of in this book, it should and would be all our life lived till yesterday. All that we have learnt, all that we have acquired, and all that we have prized is threatened with extinction. We do not know how the end will come, whether through a cataclysmic holocaust or slow, putrid decay. But regarding the eventual extinction there does not seem to be any uncertainty" (131).[1]

The high seriousness of Chaudhuri's approach to life enables him to recognize the complexity of life, the interdependence of character and environment, and the simultaneous existence of contrarieties in life. Man's life, according to him, is not a story of mere growth or mere decay but that of both. "For us," says he, "the irony of the situation lies in the fact that the very existence, which has created the values whose passing I regret but also created the agencies, which are destroying them. The catastrophe has unfolded inexorably from the environment I have described and the experiences I am going to relate. There is a unity, an unbroken chain of cause and effect, running through the whole process which if it is a fatalistic cast is fatalistic only in the sense that characters is fate. We began the journey towards where we have arrived from what we did and experienced in our earlier years, which is only another way of saying that in this autobiography I shall have no phase of pure growth to set against a phase of unrelieved decay. In our existence, growth and decay have been intermingled in an inseparable embrace. We have lived with mirth in funeral and with dirge in marriage. But the hour has come when life, if there has ever been any principle of life in us, must part company with its baleful mate and go its way. The marriage can no longer endure. Either we end it to be resorted to cleanness, or it ends itself in a witches' Sabbath" (131-32). Thus, Nirad Chaudhuri wants to picture the double-faced nature of life. Besides that his main aim is to highlight the environmental condition determining the character of the individual. In spite of the philosophical awareness of the paradoxes of life, Chaudhuri, as far as possible, wants to portray an objective picture of life around him. Since Chaudhuri is not a writer of a textbook on ethnology, his selection of material is decided by the writer's point of view. His scientific views may be borrowed from anthropology, ethnology and history, etc. But his distinctiveness and forte as autobiographer lie in his empirical confirmation of the scientific theories. This is evident in his words, "Since it has been laid down as the basic principle of this book that environment shall have precedence over its product, I shall begin by describing three places, which exerted the deepest influence on my boyhood and form, so to say, the buried foundations of my later life" (xiii). The *Autobiography of an Unknown Indian* not only offers the story of Chaudhuri's individual life but it also creates a vivid picture of Bengali culture with all its diverse strains. Hence, the justification of the author's designation of his work as 'descriptive ethnology'.

That man is the product of his environment has become a commonplace truth in social psychology. Man's behaviour is decided by the hereditary factors and environmental circumstances. That is the reason why man's thinking, feeling and action differ from nation to nation, race to race and time to time. Human culture is nothing but the manifestation of the highest form of his thoughts, feelings, customs, beliefs, entertainment, occupations and artistic impulses, etc. Thus, the term 'culture' includes everything that belongs to a particular race or community of human beings. Whereas the study of the culture of a major community or race is known as cultural anthropology, the study of the culture of a minor community has come to be known as ethnology. The relationship between man and his environment is so thick that they can hardly be separated from each other. Nirad Chaudhuri wants to delineate his own character in relation to the environment which includes Bengali culture, Muslim culture and British culture and so on. His interest is not in the isolated individual but in the relationship between cultures, which are brought together by historical forces and affect the individual life. Chaudhuri makes it clear. "The story I want to tell is the story of the struggle of a civilization with a hostile environment, in which the destiny of British rule in India became necessarily involved. My main intention is thus historical, and since I have written the account with the utmost honesty and accuracy of which I am capable, the intention in my mind has thus become mingled with the aspiration that the book may be regarded as a contribution to contemporary history" (ix).

A brief outline of culture may be helpful for the clear understanding of the problem. In spite of the innumerable definitions of culture, one of the best early definitions was offered by E.B. Tyler. According to whom, culture is "that complex whole which includes knowledge belief, art, morals, law, custom and any other capabilities and habits acquired by man as a member of society".[2] In other words, culture is the sum total of everything that is to be seen in life. It is the quintessence of all that a man thinks, feels, does and creates. To borrow that famous phrase from Matthew Arnold, culture consists of sweetness and light of a particular community of people. The study of minor cultures and 'contemporary primitives' has been growing very popular in the countries like America in the recent years.

The significance, the novelty, the charm and the limitation of a particular culture may be understood only when it is compared with other cultures. The distinction of a culture becomes clear only when it is contrasted with other cultures. But before a comparative study of cultures is attempted, it is mandatory on the part of anthropologists and anthropological writers to observe the cultural traits of a group minutely and enumerate them consciously and explicitly. The study of human cultures, regardless of their being large or small, is based upon the supposition that culture is meaningful and throws light upon the nature of human life. The ethnological study of a culture is interested not so much in recording the traits of a culture for themselves as in revealing the cultural universals through the cultural peculiarities. That accounts for the life-long devotion of the great anthropologists like Malinowski, Levi-Strauss, Ruth Benedict and Margaret Mead, etc., for the study of the 'contemporary primitives' like the Peublos and Mexicans, etc.

Nirad Chaudhuri is undoubtedly the first Indian writer to attempt the ethnologically oriented works. It is through this rare combination of literature and science that Chaudhuri has been able to give a clear and convincing picture of the Indian society in his works. That explains his popularity in the Western countries and unpopularity in his native country. His unpopularity in India is ascribable partly to his realistic way of writing and partly to the readers' ignorance, Puritanism and fanaticism. Once again it has to be clarified that what irritates the Indian reader is not so much the scientific data (however paltry it may be) that he provides as the dispassionate way in which he analyses and interprets the human problems.

The Bengali culture, if there is one such accepted by anthropologists, chosen by him for the ethnological description and analysis becomes interesting for only those who are aware of such an approach to culture. Freeing himself from the indifference resultant upon the unfamiliarity Chaudhuri adapts the travelogist's eye for minute details of life. A travelogist can easily do this because of his previous unfamiliarity with the people he meets. But for a native it is not so easy to do. If at all he wants to do so, he has to forget that he is an insider and adapt the psychology of an outsider as far as the minute observation of things is concerned. In my opinion, Chaudhuri has done this job successfully and superbly.

The Bengali culture, as depicted by Chaudhuri stands out as distinct from other cultures or groups of the Indian sub-continent. Though Indian culture is loosely referred to as a single entity, ethnologically speaking, it is a strange mixture of diverse ethnic groups. Though it is true that such ethnic distinctions are not studied as systematically in India as, for example, in America, the fact that the diverse ethnic groups remain different from one another may be felt by all those who employ an ethnologically oriented approach to the problem. In spite of being part of Hindu culture, the Bengalis have developed their own particular customs, habits, and beliefs, etc., which are geographically and historically conditioned. Whereas history may denote the essential oneness of culture, geography definitely shows the apparent diversity of culture. The so-called apparent diversity assumes great importance in ethnic studies because we have to study the invisible values only through the visible manifestation of them.

For the sake of clarity and convenience the ethnological idiom may be employed in the present analysis. The word 'culture' may be replaced by the word 'group'. According to Jerry Rose, "It is an ethnological truth that a group of people becomes conscious of itself only when it comes into contact with another group due to a variety of reasons like the political, the economic and the social, etc. Two or more than two groups begin to react, respond, rebel or reconcile only after coming into contact with one another. Again 'coming into contact' may be of two kinds: one mental; and two physical. The contact between two groups may result in four kinds of relationship. One, whenever two groups come into contact with each other the native group may be attracted towards the alien group and learn some of the customs and habits of the latter. This is known as acculturation of the native group. Two, the native group may be fascinated by the alien group to such an extent that it may set out to imitate the latter in toto thereby forgetting its own native tenets. This process is known as de-culturation of the native group. Three, the native group may try to preserve its distinction and identity consciously from the very beginning of its contact with the alien group. This process is said to be the enculturation of the native group. Four, the native group may first imitate the alien group and then after a few decades decide to go back to its original customs and habits. This process is said to be the re-culturation of the native group."[3]

The ethnic processes of acculturation, enculturation, deculturation and re-culturation are connected with historic forces and movements in Chaudhuri's autobiography. The *Autobiography of an Unknown Indian* offers a picture of not merely a bi-cultural confrontation but even a more complicated tri-cultural encounter. The Bengalis (Hindus), the Muslims and the British (Christians) are involved a triangular love-hate relationship in Chaudhuri's world. If, for the convenience of discussion, the three communities are accepted as three groups, Chaudhuri's delineation of the multi-cultural phenomenon becomes clearer to the reader. The Bengalis (Bengali Hindus) are the 'native group' whereas the Muslims and the British are the 'alien groups' with one difference, i.e. the Muslims are not as alien as the British in India. Naturally, when the three groups are brought together by historical forces, the problems, the advantages and disadvantages of diverse kinds are created in the social intercourse among them. Nirad Chaudhuri with his ethnologically oriented approach to life records many of the details of human life generally unnoticed by non-ethnological writers.

Nirad Chaudhuri himself is a product of the environment in that he is a Bengali whose life is strongly affected by his social intercourse with Muslims and the British which is again decided by the historical forces of the world. Thus, an obscure and hence 'unknown' Indian like Nirad Chaudhuri living in a corner of Bengal situated in a corner of a vast country, again situated in a corner of a sub-continent is the product of the hereditary and historical forces and geographical surroundings. Chaudhuri wants to reveal the environment in revealing the individual character. But one specialty of his is to be noted by the reader. Far from going from environment to the individual like a textbook writer, he follows the creative writer's method of going from the individual to the environment. Since the 'individual point of view' is kept up throughout the work, it cannot be mistaken for a tract. The complaint of some critics about Chaudhuri's lack of originality in borrowing his views from sociology and anthropology can easily be dismissed as unsympathetic unintelligent and uncritical accusation.

If ethnology means the study of 'culture' of any race or community however minor it may be, Chaudhuri is really interested in the ethnic description of 'Bengali' culture. He has tried to enumerate in his *Autobiography of an Unknown Indian* many of the details of culture elaborately defined by Herskowitz, who says, "A short and useful delineation of the concept is: culture is the man-made part of the environment. Implicit here is the recognition that man's life lived in a natural habitat and a social 'environment'. It also implies that culture is more than a biological phenomenon. Culture includes all the elements in man's mature endowment that he has acquired from his group by conscious learning or by a conditioning process—techniques of various kinds, social and other institutions, beliefs and patterned modes of conduct. Culture, in short, can be contrasted with the raw materials, outer and inner, from which it derives. Resources presented by the natural world are shaped to meet existing needs, while inborn traits are so molded as to derive out of inherent endowment the reflexes that are preponderant in the overt manifestations of behaviour."[4] Culture can thus be said to be the efflorescence of every kind of potentiality that man is endowed with.

Chaudhuri, with his ability for vivid description of the environment, creates the local colour in a very precise manner. He gives almost a photographic, precise and microscopic view of the picturesqueness of the geographical life around him. He creates the local atmosphere by enumerating all things and items that have captured his attention. The elephants disporting in the river, the monsoon-affected landscape, the frogs, the crows, the ants, the centipedes and the Night blooming Flower of sadness offer a picture of the Bengali atmosphere. He refers to the common animals of Bengal like snakes, cats, leopards and tigers.

The geographers and the anthropologists declare that the house patterns and structures are decided by the geographical conditions of the area. Our commonsense tells us that whereas the houses of the rainy belts have sloping roofs, those of the plains have flat ones. Even the material used for the construction is the one supplied by the immediate geographical resources like wood, stone, bamboo, etc. Chaudhuri gives a detailed picture of the Bengali houses, which had mud-floors. He describes his birthplace Kishorgunj as 'a country town' and differentiates it from the English country town that he has been able to guess from his reading. It was "only a normal specimen of its class. The village had the thatched cottages slowly giving place to the huts with corrugated iron roofs. These were flimsy huts and there was not much difference between the country and the town" (155). The architecture and the maintenance of houses reveal the aesthetic taste of the people of a particular culture. They throw light upon the history, the geography, the sociology and the economics of their life. According to Chaudhuri, the aristocratic mansions were quite commodious and were modelled upon the European styles and contained the most important thing, i.e. the drawing room. "The most ambitious piece in these houses was always the drawing room" (128). But the houses of the middle-class people differed from the aristocratic mansions and are referred to by Chaudhuri as 'human hives' consisting of three groups of members of the family. Sometimes the same room was used as kitchen, storeroom and lumber-room. Whereas the entrances of the aristocratic mansions were ugly, the entrances and the insides of the middle-class houses were tidy. The culture of a community can be understood by the pictures and photos with which they decorate their houses. The Bengalis, says Chaudhuri, were habituated to using the religious and mythological figures. "These were mostly coloured pictures of the gods and goddesses, very alluringly amatory, if of Krishna and Radha, and if of Kali very minatory and blood-curdling, in spite of her nudity" (391). Another photo inevitably to be seen in every house "would be the portrait of the departed father or mother" (391). These photos testify to the Bengalis' religious bent of mind and their reverence for the ancestors respectively.

Cultural anthropology studies even the physiognomy of the different races of world. Such a study is based upon the scientific theory that the physiognomy is suggestive of the historical, geographical, genetic and economic factors deciding the culture of a particular race. Even in the same race the physiognomic differences can be seen due to the geographical diversity. This is especially true of Indians or Hindus. The modern Hindus, whatever may be the extent of the hybridization between the Aryans and the Dravidian in the past, are not physiognomically identical all over the country. A Punjabi is definitely different from a Madrasi and a Kashmiri, from a Karnatakian. One can easily identify the locality of a person by studying his physical structure. Such a study assumes great importance in ethnology. Chaudhuri's photographically minute observation has captured these details. An average-Bengali, according to him, will be tall and fair. Though Chaudhuri has not cared to offer the details of the male physiognomy, he has not forgotten to study the female one. The Bengalis share with other Indians the mythological habit of comparing human beings with gods and goddesses to denote the height of beauty or virtue. Referring to the female beauty of Bengal Chaudhuri says, "The traditional type of female beauty accepted as the ideal all over rural Bengal, was derived from the iconography of Mahayana Buddhism and Puranic Hinduism. By this criterion, a Bengali beauty was likened to a goddess, which meant that she had an oval face, wide at the forehead and pointed at the chin, long and rather narrow eyes with a perceptible slant, thin but fully modelled lips and a complexion pronouncedly yellow with no tinge of rose, rather like beaten gold. Even now one can pick out Bengali girls who are exactly true to this type" (378). And Chaudhuri continues, "But the Calcutta type was different. It was rounder, fleshier and rosier" (378). The truth of these words can be understood only when Bengalis are compared and contrasted with other Indians. The Malayalis, for example, are dark with their receding foreheads and protruding chins and dark and thick lips. Whereas the Madrasis are dark, fat and have round faces, the Karnatakians are, by and large, brownish, lean, and lank and have relatively round faces.

Familial life is an important part of the wider, i.e. social life of a particular race or community. In fact, family is a mini society in itself. It contains all that is to be seen in the wider world of human beings. Chaudhuri, who has an ethnological awareness of this factor, has enumerated innumerable traits of the Bengali family life. The Bengali child seemed to be too serious to be playful. "The children of the wealthy in Calcutta appeared to be un-endowed even with boyish playfulness" (385). This is probably attributable to the puritanical attitude passed on from parents to children. Biologists can explain why of this phenomenon. It was customary for a Bengali young fellow to address his father by the honorific 'sir' and not by the simple father. The Bengali familial code of behaviour was obsessed with extreme Puritanism. "Nothing disappointed me," says Chaudhuri, "more in 1907 at the age of nine than not to have been permitted to go near a bride, in fact to have been turned out after having sneaked into the room in which she was, because her status in relation to mine was that of a daughter-in-law. I saw not only relatives but relatives two generations in advance of me" (51). Because of the ridiculous extremity of Puritanism, Nirad at the age of nine was not allowed to be near a bride. It would be a sin if he did so. The joint family system of India creates a good deal of confusion to the non-Indians. The diversity of familial relation in a family provides a good humour for the westerners. "At five years old" says Chaudhuri, "I was the uncle of half a dozen grown-ups and was addressed as such by them. At twelve I became the granduncle of a baby which was not so very far removed from me by filiation" (51). The diversity of blood relation created confusion in the minds of the children, who consequently addressed their fathers as 'brothers' and brothers as 'uncles', etc. The parental selfishness is another striking feature of the Bengali family. Whereas the women and children had to live on "the plainest and the most monotonous diet, while the elders savoured no end of delicacies, in their private room" (71). Another allied feature of the Bengali family is the absence of natural affection between parents and children. Both the parties appeared to be too serious to be amicable. Since Nirad belonged to the poor family his parents did not care to preserve his horoscope. Therefore, his date of birth was not recorded at all. The aristocratic families were very particular about the preservation of horoscopes of the children. The young women of Bengal had to go through the pre-delivery purificatory rites. This ceremony had "to be performed only after the first monthly course of a girl after her marriage and was euphemistically called the 'second marriage'" (138). "When the same woman was carrying, she had to go through another ceremony called the 'wish-ceremony' in which the women relatives would invite the young expectant girl for partaking of milk pudding and receipt of presents. The Bengali father resembles the Ben Jonsonian type called the 'tyrannical father' whose son was only too eager to get rid of him. The plight of the Bengali son-in-law is pitiable indeed." As to the young husband, he bad no *locus standi* whatever except to sneak at night to his wife. Nobody took any account of him for any other purpose" (141). The jealousy and hatred between the mother-in-law and the daughter-in-law are very common in Indian society. In Bengali families also the archetypal figures of mother-in-law and daughter-in-law are the dominant ones who have to 'reign' or to 'serve' by turns. The private life of the parents was taboo in Bengal as also in other parts of India. "...it is implicit in the very nature of the relationship that large parts of a father's or a mother's character, personality and life should remain as unknown country to the son and that he should shrink from probing into these parts with a reluctance which is somewhat akin to a healthy man's revulsion from incest" (143).

Every race has its own distinct social code of behaviour, comprising social habits, manners, etiquettes, etc. The social behaviour changes from race to race and nation to nation. This is borne out by the researches in the field of sociology and social anthropology. The Bengalis also had their own indigenous social life, which was distinct in spite of being similar to that of other Indians. The following are few strands of the Bengali society enumerated by Chaudhuri. In spite of the ubiquitous class-consciousness, the Bengali society was also ridden with communal consciousness. Bengalis shared this malady with other Hindus. Staunch believers in *varnsrama* as the Bengalis were, their social behaviour was deeply affected by this kind of obsession. "...at Banagram," says Chaudhuri, "we felt conscious of our birth. This is not wholly correct. For the blue blood of a Chaudhuri of Banagram was acknowledged as readily at Kishorgunj and elsewhere as it was taken for granted at Banagram" (55). In spite of the inter-caste marriages in Bengal, the communal consciousness was very powerful in that society.

Pitying was one of the widely practised and appreciated social manners in Bengal. Sometimes pitying resulted in self-pity. One day his friend's wife said to Mrs. Chaudhuri that the latter did not look well. Chaudhuri offers a socio-psychological explanation of the custom, "...to say 'You do not look well' is the most polite, friendly and considerate remark that we can make on meeting an acquaintance, and one which will be appreciated by the person addressed with almost a lump in his throat. On the other hand, to ignore his self-pity and assume that he is hale and hearty is to rival the heartless gruffness of the Gryphon in his attitude towards the Mock Turtle" (137). According to the social etiquette, the male friends were received only at the front rooms, whereas the female friends were allowed into kitchens and bedrooms. Chaudhuri's keen and subtle observation makes him remark that there was no real social life in Bengal. What the Bengalis had was gregariousness rather than sociability. It is very difficult to be clearer than Chaudhuri who says, "There was very little social life among the Bengalis of Calcutta, as understood even in the more frivolous connotation of the words 'society' and 'monde'. No afternoon parties, no dinners, no at home and of course, no dances, enlivened their existence. The heaviest social exertion in this sense that they could or would undergo was to pay formal calls. But there was something to offset this deficiency. What the native of the city lacked in sociability he made up in gregariousness. "Another feature connected with the Bengalis' gregariousness is garrulity. They were very facile in their speech and gossiped endlessly. In this respect, they resemble the South Karnatakians. Garrulity in itself is not bad. But what is annoying about it is that in Bengal it is not accompanied by real heartiness. Garrulity is unfortunately clubbed with heartlessness, which is the result of herd instinct and callous urbanization. Opportunism and power-mongering are the worst traits of Bengali society. Chaudhuri's bitterness about them is vented out in his words. "The Bengalis, more especially the Bengalis of Calcutta were and still remain some of the finest *virtuosi* of facetiousness. There is hardly any activity into which they do not practise, and hardly any activity into which it has not wormed its way. Municipalities, universities, learned societies, political parties, public offices, business concerns, clubs and even schools are rent by cliques, and are always splitting up like protozoa. To be in the ruling clique means a temporary monopoly of all the advantages that these institutions offer and to be outside it is to be deprived for the time being of all opportunities, rights, facilities, in a corresponding measure" (401).

Religion, whether organized or unorganized happens to be one of the important features of every culture. Though Bengalis had their regular religion called Hinduism, they differed from other Hindus in the practice of that religion because of their ethnic peculiarities. Religion, in fact, had permeated every field of their life. It is extremely difficult to distinguish between their religious activities and secular ones. They followed their religion at all the levels, i.e. the ritualistic, the philosophical and the metaphysical. Especially, the ritualistic aspect of their religion was very popular with the Bengali masses. The photos and pictures in their houses were mostly of gods and goddesses. Besides, they worshipped different deities at different temples and conducted fairs and festivals at different times of the year. Goddess Kali is a favourite deity of Bengal. The car festival of Goddess Kali, the ear festival and the swing festival of Krishna, Ganesh and Kartik Festival and Durga Puja were the most famous religious festivals of Bengal. Especially during Durga Puja and Kali festival, goat and buffalo sacrifices were conducted with great enthusiasm. The religious superstitions also played a great role in their life. One of the superstitions believed in by them was to avoid the calamity foretold in the horoscope by giving the widest possible publicly to it. The Bengalis, like the other Hindus, were very proud to know that their religion was so great that it lent itself to the scientific analysis by the Western scholars. Their religious fanaticism went to the extent of 'grotesqueness' and 'scientific claptrap'. "Every Hindu custom and every Hindu taboo", says Chaudhuri, "found its justification in some theory of electricity and magnetism. At times even the science of bacteriology, new at the time, was invoked. It was proclaimed that if a Hindu kept a pigtail it was only as an electro-magnetic will; if he bathed in the Ganges it was because an unspecified European (for preference German) scientist had demonstrated that Ganges water killed bacteria instantaneously; if he fasted at full and new moon it was only to counteract the gravitational forces of the sun and the moon; the Diwali illumination was supposed to be a collective lighting of fire for burning up poisonous gases given off by the earth on that evening" (208).

This indeed is the line of demarcation between the religious activities and the artistic ones in Bengal. Sometimes they overlap each other. The artistic sensibility always had a religious tinge about it. They had a special liking for the religious and mythological themes. That is the reason why Michael Madhusudhan Dutt composed his famous epic called *Meghanada Vadha Kavya*. Similarly, R.C. Dutt wrote the English versions of the *Ramayana* and the *Mahabharata*. Among the mythological plays staged in Bengal, *Vilwamangal* was the most famous one as *Sri Krisna Parijata* is very famous in Karnataka. Even their music was devotional in nature and was used for the glorification of gods and goddesses. Besides these, there were also folk music, folk-drama and folk rituals.

The life of the Bengalis was deeply affected by their philosophy. Their staunch belief in the theory of *karma* sometimes degenerated into fatalism. Sometimes their religion appeared to be a mere farce because of the essential spirit missing in it. These were some of the striking features of Bengali culture enumerated by Chaudhuri. But Bengalis were not the only group in Bengal. Historical forces had made it inevitable for them to rub along with the other alien cultural groups like the Muslim and the British. The Bengalis had naturally to undergo the stages of acculturation, de-culturation and re-culturation in their relation with the alien groups. They did not mind living with Muslim friends in their neighbourhood. Chaudhuri used to address a Muslim friend of his as Dulaha Sahib Diwan Alimdad Khan. The Bengalis even went to the extent of preaching communal harmony. But they would hate the Muslims only because of the historical memories. They had a historical hatred for the Muslims who, according to them, had harassed the Hindus in the past. Besides, the Bengalis did not like certain habits of the Muslim race. They, for example, did not like the Muslim habit of circumcision. Thus, the Bengalis had an ambivalent attitude towards the Muslims.

The same kind of ambivalent attitude towards the British was cherished. When the British had come into Bengal, the Bengalis had a liking and fascination for the alien culture, which appeared to be new and strange. Hence, their imitation of certain traits of British culture. As part of the process of acculturation the Bengalis assimilated the following features of the English culture in their own life. Many of the Bengalis were attracted by the British things like the steel trunks. They came to like the British games like cricket and billiards. The battleship was one of the symbols of British culture. It had become a fashion for the Bengalis to hang on their walls the photos of British leaders and officers, who were connected with the Indian administration. The acculturation of Bengali culture was not confined to the assimilation of the physical items alone in their culture but it extended to the psychological level also. Language, which is the instrument of communication, plays a great role in the interaction of two cultures. As a result of the colonial relationship with the British, the Bengalis had inevitably been drawn towards the English language. Since language is inextricable from culture, the Bengalis, in the process of learning the English language, came to acquire the British way of thinking also. As the British culture had the attraction of novelty for the Bengalis, the latter had begun to admire everything that was British. They, not excluding Chaudhuri, were attracted by the glamour of the magnificent names of British personalities of diverse professions. These personalities included great litterateurs like Shakespeare, Milton, and Burke, etc.; regal dignitaries like Queen Victoria, Napoleon and Prince Albert, etc.; great politicians like Gladstone, Lord Roseberry. Such British men and women became the symbols of highest achievements of British culture for Bengalis. In spite of the difficulty of mastering the English syntax and phonetics, they struggled hard to study that alien language colonially handed to them. The most attractive item of British culture that captured their attention was the British, i.e. fair complexion. The British garments like suits, hats and skirts appeared strange and bewitching for them. The English woman was a matter of great curiosity for the Bengali youngsters. Her physical appearance was something very strange and unusual for them. "Mrs. Nathan...gave us our first sight of an English woman after we had become old enough to remember things. The resultant excitement was indescribable. We hardly talked about anything else but her blue eyes, her flaxen hair, her dress and her hat for the whole day" (121).

After the attraction of the British novelty had worn out, the acculturation of Bengali culture began to decrease gradually. Slowly, the Bengalis started analyzing the motives and intentions of the British rulers in India. As they steadily realized the underlying imperialistic policy of the rulers, they began to shed their illusions. Their realization that the relation between themselves and the British was not one between friend and friend but one between master and servant, i.e. between the colonizer and the colonized, their attitude towards the alien culture underwent a change. Their love for them started reverting to hatred. Hence, there was a change from understanding to misinterpretation, blackmailing and malicious mythifying. Their judgments of the British life came to be coloured by their own raw emotion of hatred for them. This kind of reversal of attitude is a very common stage in the relation between the colonizer and the colonized all over the world. The native culture, far from appreciating the traits of the alien culture, begins to misinterpret them and tries to keep itself from contamination by the alien culture.

The Bengalis' depreciation of the British culture may be seen in the following details. The first thing that struck the Bengalis as peculiarly English is the fair complexion. Because of the robust physiognomy and corpuscle, the British looked like 'monkeys' or '*bunder log*' to them. "This monkey analogy had deeper and less innocent antecedents." The jealousy expresses itself in the invention of ridiculously ingenious and malicious myths. One of the old teachers of Chaudhuri goes to the extent of declaring in the classroom that "the English race was of a she-monkey by a demon born" (119). Chaudhuri is very clear in his analysis of the Indian attitude towards the British. "The prevalent attitude towards Englishmen of our people was one of irrational and unconquerable hatred" (119). The 'tiger' analogy also is very common. The jealousy, the hatred, the helplessness and the wishful thinking of the Bengalis have been beautifully captured by Chaudhuri in the following similes, "A meeting of Englishmen is represented as a meeting of tigers, but the indigenes are shown as monkeys discreetly hiding themselves among the branches and leaves. When the tigers disperse, the monkeys swagger out and declare that they will now hold their meeting and abuse the tigers and they do so. Finally, the meeting is closed with the observation that after getting such a fusillade of bad language all the tigers must be dead in their lairs" (119). The Bengalis' jealousy of the British complexion expressed itself in the construction of a malicious myth according to which the British children are black but later on they are fried in wine and consequently become white ones. Another way of satisfying the Bengali ego was to compare the fair-coloured race to the leprous. The malicious comparison was most enjoyed by the patriotic fanatics: "One knee of Mother India is adorned by Tilak, the other by Das, but the white are spread all over her body as a disfiguring skin-disease" (125). Similarly, the Bengalis' purity-mania made them wrongly believe that there was not a single chaste woman in the entire British country. Sometimes the Bengali misinterpretation of the British culture was the result not so much of malice as of ignorance. When the picture of Mr. Churchill was shown to a nephew of Chaudhuri, the latter designated the former as a 'band-master'. Chaudhuri's analysis of the Bengali psychology in relation to the British is as true as objective. Referring to the Bengali, he says, "His deep-seated xenophobia is roused. He is intolerably humiliated and in his unforgiving envy and hatred he seeks to obliterate the foreigner's superiority by casting on it the shame of the most loathsome disease, which can afflict a man. The demented creature tries to console himself with the illusion that if in this world there is a foreigner fairer than he, it is only because the foreigner is a leper" (130).

When the native culture realizes that it should not imitate the traits of the alien culture any longer and that the alien culture is not *really* interested in the welfare of the native culture, it either begins to cleanse itself of the contamination by the alien culture or to maintain its own purity by acquiring a new consciousness of the greatness of its own culture and tradition. This is known as 'revival of culture' or 'renaissance'. The Bengalis did not go to the extent of unlearning and dispossessing whatever they had learnt and acquired from the British culture. But they became aware of their own indigenous and distinct culture. The process of cultural reawakening was expedited by the social reformers like Raja Ram Mohun Roy and proselytizers like Swami Vivekananda. Especially, Swami Vivekananda did a lot of missionary work for whipping up the latent patriotism and self-respect in Hindus of those days. This kind of propagandistic exhortation was complemented by the artistic activities of Rabindranath Tagore and the philosophical writings of Sri Aurobindo. A greater fillip to this revivalism was provided by the political awakening throughout the country led by Mahatma Gandhi and other leaders in India and by Subhas Chandra Bose outside the country. As a result of all these happenings the Bengalis like other Indians began to hanker for political independence. Hence, the permeation of political consciousness in many a field of their life. They made literature a mean of patriotic propaganda and wrote patriotic songs and novels. Bankim Chandra Chatterji was the greatest Bengali novelist who wrote with the keenest possible contemporary consciousness. They employed even music to sing the patriotic songs. Inspired by the European Orientalists they began to study the Indian religious scriptures like the *Vedas*, *Upanishads* and others with a new zeal, confidence and consciousness.

Thus, The *Autobiography of an Unknown Indian* offers us not only the life-sketch of an individual but an ethnological picture of a culture. Since ethnology is said to be the autobiography of a race or a culture, Chaudhuri's work provides a description of a culture seen through the individual's point of view, the author is perfectly justified in designating his work more as an experiment in descriptive ethnology than as an autobiography. Obviously, Chaudhuri has extended the frontiers of the Indian English autobiographical writing by showing the influence of environment on the individual. His autobiography is comparable to Nehru's in the sense that the latter also reveals Nehru's personality in relation to his political involvement with India.

Notes

1. Nirad C. Chaudhuri, *The Autobiography of an Unknown Indian.* New Delhi: Jaico Publishing Company, 1972. p. 131. (All the subsequent references are to this edition.)
2. Quoted by Melville J. Herskowitz in *Cultural Anthropology.* New Delhi: Oxford and IBH Publishing Co. 1969. p. 305.
3. Jerry D. Rose, *Peoples: The Ethnic Dimensions in Human Relations.* Chicago: Rand McNally College Publishing Company, 1976. pp. 41-51.
4. Melville J. Herskowitz, *Cultural Anthropology.* pp. 305-06.

Chapter 3

A Passage to England[1]: A Travelogue

Travelogue as an art-form is conspicuous by its absence in the realm of Indian-English letters. The lack of this art-form in Indian English literature is probably the result of negligence and lack of recognition that is due to this form. One of the implicit reasons for the negligence of this literary form seems to be rooted in the Indian view of life which is conditioned by the Indian, i.e. Hindu philosophy, which enjoins upon the believer the inward or spiritual journey and indirectly prevents him from travelling in the external world. In other words, the Hindu philosophy holds the view that the best knowledge that is possible for man is the self-knowledge, which can be had wherever one is born or exigently made to stay. Unlike the medieval European, the traditional Indian does not believe in the knowledge that can be acquired through journey or travel. The medieval Europeans believed that travel is part of education. It is on account of this basic cultural difference between the East and the West that the travelogue as a literary form is discouraged or encouraged according to the philosophical attitude of a particular nation. The journey or travel in its secular aspect is quite absent in traditional Indian culture, although it comes as part of the religious activities. The journey or pilgrimage to the holy shrines and places has an explicit religious intention behind it. Moreover, the journey or pilgrimage comes only at the last stage of a Hindu's life and gives him a sense of fulfillment and completeness. This journey is generally not encouraged as a secular programme of the acquisition of knowledge in traditional India. One might even risk an opinion that the travelogue which is the result of the travel that is not encouraged in Indian English literature mainly because of the hangover of the traditionalism of Indian philosophy or religion. It may be a matter of surprise to note that even the best educated but traditional Hindus, sometimes, do not want to cross the black waters in spite of being offered prestigious scholarships from Western countries simply because their tradition interprets such a travel as a sin or sacrilege. That explains the strong influence of superstition upon the traditional Hindu and accounts for the lack of sufficient growth of the literature of travel in Indian English letters.

Nirad C. Chaudhuri is an exception to this phenomenon partly because he is not a traditional Hindu and partly because he is a man of remarkable originality and courage. *A Passage to England* is an important landmark in the form of travelogue and as such invites comparison with other famous works of travellers of the world like Fahien and Huen Tsang, etc. But what is more noteworthy about *A Passage to England* is that it has certain other qualities in it, which are not normally found in other travelogues of the world like, for example, critical analysis and scientific description in addition to poetic and philosophical observation. The characteristic features of Chaudhuri's remarkable travelogue may be analyzed at some length in the following paragraphs.

A Passage to England is, of course, the result of Chaudhuri's trip to England during his fifty-seventh year at the invitation of the British Broadcasting Corporation. The trip obviously is of very short duration of five weeks in the spring of 1955. The first thing that strikes the attention of the reader is the brevity of the journey, which therefore automatically sharpens the traveller's sensibility and intensifies his experience with the strange atmosphere. Unlike the famous travellers like Fahien and Huen Tsang, who spent months and years together in the foreign countries, Chaudhuri is compelled by the exigencies of modern life to avail himself of only thirty-five days for his foreign trip. It is this brevity of trip that causes an extraordinary alertness in Chaudhuri and enables him to absorb the maximum possible experience of the strange country, customs, manners and government and so on. It is this great intensity of experience caused at least partially by the brevity of his trip that he describes when he says, "In that short space of time I saw more paintings, statues and works of art in general, more plays, fine buildings, gardens and beautiful landscapes, heard more poetry and music, ate and drank better, and altogether had a more exciting and interesting time than in all the rest of my life" (9). Mere intensity of experience is not the sole feature of this travelogue. It is ideally matched by the wide range of variety, which smacks of the encyclopaedic. A man of variegated interests as Chaudhuri is, his sensibility can absorb anything and everything that is presented before him. The bewildering variety of themes (in comparison with the relative brevity of his trip) in *A Passage to England* is the product as much of richness of the objective world as of that of the subjective capacity of the author. Chaudhuri's mind can, in this sense, be compared to a colour-camera as contrasted with an ordinary black-and-white camera, which is able to capture the variegated colourfulness of the world only because of the presence of the ingredients of colour in its film.

One of the most striking features of *A Passage to England* as also of other travelogues is the immediacy of experience, which is intensified by the novelty and the contrast that it provides to the traveller's native experience. This is matched by Chaudhuri's sensibility, which is sharpened by his encyclopaedic reading of a wide range of subjects from art to ammunition and from poetry to politics, etc. It is because of this rare combination of a rich sensibility encountered with a rich atmosphere that Chaudhuri is able to produce a work of art of substantial worth. The first impression of Chaudhuri when he lands in England is that of the British weather which provides a sharp contrast to the Indian weather in which he is brought up. Chaudhuri is so sensitive that he notices it at the earliest possible opportunity. The strange combination of light and temperature creates an illusion of unrealistic strangeness and oddity for Chaudhuri. The geography of England obviously makes a very deep impression upon him. He therefore says, "Everything in England presents itself to our eyes in a manner different from visual phenomena on the plains of India. We get a curious sense of the reality of the third dimension which is perhaps most easily illustrated with reference to trees" (26). Similarly when Chaudhuri walks to the

Hyde Park he notices a place near Albion Gate and notices its strangeness again. He says, "But the whole scene affected me in a very queer way and trying to account for this sensation of strangeness and even oddity. I found that to my eyes the houses were rising more steeply and perpendicularly from the pavement, forming a skyline and altogether standing more four-square than anything in the way of houses I had seen doing in my own country, even in a big modern city like Calcutta" (27). He further continues to say that "The impression of solidity was so strong that if I had had a hammer in my hand I should have walked along unconsciously tapping the houses with it, and in a mood of impatience, which endless rows of brick and stone often generate" (27). All this strangeness of atmosphere is not only noticed by Chaudhuri's keen sense of observation but is even rightly designated by his knowledge which is informed by the encyclopaedic reading of art and architecture and so on. That explains why he describes the impression of depth and solidity of the British weather in terms of art-criticism, when he refers to the "three dimensionality of the western buildings" (27). The thick fog and cloudiness of the British weather gives depth to the human perception of them and makes the buildings appear more solid and sturdy and concrete than they really are. This phenomenon is rightly described by Chaudhuri as cubist. *A Passage to England* therefore attains the height of a standard travelogue as it combines the author's unusually sharp sensibility, sense of minute observation and encyclopaedic reading and shows his ability to relate all of them relevantly to the external world into which he is thrown. Like other writers of travelogues, he describes the scenery very minutely but unlike them, he goes a step ahead in critically evaluating them also.

Once the unusualness of the British weather is noticed by Chaudhuri at the very outset, he goes on observing the different aspects of English life like geography, people, art, architecture, economics, politics, religion and love, etc. in coarse of his tour. That explains the comprehensive range of his vision and the sharpness of his sensibility. He, for example, notices the striking features of the geography the British country. His remark about the density of English weather has already been discussed. Next, he observes the close connection between man and Nature and the intimacy between village and town. He also notices that the greenery of Britain is not one of trees or shrubs but that of the grass. He is obviously fascinated by the British greenery of grass. He finds that there is more peace in the English woods than in the Indian ones. His keen observation of the salient features of London is very significant. He designates London as an archetypal city, which is in his opinion, conscious of its appearance like a man. This city is big and complex and historical and modern at same time. It contains mist, domes and cupolas and closely connected with the industrial order and is known for immensity, gravitation and mass. He also points out the unpredictability of the British weather.

Chaudhuri observes the economic aspect also of the British life. He finds that the British markets contain a bewildering variety and abundance of goods from the highest to the lowest quality and importance. Similarly, he notices the great variety of food also. A man of keen observation as he is, he cannot be blind to the snobbery of the Bond Street in London.

Chaudhuri's observation is equally keen in the field of British politics also. He rightly remarks that an average British man is a John Bull at heart, with his double face of conservatism and radicalism. Chaudhuri cannot help appreciating the concept and practice of the Welfare State in Britain. Likewise he also comes to admire the advanced agriculture and animal husbandry encouraged so much by the British Government. He is really impressed by the unassuming nature of Churchill. The architectural pieces of England have a special fascination for Chaudhuri who is quite well versed in this field. He is careful enough to notice the incongruity of the fusion of different architectural styles like the Roman and the Mediterranean, etc. He points out how the Roman basilica and the Italian palazzo had been transformed by the British into the Gothic cathedral and the country-house respectively.

Similarly, Chaudhuri absorbs the cultural life of Britain expressed in terms of various arts like antiquities, painting, music and drama. He, for example, visits the Fitzwilliam Museum among others, sees a variety of paintings including *The Nativity of Francesco*, hears a number of musical compositions including *Messiah* and sees the famous incunabula. Besides he witnesses a number of plays of Shakespeare enacted on the British stage and appreciates the excellent spectacle and beautiful language of the same. But he does not forget to mention the unfortunate commercialization of Shakespeare in Stratford-upon-Avon. He also admires the excellent enactment of Racine's plays like *Athalie*. He even visits a Savage Club in Bristol. Thus, Chaudhuri acquaints himself with the panorama of British culture.

As for religion, Chaudhuri visits many churches and notices the fact that religion and economics are separated in England unlike in India. He also observes that in England the upper-classes are more religious than the common people are. He even sees the religious significance in the secular activities of British life. Coronation, according to him, is a secular ritual and games and sports are a ritualization of physical exercise.

The British love, of course, does not escape Chaudhuri's attention. His observation shows that love was going on everywhere and at all times in England. Love was of self-abandoned kind. He remarks that lovemaking is as much social as biological in the West. He further remarks that whereas the idealization of sex-relation is the work of man in Europe, it is the work of woman in India.

All these physical details testify to the fact that *A Passage to England*, like many other travelogues in many other languages, is an important work in that it has captured the picture of the contemporary England which no doubt assumes an inevitable historical significance and enables the non-British reader to visualize the image of the country which he has not visited. Chaudhuri has obviously absorbed all the major features of British life through his photographic and panoramic observation. But Chaudhuri will not be Chaudhuri if he were to remain content with this much only. His greatness lies in the fact that in spite of his meticulous record of the fleeting life of Britain, he attempts to offer a picture of the timeless England through the description of the relatively permanent features of the British national character. In this regard, he grows from the level of a mere journalist to the height of a philosopher. One of the significant features of Chaudhuri's personality as also of his writing is that he never imitates others or their views however fascinating or repulsive they may be. He is always willing to respond to a situation or phenomenon in a fresh and first-hand fashion. That is the reason why he is only too willing to revise his opinions he had borrowed from books about the English people and their culture when he is made to encounter the same empirically. He has neither the cowardice nor the hypocrisy nor the snobbery of aligning his first-hand experience with the preconceived notions acquired through the reading of English literature and writing. A romantic realist as he is, he does not mind seeing the harsh reality in the face and tries even to see the beauty in it. One of the most important instances of this habit of Chaudhuri may be seen with regard to the British complexion. He, like all Indians, had developed a notion about the British people from reading their literature that they are very handsome and pretty and even ethereal and very impressive, etc. But his face-to-face encounter with them shows him the falsity of his preconceived notions. He finds that there is nothing special about the appearance of Englishmen, and that they are not remarkable in any way but look like clerks and workmen. "Judged by their clothes they could have been anything from clerks to high officials in India, but I assumed that they were English workmen" (79). Nor is Chaudhuri impressed by their complexion. Like an art-critic analyzing the chiaroscuro of a painting, Chaudhuri attributes the unimpressiveness of the English complexion, which is nothing but a combination of white and pink colours and which therefore upsets the balance between light and shade on the face and appears like one block of light, which is not a mark of beauty. "The pink Western faces send out, at least to our eyes almost equal light from all points and surfaces, and thus the features tend to be flattened out" (85). Similarly, he is disillusioned about the English ladies also. He feels that the British chambermaids are better than the men-sahibs are. That is why he is impelled to ask, "But where are your beautiful women, whom old painters painted and the poets raved about? Where are they to be seen?" (83). He is frank enough to point out that the English women are plain and dowdy in spite of their furry and other elegance. He is rather disappointed by the dull and flattened out effect of their white faces into which lipstick and rouge merge. These observations by Chaudhuri illustrate his ability, sincerity, courage and willingness to revise the *a priori* knowledge in the light of the *a posteriori* one, which contradistinguishes his travelogue from a textbook of anthropology of the British people.

After recording his impressions about the external appearance of the English people, Chaudhuri goes on to comment upon the general features of the English character, which naturally contradistinguish them from the natives of other countries. In fact, they even provide a sharp contrast to the Indian character of which Chaudhuri is only too keenly aware. Some of the major features of the English national character may be expatiated here. Lack of inhibition in the matters of sex or love is one of the most striking features of English life. The main reason why Chaudhuri notices this aspect so unfailingly is the fact that he comes from a puritanically inhibited country, India. He therefore clarifies it when he says, "This statement would appear to be very odd unless it is remembered that I am a Hindu and that in our society it is very difficult to observe the workings of love in human beings and to watch love-making at first hand is virtually impossible" (123). Since Chaudhuri comes from such an inhibitive background, he is instantly made to observe the phenomenon that is contrary to that of his own country. He finds that love manifests itself in an uninhibited fashion in England. There is no restriction of either time or place or rules or principles. Mr. Chaudhuri records it without any fear of seeming indecent. "I also saw that love-making was an easily observable activity. In fact, it was going on everywhere and at all times. I have seen young people falling on one another, crying, and kissing on a studded pedestrian crossing in a wide Paris thoroughfare, thundering with motor traffic...I saw the same spectacle in England, even in the Cambridge Backs, almost under the shadow of King's College Chapel. The exhibition is more self-abandoned by the standards of each nation: it makes Englishmen forget their dignity and Frenchmen their intelligence" (125). Love-making thus happens to be a socially approved public activity in England and testifies to their free behaviour.

Silence is another important feature of the English character. Mr. Chaudhuri observes this phenomenon quite keenly and says that the English young man acquires the 'negative attitude' quite early in life when he is advised constantly by his elders about the 'don'ts in life'. Chaudhuri naturally provides a contrast by referring to the Indian young man who pretends to obey his elders in their presence and follows the exactly opposite way in their absence. In England even the most rebellious youth cultivates this restraint. It is probably because of these injunctions—social, moral and so on—that the Englishman follows a restrained life later in his life. Their social life is marked by silence as they usually keep their work and social life separate. Chaudhuri, who comes from a garrulous country, is puzzled by the un-exhibitive nature of the English people. He says, "Another habit of theirs perplexes us and at times causes social awkwardness. They do not disclose their position in the world. I have met distinguished people, but unless I knew who they were I should never have been able to guess that they had achieved anything at all. If they are thinkers they do not hold forth, if they are statesmen they do not disclose programmes for reforming the world, a man who is not well up in a subject might not be able to discover that an Englishman is an expert on it. This makes it difficult for us to decide how much civility to mete out to them" (98). The importance of this feature of English character can be understood only if it is contrasted with the Indian habit of declaring one's position, degrees, achievements, views, feelings, prejudices, etc. as openly as possible with an element of pride concealed or otherwise.

The silence of English character is connected with another habit, i.e. of understatement which is typical of their life and occupies an important position in their grammar also. Chaudhuri quotes a few events to demonstrate their habit of understatement. Once he meets an English intellectual at his home and on seeing the books on the shelves compliments him by saying, "How beautifully they are bound" (98). The Englishman seems to be rather embarrassed and only says "They were presented to me by the Swedish Academy" (98) in an apologetic tone. An Indian in his position would have given the whole history of the book and book-writing in an elated fashion. On another occasion, Chaudhuri is taken by an Englishman to a lake and is shown a 'mallard' a 'gorse' and a 'braken' without explaining their meaning at all. On yet another occasion, Chaudhuri is shown the tapestry after Rubens in the hall of King's College and the Gate of Honour at Caius by two different Englishmen who never explain the meaning of the same to him. "The fact is that when an Englishman is friendly he imputes himself and considers all explanations as rudeness" (103).

Absorption in small things, love of concrete things and sensitiveness to the inherent aspects of stone and metal, etc. form part of the microscopic imagination of the English people. Chaudhuri is rather puzzled by this aspect of their behaviour. But nonetheless his anthropological imagination enables him to explain it in terms of the influence of the weather on the human behaviour. The unpredictable weather of England which restricts the Englishman's sight of the horizon and enervates his abstract imagination, enables him to accept the surprises and develop a concrete imagination, Chaudhuri explains it quite lucidly, "Now to come to the main point. I think the weather has very largely entered into the formation of the Englishman's mind, and the training of his sensibilities. It has made him responsive to changes in the environment, capable of meeting surprises of all kinds, both pleasant and unpleasant, and of taking contretemps with good humour; above all, it has made him observant of and susceptible to concrete details" (109). Chaudhuri explains further, "I was very much intrigued by his absorption in small things. A book, a knocker, a hinge, a paw foot to a chair, not to speak of a whole piece of furniture or a wrought iron gate, seemed to have an irresistible fascination for him" (109). The English exhibit the same tendency, i.e. microscopic observation with regard to the objects like wood, stone, metal or glass. They seem to prefer the naturalness of things to their improvement by man. "The same characteristic is illustrated by the extra-ordinary sensitiveness that the English people show to the inherent attributes of wood, stone, metal or glass. They seem to be drawn by them as cats are by the texture of velvet and satin. We in the tropics would never have dreamt of leaving the beams exposed in a stately room like the Solar at Penshurt Place, or of putting a bronze bushel measurer in it even though if might have been cast from the guns of the Spanish Armada" (110). The microscopic attitude of the British finds expression in their architecture also. It may be easily guessed that the geocentric imagination conditioned by the English weather is at work in almost all the fields of their life. Chaudhuri says, "The interiors of the English houses, especially the great ones, also give evidence of the love of concrete details. They are in a way possible only in that climate and weather. They were made by and meant for a people who had to spend long evenings indoors, sometimes day after day when the mind would be benumbed by its own emptiness unless it could crawl from one object to another along a continuous chain of interest—furniture, China, glass, plate, pictures, ornaments, fireplaces and other fixtures" (110). The English weather thus plays an important role in shaping the behaviour of the Englishmen. "There can be no doubt that the English weather has fostered a pronounced degree of sensitiveness to nuances and made both men and things more mellow" (111). All these details testify to the concrete and microscopic imagination of the English people, which forms part of their national character.

Spending is a positive urge in an Englishman, which is contrary to the Indian habit of hoarding. The Englishman wants to enjoy life by spending money without any hesitation because, as Chaudhuri points out, "England appeared to be a country of easy money, in the moralist's sense of the term" (116). Since England is a country of well-established economic order, which is supported by the moral order, commercial honesty and unsuspiciousness, the Englishman enjoys a sense of economic security denied to an Indian. Mr. Chaudhuri offers a few examples to illustrate this phenomenon. When he offers his cheque in one of the English banks, the clerk gives him the amount without even verifying the signature and balance. Similarly, a friend of Chaudhuri from B.B.C. gives him a large sum as an advance and asks him to write some talks for the B.B.C. in course of time. What is to be noted here is the fact that a public body like the B.B.C. trusts even a stranger like Mr. Chaudhuri with this money without having any guarantee about the fulfillment of the contract. These instances are enough evidence of the basic moral integrity, which helps the Englishman maintain the economic order without the least contamination. This phenomenon appears to be rather strange to Mr. Chaudhuri, who comes from a country where money-making is an open conspiracy" (115), and economics and commerce are conditioned by downright immorality and corruption.

Colour prejudice is another attitude ingrained in the British character. The English child, who is relatively more free than the adult Englishman from social decency, expresses the colour prejudice with more abandon than the adult does. It is interesting to know this from Chaudhuri's own words, "As I was coming out of Canterbury Cathedral I observed a little English boy of about six sitting on the grass and looking at me with an intense gaze, like a lion cub watching a distant zebra. When I came near him he began to rise slowly on his knees, and while still half kneeling raised his arm, pointed a finger at me and cried out in his sharp treble, "You're from Africa" (133). This example holds a mirror to the deep-seated colour prejudice of the English race, although it is not exhibited everywhere and at everyplace because of diplomatic nature of the human relations between people of two different countries.

Social life in England is always compartmentalized and has to be conducted only through proper channel. Mr. Nirad Chaudhuri remarks that "...English social life is still English social life, and trying to enter it is like entering a club. Physical nearness means very little there. In my London hotel, which was not large, I did not notice anyone making friends with the other inmates. An African, obviously a highly educated man, always took his meals alone, and even I did not go up and talk to him, falling in, I suppose, with the spirit of the society" (136). Unlike the Indians, who make friends within no time over the dining table or across the corridor, the Englishmen do not indulge in conversation simply because of physical nearness. In other words, the English social life is characterized by commonness of interests, equality of status and unwillingness to communicate.

The Englishmen attach a great significance to the physical exercise again, understandably, to keep themselves physically fit and to shake the numbness of limbs caused by the cold weather. The physical exercise is of course English parallel to the Indian yoga. They make a religion of the physical labour. Mr. Chaudhuri, therefore, comments that "There is something monastic in the English attitude to physical labour" (141). "When we Hindus thought of physical exertion as a means of spiritual catharsis, we indulged in yoga. Of course, in England, too, physical exercise has been ritualized in the form of games and sports, and perhaps most so in the centres of intellectual training" (142). It is the regular indulgence in physical labour that keeps the Englishmen so healthy and cheerful. This makes them extraverts and provides a contrast to the Indians who are, by and large, introverts and melancholic. It might therefore be said without any hesitation that extraversion is part of their national character.

The intellectual life of the Englishman is marked by unpretentiousness in contrast to the tall claims of the Indian intellectual. Mr. Chaudhuri says, "There is the same unpretentiousness in intellectual life so far as it forms part of general culture" (179). He supports this observation with an illustration of a blind professor of England who writes to Mr. Chaudhuri about his *Autobiography of an Unknown Indian* and expresses his frank views without any literary pose or diplomacy. "Time after time I wanted to rush off to you and say, 'I thoroughly agree with you' or 'I don't believe that'. Indeed, at one time, I thought of making notes in order that in writing to you I could mention all the points that occurred to me, but the only way is really more discussion, preferably at the Savile Club, over a bottle of the best" (179). The unpretentiousness of the Englishman as experienced by Mr. Chaudhuri could be understood only if one has any knowledge of the conceited behaviour of an Indian by contrast.

Politically, the Englishmen seem to live in the present life only and have very little thought of the future. Mr. Chaudhuri, who asks the question about the national destiny of England repeatedly, at last gets an answer from a British lady, who explains the loss of the English political ambition as follows: "You see, Mr. Chaudhuri, we have had very bad times and we have come through, though we hardly knew how to. We have also recovered more rapidly than we could have believed to be possible. I think that is why we are enjoying the present for a little while. I am sure we are not really thoughtless about the future" (214). The generality of the English seem to have lost their political zest and ambition and provide a good contrast to the Indians, who want to involve themselves with political life actively either pragmatically or ideologically, because in India the political order is the highest one and influences all other orders of life.

The English political life is marked by a dualism. This dual aspect of English political character is, according to Mr. Chaudhuri, represented by John Bull who "like Janus, always had two faces, the conservative and the radical" (137). Although conservatism and radicalism are antithetical to each other, they are professed together by the Englishman and add irony to his character. This quality is found not merely in political leaders, but in the working class also. It is expressed not only in public international life but in private local life also. That is why Mr. Chaudhuri is compelled to say that John Bull is 'Made in England,' "But if I think that John Bull lives on, I have something else too in mind, and John Bull, not in his relation with foreign people and the outside world, but John at home in his private capacity, as an English personality" (138). The Englishman cannot overcome this dualism and cannot be a typical Englishman without it.

The love of historical civilization seems to be another dominant feature of their culture and hence character. That explains their great historical sense and their unwillingness to think of the future. Unlike the Indians, who have a great history with little historical consciousness, the English have a great history with a greater historical consciousness.

Mr. Chaudhuri therefore remarks that the enormous man-power that they have created with their science has made them recoil from it and immerse themselves in historic civilization by way of self-protection. "This leaves to all western nations, and Englishmen among them, only one thing to fall back on: their historic civilization. As soon as I came to this point in my thinking I also understood the real meaning of all that I had seen in England and France—the crowds at the classical plays, concerts, picture galleries and exhibitions, the interest in architecture, gardens and landscape, loyalty to religion and the *mos majorum*; the care bestowed on the interpretation and preservation of the national heritage; the love and piety inspired by all the aspects of the historic civilization including even its politics" (230). Sometimes this preoccupation with historic civilization turns out to be only a snobbish interest in old things. Their culture-vulturism is expressed in their turning away from the modern civilization created by material progress towards the historic and cultural life. "It is the number and prosperity of the shops dealing in antiques, old books, and second-hand furniture. Judged by this test the people of England are very civilized, for I found these shops everywhere stocking goods for all purses" (173). Historic consciousness to be expressed now in genuine and now in snobbish manner happens to be an important ingredient of the English character.

Insularity can be said to be one of the moat typical qualities of the Englishman. The English insularity is easily comparable to the brahmanical parochialism in India. That probably gives them a psychological consolation in the modern world, which is slowly moving towards the international way of life. Mr. Chaudhuri says "...the Englishman is at his strongest and best when he is most insular. Even in olden days this made a thoroughgoing English imperialist a man of two minds, and the Little Englander trait has won" (204). Whereas the Englishman's relation with the outside world is marked by insularity, his relation with his own, i.e. English world is characterized by grumbling. Mr. Chaudhuri rightly opines that the national habit of grumbling is alternated with irritation, moodiness and gaiety.

Mr. Chaudhuri thus offers a descriptive picture of English environment and an analytical picture of the English character. In spite of the extreme shortness of his travel in England, he has shown the maximum possible operation of his perceptive and cognitive faculties supported, of course, by his encyclopaedic reading, historical imagination and remarkable memory, the result of which is the creation of the picture not only of the temporally and spatially bound variegated England but also of the timeless, spaceless and universal England. Chaudhuri the painter and Chaudhuri the philosopher have joined hands to produce *A Passage to England* which is undoubtedly an excellent product of his panoramic as well as microscopic observation of life and which as such, attains the stature of not merely the best travelogue but of the best treatise on English character.

Note

1. Nirad C. Chaudhuri, *A Passage to England*. Bombay: Jaico Publishing House, 1974. (All the references to the text are from this edition.)

Chapter 4

Essay as Satire: *The Continent of Circe*

There is no sensible Indian who is not delighted, shocked and irritated by the powerful satire *The Continent of Circe* written by one of the most solid thinkers that India has ever produced. Nirad Chaudhuri is like a highly sensitive musical instrument, which cannot help responding to the slightest possible whiffs of air. This does not mean that he inherited it from his birth. Though the essence of it is a matter of inheritance, the rich variety and subtlety of it is the result of conscious effort on the part of Chaudhuri to absorb the phenomenal world through his senses and train himself to look at the world with extreme alertness. That is why Chaudhuri is said to be more Indian than the Indians are and more British than the British themselves as far as his sensitivity is concerned. K.R. Srinivasa Iyengar is right in describing him, "He is the gadfly, he is the Geiger counter looking for hidden obliquities of self-deception, he is the fiercely honest and unsparing critic of men and morals and manners in contemporary India. The truth about him seems to be that he is at once more Indian than most Indians and more English than many Englishmen."[1]

A highly sensitive soul as he is, Chaudhuri could not help looking around him and recording his responses to them. *The Continent of Circe* is the product of very keen observation, contemplation and analysis of the nature and problems of the vast subcontinent called India consisting of a variety of countries in it. It can easily be considered as a powerful satire because of the presence of the many strains of satirical writing in it. Satire may express itself in a diversity of literary forms like poetry, prose, fiction and drama, etc. Similarly, satire may be expressed in a variety of techniques also like the allegorical, the symbolic, and the realistic, etc. Satires may be written in different styles also. There may be descriptive satires or analytical satires, or descriptive-analytical satires. Similarly, there can be crude satires and sophisticated satires also. There can be satires proper and satirical works. Chaudhuri's *The Continent of Circe* may be designated as a descriptive-analytical satirical work. Chaudhuri does not want to call it a satire because his intention is to try to 'understand' the bewildering continent called India. That is the reason way he defines his work as an essay. "This book", says Chaudhuri, "is an essay in the primary meaning of the word, a trial in exposition which cannot but be sketchy and tentative."[2] The confession here only testifies to Chaudhuri's tongue-in-cheek humility and therefore should not be taken on its face value. The form of the 'essay' should not be taken to mean the essay of Bacon or of Montaigne or of Emerson. The essay that Chaudhuri writes is not of the length of two pages to twenty-five pages but runs into three hundred and seventy-six pages of close print. Naturally, Chaudhuri's 'essay' resembles Hobbes' *Essay on the Human Understanding* in its length. He justifiably calls it an essay on the peoples of India. Chaudhuri is right in designating his work as an essay because his main intention is to endeavour to understand the mysterious and puzzling country of which he himself is a native. To live in a country is not to understand it. Even when one wants to understand one's country, there is no guarantee that one understands it properly if at all one can do so. This is especially true in the case of India, which is known for its contradictions, riddles, and peculiarities. India defies understanding. In this context trying to understand it becomes one of the greatest challenges of life for an Indian. Chaudhuri deserves congratulations on his bold venture of trying to understand his country. He is, therefore, perfectly right in calling his work 'an essay'. It easily fits in the definition of the essay. "In general, it is a composition, usually in prose...on a restricted topic."[3]

Though the 'essay' that he has written is half-descriptive and half-analytical in its style, the metaphorical title of the work offers us the picture of its satirical nature. It easily reminds us of the other famous satires of the world like *The Gulliver's*

Travels, The Animal Farm, The Battle of Books, Erehwon, etc. *The Continent of Circe*, obviously, reveals the fact that the vast continent of India is identified with the demoness, Circe. Nobody can fail to understand its satirical undertones. But the main difference between *The Continent of Circe* and other satires like *The Gulliver's Travels* is also to be noted. Whereas Jonathan Swift follows the method of allegorizing the characters, situations and places, Chaudhuri follows that of realistic description, and analysis. In other words, *The Gulliver's Travels* is a purely satirical allegory, but *The Continent of Circe* is a satirical and discursive essay containing occasional metaphorical references. Nonetheless *The Continent of Circe* may be studied as a satire as it contains a great deal of satirical attitude and stuff in it.

All over the world satires are written only when and because the authors are disappointed with the prevalent conditions of life, be they social, economic, political or religious, etc. But those who are happy with the conditions of life will prefer to write patriotic and even chauvinistic stuff and never think of venturing into the challenging, though negative, form of satirical writing. "...it criticizes, unmasks, subverts the world we know. Satire attacks because man is, or least some men are, engaged in a ceaseless battle against evil or dullness or (Frye) against some 'form of romanticism or the imposing of over-simplified ideals on experience'. Man may not win, but he must go on fighting; in the fight is life. Thus from mockery to despair—and by the very battle proving hope—directly or indirectly satire wages war against Chaos, the mighty Anarch."[4]

Having accepted *The Continent of Circe* as a satire, one has to examine as to what kind of a method the author employs in satirizing the people of his choice. Broadly speaking, there are two methods of satirical writing. One way is to satirize the life of a people by transferring them to an imaginary world so that the satirist may escape the danger of being harassed, or punished or imprisoned or even killed by the people he has criticized. The method of creating an imaginary world is decided by a variety of factors like the temperament of the writer, the nature of the society that he lives in and the demand of the burning problems of his country, etc. The second way to satirize the people is to lay bare all the weaknesses and dark spots of a people in a direct fashion, i.e. not by creating an imaginary world but by being historical, scientific and realistic. This method also is decided by the temperament of the author and the nature of the people chosen for satirization. Of the two methods Chaudhuri, undoubtedly follows the second one. The reason for this is obviously and mainly ascribable to Chaudhuri's bent of mind. In other words, a man of sterling quality as he is, Chaudhuri cannot help having solid scholarship of almost encyclopedic range. Again, as Chaudhuri is a student of history and anthropology he could not help using them in his own keen observation and contemplation of life around him. As a result of the rare and strange combination of these elements in his personality Chaudhuri could, without doubt, acquire a highly sharpened sensibility, which has become an object of envy and admiration in Indian literary circles.

Satire is invariably occasioned by the author's disappointment with the prevalent conditions of life. It does not however mean that a satirist is always a pessimist. On the contrary, the satirist is always an optimist at heart and his so-called pessimism is only the apparent product of the failure of society to live up to its ideals. Even though the satirist finds fault with the society and seems angry at it, his implicit intention is to point to the ideal society or Utopia that he is so much secretly in love with. This principle is especially applicable to Chaudhuri because of the frequent accusation of him as a pessimist and a cynic by the Indian critics. But to dismiss one as a pessimist or cynic is not to understand one. The aim of criticism is not to dismiss the author with half a dozen catchy words and phrases but to analyze and understand the subtle and sophisticated pattern of meaning supported by the underlying motives and intentions. The business of criticism that is responsible is to help the reader to enter into the spirit of the author's work of art and not to turn away from it. This is no less applicable to satire than to other forms of literature. An attempt, therefore, has been made in the present article to understand through analysis Chaudhuri's satire *The Continent of Circe*.

Chaudhuri subtitles his work as 'an essay on the Peoples of India'. This is quite in keeping with the anthropological view of India not as a country consisting of a people but as a subcontinent with a multitude of peoples or ethnic diversity. Obviously, Chaudhuri's aim is to try to understand the varied society of India. In his attempt to describe through analysis the conditions of Indian life he cannot help making incisive remarks on Indian life and character which contribute to the satirical atmosphere of the work. His views may be examined in the following paragraphs.

Chaudhuri begins his book with a note about the justifiable curiosity of the foreigners to know the Indian culture and character. That explains the perpetual flow of foreign tourists, journalists, travellers, diplomats, novelists and photographers into the Indian continent. But Chaudhuri points out the unfortunate failure of all these foreign enthusiasts to understand the puzzles and riddles of the Indian life in spite of their remarkable sense of observation and sympathy. Chaudhuri points out the epistemological difficulty in understanding the great country. He even suggests an epistemology for all those who want to understand India. The epistemology suggested by Chaudhuri is more relevant to the foreign admirers of India than to the Indians themselves. For, it is the foreigner and not the Indian who wants to know India. Chaudhuri borrows an example from *The Arabian Nights*, in order to illustrate his epistemology. Just as the Prince Diamond had to carry with him the magic weapons offered by the king's daughter with the help of which he could survive the terrible blasts of Flying Simurg's bum and finally reach the city of Wakak, the foreigner should, Chaudhuri suggests, arm himself with various weapons in order to overcome the difficulties in 'knowing' the bewildering country. But once the basic hindrances are overcome, the foreigner is sure to have a vision of the panorama of the Indian landscape. "I think," says Chaudhuri, "the genie, who guard the secrets of our country, life, and civilization put us to the same test before they will allow us to see real India. But when they do carry us up what a vision it is!" (25). Those, who want to understand India should overcome their intolerance of filth, squeamishness, contradictions and riddles of the country before they can, ever have an overall view of the Indian life. Many a time, the knowledge seeker will be stuck up at the very beginning stage of his quest and there is no guarantee that he will have a comprehensive if not a complete or final view of the huge country. The epistemology suggested by Chaudhuri is really very difficult to practise for a variety of reasons.

Chaudhuri himself has arrived at the already suggested epistemology after undergoing a number of such difficulties. He is in fact said to be in a fix because he has to act as an inside-outsider in the sense that by virtue of his birth he is an insider and has the first-hand experience of the conditions of life in his country and by virtue of his so-called, 'Anglomania' or the consciously acquired English sensibility he is an outsider who wants to look at the country from a pragmatic and rational point of view, which is ill-suited to a country which can, at best, lend itself either to sub-rational or supra-rational interpretation. Nonetheless Chaudhuri ventures into the challenging, though exhausting odyssey of trying to know the heart of India. He is sufficiently well armed to carry on the task. In the process of this adventure Chaudhuri cannot help formulating his own opinions into principles which correspond to those of social psychology and anthropology. The intention in this article is to concentrate on the satirical aspect of *The Continent of Circe* and examine Chaudhuri's observations and opinions about the Indian life and character. An original and a clear thinker as he is, Chaudhuri offers a very clear-cut analysis of the Indian society, which may be examined in some detail here.

After a great deal of patient and careful observation of the life in his country Chaudhuri arrives at certain conclusions about the national culture and character. At the very outset, he clarifies the confusion between the words like 'Hindu' and 'Indian'. He is right in pointing out how the adjective 'Indian' is merely political in its connotation and is inadequate to convey the other implications. He, therefore, rightly prefers the adjective 'Hindu', which conveys the cultural traits of the dominant community of India. Consequently, Chaudhuri's observation of Indian life becomes synonymous with that of the Hindus' life.

Having established the basic hypothesis of his book, Chaudhuri goes on examining the society and its dominant traits. The first feature that strikes his attention is the Hindu duality, which is irreparable. Says he, "...the duality of the Hindu existence is like the cat-and-dog life of maladjusted married couple, who can neither separate nor live together" (1). In as much as Chaudhuri is himself a Hindu he is also a victim of this duality. The Hindu has been making the duality more and more pronounced with the march of years. He is very sour about the ever-widening gap between the Hindu ideals and the Hindu practice and the consequent compromise and hypocrisy that have become the dominant strains of the Hindu's personality and hence culture.

Chaudhuri satirizes the Indian society by showing the contrast between the cherished ideals of Hinduism and the actual day-to-day practice of the Hindus. In a country where the ideals of Hinduism are expounded so prominently in the *Vedas*, the *Upanishads* and the *Bhagavad Gita*. The people are naturally expected to live up to them. But on the contrary, as Chaudhuri points out, the Hindus are the stark materialists and can be more materialistic than the so-called materialistic society of the West itself. That is the reason why money and official position count far more than any spiritual height or achievement in India. Chaudhuri offers himself as the living example of a man, who is not likely to be respected in his country for, lacking both money and power, the two great pillars of Indian materialism. When interviewed by an American lady about non-fiction, Khushwant Singh replies, "In non-fiction? Without a doubt Nirad Chaudhuri.... A bitter man, a poor man. He doesn't even own a typewriter. He borrows mine a week at a time" (2). Chaudhuri continues, "My poverty is, of course, well known in New Delhi and much further afield, and therefore I was not prepared to see it bruited about by so august a body as the American Women's Club of Delhi. Why did the impressive board of twelve American women, who were jointly looking after the magazine think it necessary to publish such small talk about a man, who was even smaller by their standards, who had neither of the two things they understood and respected: namely, money and official power?" (2). In fact, this satire is more applicable to the Indians, who never cared to notice him than to the American ladies who had at least the courtesy to interview him.

Chaudhuri is absolutely right in his satirization of the commonest malady that Indians have cultivated, i.e. their dependence on white experts for everything ranging from cosmetic to the cosmic. In fact, it is an indirect and sometimes even direct recognition of their own inability and of the superiority of the Western talent. Sometimes this madness of Indians reaches ridiculous height. They never trust the authenticity of Indian talent and the durability or quality of Indian things. Books and books can be written on this subject. Chaudhuri is very bitter about this aspect of the Indian character. He says, "But there is nothing which frightens the present Indian ruling class more than the idea of doing anything without the advice and help of white experts. So we have them, and they range from the specialists, who advise us about taxation and contraception, to those, who build our dams and steel plants. Even a Japanese gardener was brought over to convert a public park, which was being grossly neglected by the Delhi municipality, into a Japanese garden, why, the Japanese himself could not understand" (11). Obviously, Chaudhuri's attack is on the Indian lack of confidence in themselves as a nation.

Indians are not consistent in their behaviour, because on the one hand they depend upon the foreigners and on the other, they dread them. Thus, xenolatry and xenophobia are found simultaneously in Indian character and culture. When the barbarians of the Central Asia came and attacked the Indians, the Hindus were utterly humiliated. "Their domination intolerably humiliated the proud Hindu order and it was in dealing with them that it added to its intense pride of race and culture, that violent xenophobia, which henceforward became a fixed trait of the Hindu outlook. The compound of fear, hatred, contempt and humiliation was embodied in the notion of Mlechha, the unclean and uncivilized foreigner" (56). Consequently, the Hindus became conceited and began to hate all the foreigners regardless of their being barbarians or Muslims or others. The radical change from the historical xenophobia to the modern xenolatry is ridiculous and absurd. Chaudhuri has rightly satirized these qualities of Hindus by showing them through his perceptive historical observation.

Chaudhuri's keen observation and subtle analysis of the Hindu life helps him lay bare the pseudo-trappings acquired by the majority of the Hindus. He points out the hollowness, the superficiality and artificiality of the Hindus' Westernization. He is perfectly right when he says that the Hindu Westernization is purely technical. The Hindus have not really assimilated the Western scientific spirit in their blood system. Their westernization is confined only to certain exteriorities of culture such as the Western clothes, eating manners, sports, entertainment, etc. It is very intelligent of Chaudhuri to have pointed out the paradox of the Hindu Westernization. The Indians, who have not gone abroad, are more westernized than those who have. "In fact, I do not meet more Hindus with a Westernized mind among those who have been educated in the West than I do among those who have remained in India" (340).

The pseudo-Westernization of the Hindus is allied to their Anglicization also. Chaudhuri is very bitter about and angry with the anglicized middle-class Hindus, who in their madness for Anglicization do not mind de-Hinduizing or de-Indianizing themselves. Such Anglicized Hindus are found in the following four categories: (1) The Officers of the Armed Forces, (2) The Bureaucratic, Managerial and Professional Elite, (3) The Technicians, and (4) The Youth in schools. What Chaudhuri says about the Officer corps is applicable to all the Anglicized Hindus. "But they are the most Anglicized Hindus today in their behaviour and manner of living. They are also the Hindus who know least about Hindu way and traditions and are the most indifferent to all things Hindu so far as these can be present in the consciousness" (341). Chaudhuri attributes this lack of cultural and national awareness of Hindus to the alien education they receive at the convent schools and other English medium schools, which deliberately or otherwise teach the British manners, etiquette, habits and styles, etc. and de-Indianize them thoroughly. Chaudhuri attacks that even the imitation by Hindus of such British traits is not really genuine, because the military education is not suited to the national character of India. Even the British traits like self-restraint, reticence, fair-play and strong will are not cultivated by the Hindus in the real sense of the term and remain rather skin deep. The Anglicized Hindus are notorious for their madness for 'Scotch' whisky. Chaudhuri castigates the terrible class-consciousness of the Anglicized officers and their 'I know, I know' philosophy. The Anglomania is not confined to military officers alone but extends to the entire middle-class society of India. Chaudhuri satirizes the Hindu girls' madness for convent schools and their desire to marry the IAS Officers. Chaudhuri's observation about the Anglicized Hindus is as bitter as true, "All these men combine the Hindu pride of caste with the English pride of class and they can be very unpleasant" (353). Chaudhuri's perceptiveness may be seen in his satirical enumeration of the general features of the Anglicized Hindus' timidity, madness for English clothes, especially the tie, use of English language, delight in the mass-made popular amusements. Western vulgarity and viciousness are the dominant features of this snobbish class. Besides, they are revolutionary only in the reverse gear and have no principles. Chaudhuri is frank and bold enough to say that the person who was responsible for the dominance of the Anglicized middle-class Hindus was none other than Jawaharlal Nehru himself. Says Chaudhuri, "Nehru would not be Nehru without that language" (357), i.e. the English language. Chaudhuri's satire on the un-Hinduness of the Hindus or the un-Indianness of the Indians is quite clear and obvious.

The Indian's madness for the alien language is again something that poses special problems. Many Indian writers desire to write about their country in the English language. But this venture more often than not turns out to be a failure, because of two reasons: one, the Indians cannot achieve the mastery over the alien tongue in the real sense of the term, because as Chaudhuri points out in his *Autobiography of an Unknown Indian* they can manage to enrich their vocabulary but can never overcome the difficulty with regard to the English prepositions and structure as they are accustomed to the inflective languages of India; two: even when they acquire a tolerable mastery over the English language they will not be able to write typically Indian novels because in the very process of learning the English language (mostly in convent schools) they will have de-Indianized and anglicized themselves so much that they fail to capture the true Indian spirit in their works. These two problems have to be faced by every Indian writer, who cares to be sincere in his profession. Says Chaudhuri, "Over and above in order to be novelists in English, these Indian writers are faced by a problem of writing for tackling which they have neither the knowledge nor the strength of mind. The life, the mind, and the behaviour of Indians are so strange for the people of the West that if these are described in ordinary English the book would be unintelligible to English-speaking readers, and unacceptable to British or American publishers. Most Indian writers solve this problem, not by choosing a genuine Indian subject and creating an adequate Western idiom to express it, but by selecting wholly artificial themes which the Western world takes to be Indian, and by dealing with them in the manner of contemporary Western writers. To put it briefly, they try to see their country and society in the way Englishmen or Americans do and write about India in the jargon of the same masters. The result is an inefficient imitation of the novels about India written by Western novelists. India is far too big a subject for such frippery" (14).

Chaudhuri attacks the Hindus ever readiness to imitate anything that is un-Hindu or un-Indian; because of their crass ignorance of their own culture. Another malady the Hindus suffer from is the Americanization. As Chaudhuri points out, the modern Indians, unlike the ancient and medieval Indians, have lost their sense of cultural identity and are only too willing to surrender themselves to the alien lifestyle which came in their purview. The industrialization of India an "underdeveloped country" has easily paved the way for the Americanization of Hindus.

The Indians are guilty of neglecting the two most important features of their country, i.e. Hinduism and agriculture. Chaudhuri is absolutely right in his attack. In the India of the present days, the Hindus have come to acquire a view that following their religious practices or trying to understand them or cultivating the land are below their dignity and are supposed to be meant only for the illiterate. The Hindus will not turn their attention to these things until some foreigners recommend them.

Chaudhuri's rational attitude to life easily detects the riddles of the Indian continent. India is a land of riddles for all those who want to 'think' about it. Chaudhuri shows how the Indians, by and large, are 'lackadaisical in action as well as thought'. There seems to be no connection whatever between the Indian's tall talk and the squeamish and ugly existence. The Indian suffers from an indefinite sickness of heart. India is 'a country which exacts robustness or inflicts neorosis'. Chaudhuri's anger, bitterness, and concern are expressed in his words, "I declare everyday that a man who cannot endure dirt, dust, stench, noise, ugliness, heat and cold has no right to live in India. I would say that no man can be regarded as a fit citizen of India until he has conquered squeamishness to the point of being indifferent to the presence of filthy lepers in various stages of decomposition within a hundred yards, or not minding the sight of ubiquitous human excreta everywhere, even in a big city" (22).

Chaudhuri attacks the supreme fanaticism of the Hindus, which has prevented them from growing in the social and cultural sense. "They", says Chaudhuri, "suffer from a sense of genetic superiority." There is nothing wrong with the fanaticism if it does inspire a race to do something creative and progressive. But the Hindu fanaticism is negative in the sense that it enables the Hindu to rationalize or slur over his mistakes and weaknesses by holding a picture of the golden past before him. The Aryans, i.e. the ancestors of the modern Hindus, believed that "they were not only a chosen people, but the people; that their way of life was divinely ordained and eternal; that it was superior to all others; that there was an unbridgeable gulf between them and the older inhabitants of the country, as well as foreigners" (28).

Talking as contradistinguished from acting seems to be the common quality of the Hindus. The Hindus very generously indulge in talk, small talk and tall talk because they have lost their zest for action. Everyone in India from the highest to the lowest fields of life indulges talking. The Hindu politicians, religious leaders, and other social reformers set the example. Chaudhuri satirically says that all these categories of men are trained in the same institute. Whereas the *gurus* offer *bhang* to their *chelas*, the secular *gurus* offer something similar to the nation. Says he, "The secular Hindu *gurus* have not given up the tradition, but the drug they offer is different. It is the most harmful drug made in India today, which if taken in large quantities and the quantities administered are large—completely destroys the faculties of thinking and observing. I shall call it Logosane, a meaningless, tasteless, colorless, but intellectually asphyxiating substance, turned out from the only really efficient mass-production factory established in India since independence, namely the Nationalized Factory of words" (31).

There is nothing wrong with talking provided talking involves thinking. Talking means talking sense and thinking means right thinking. But Chaudhuri's satire consists in showing the irony of the Hindu (or Indian) talking. In India, one (including the foreigner) is made to listen to the torrent of words. Most often the Hindus mean the opposite of what they say. The meaning of the words is inversely proportionate to the quantity of the vocabulary they employ. That is why Chaudhuri wants to warn the foreigner not to take these words on their face value. "I only caution him against the *anexetastos logos*, the unexamined word. He can listen to everything so long as he is exercising criticism" (31). Obviously, Chaudhuri implies that the Hindus or Indians in general do not show the signs of serious or rational thinking in their talking. It may be said that they suffer from logorrhea. Chaudhuri's anger at the superficiality, emptiness and glibness of the Hindu talkativeness is as obvious as justified.

That India is a land of contradictions is a basic hypothesis of the Chaudhurian satire. In every field of Hindu culture and at every stage of Hindu behaviour contradictions loom large in number. For every value that the Hindu teaches there is a counter-value that he practises. This phenomenon may be seen in everything that the Hindu is and does. Chaudhuri points out the ambivalent view of the aboriginals by the Hindu, and the element of contradiction in the Hindu behaviour. The Hindu does not have any affection or appreciation for the aboriginals of his country. He has nothing but utter contempt for them. But the paradox is that the Hindu has always shown a special weakness for the aboriginal women. "The Hindu contempt for the aboriginals in modern times was not softened even by their notorious lust for their women" (73).

Chaudhuri exposes the Hindu snobbery about the fair complexion. The ancient Hindus did not abhor the dark complexion. On the contrary, dark complexion was considered a mark of beauty. The Indian epic the *Mahabharata* shows how Lord Krishna was deemed as handsome because of his dark complexion. But in the modern days the Hindus probably because of their contact with foreigners, have developed a snobbish partiality for the fair complexion, which has added to the social problem in India. This problem becomes acute especially in the case of dark girls who are "the unsalable goods in the marriage market" (25).

Contradictions like chauvinism and servile imitation are again to be seen in Indian life. Chaudhuri points out the failure of the Indian to follow one of these two consistently. On the one hand, the Hindu tom-toms about his golden age of the past and pretends to look down upon the so-called materialistic progress of the West. On the other hand, he wants to prove his modernity and assert his self-respect by industrializing his own country, which gives him a stature in the international world. The result of this contradiction is that he is neither really patriotic nor really internationalist in his attitude. Chaudhuri satirizes this aspect and attributes it to the Hindu's 'insatiable greed for money'. The Hindu, who is proverbially known as a spiritualistic man, is at heart a Mammon worshipper. He wants to forget his inferiority complex by possessing as much money as possible. There is an inevitable connection between the Mammon worship and industrialization in India. Chaudhuri satirizes this malady through an historical analogy, "Hindu nationalism is indeed a very powerful force behind the industrial revolution in India, but it is not the most powerful, and indeed cannot be because it is basically negative. A far stronger force, in actual fact the only positive force, is the Hindu's insatiable greed for money. King Dollar who is inciting King Paisa does not know either himself or his new 'Royal Brother'. The American industrialist, even when he is aware of no other motivation except acquisition of money, is the old European Conquistador in a new incarnation. He is the Genghiz Khan of the age of economics" (84). Chaudhuri's bitterness and anger are evident in his summarization of the true Indian spirit, "His spirit is best symbolized by the adulteration of food, medicine, and whatever else can be adulterated" (88). The unscrupulousness and lack of purity in all the fields of the Hindu life are too familiar to be illustrated.

India is no doubt known as the land of spirituality, of innumerable gods and god-men, etc. All that is true but in a reverse gear. That the India of ancient days was a country of the highest kind of religious consciousness to be expressed in her logic, philosophy and metaphysics, etc. is beyond controversy. Chaudhuri does not deny that at all. What Mr. Chaudhuri wants to point out and that bitterly too is the conspicuous gap between the ancient Hindu spirituality and the modern Hindu superficiality and farce. Chaudhuri is often mistaken by Indian critics for a cynic, a pessimist and a hater of Indian religion and philosophy. A bit of clarification is needed here. Mr. Chaudhuri's complaint is not so much against the Hindu religion and philosophy (i.e. ideals) as against the Hindus, who do not unfortunately live up to those ideals in the real sense of the term. Mr. Chaudhuri's point of view is similar to that of Soren Kierkegaard, who attacks not Christianity but Christians, who do not really live up to the Christian ideals. Mr. Chaudhuri shows the modern Hindus' double-guilt: either the Hindus follow the values that are opposed to their professed ideals or make a farce of the ideals by clinging to the ritualistic aspect of them without following their intrinsic worth. The result of this phenomenon is the ridiculous and absurd blankness and hollowness of the Hindu existence. Any sensible man could perceive these contradictions, illogicalities and irrationalities. Dr. Mulk Raj Anand and Mr. Khushwant Singh have castigated these features in their works. Mr. V.S. Naipaul also has done it in his *An Area of Darkness*. Mr. Chaudhuri's keen sense of observation has enabled him to enumerate them and hold them responsible for the behaviour of the modern Hindu.

The fanaticism of the Hindu, ancient or modern, is a very familiar feature. The Hindus have always deemed themselves to be superior to other races genetically, socially and culturally. The Hindu fanaticism or superiority has been noticed by many a foreign traveller. Mr. Chaudhuri quotes Alberuni, who visited India in the eleventh century and who says, "Their haughtiness is such that, if you tell them of any science or scholar in Khurasan and Persia they will think you to be both an ignoramus and a liar" (211).

The Hindu philosophy, which was the result of the actual life and not a mere theory, has obviously depth and stature to it. Mr. Chaudhuri points out how in Indian religion there is a philosophization of suffering. But the main target of his attack are Hindus, who employ this philosophy for the rationalization of their mistakes and weaknesses, which accounts for their lack of progress in all the fields of their life. The justification of the suffering both of body and of mind was the cause of the cultivation of other allied religious virtues. The mortification of flesh is such a value according to which man is supposed to defy all the comforts of life. The naked *sadhus* of India are an example of this practice, and are called 'gymnosophists' by Alexander the Great. Mr. Chaudhuri is not blind to the causes of such practices. Enabled by his anthropological approach, he offers the scientific reason for that. "What, however, nobody seems to suspect is the possibility that this impressive mortification of the flesh through the sacrifice of creature comforts, cleanliness, and appearance might have been due to the climate and weather of India" (211). Chaudhuri quotes the examples of Naga *sanyasis* and naked *sadhus* and shows how the mortification of flesh results in the defiance of filth, "...the Hindu holy men made indifference to filth an essential attribute of saintliness" (211). It is because of the influence of this philosophy that the Hindu has been desensitized and hardened to the ubiquitous dirt and squalor and made to live a life of supreme resignation. It does not mean that Chaudhuri finds fault with their religion but he castigates Hindus for making a farce of their religion by employing the religious principles for the wrong purposes. That is why he says, "In India, owing to the climate and weather, the correlation between space, solitude, beauty, and human dignity has been even closer. Here crowding mercilessly piles up squalor, while immensity and starkness can raise even the irresistible and choking dust of the Gangetic plain to the height of a sad and ascetic majesty, and make it look like grey snow or hoarfrost, as if it were the material counterpart of that ashen resignation, which is perhaps the Hindu's purest mood" (81).

Chaudhuri rightly shows how in India everything is ultimately connected with religion. The Indian sociology, politics, economics are all affected by the religion. In *To Live or Not to Live,* Chaudhuri makes a bitter and jocular remark that in India a man would not hesitate to murder another man if you said to him that it is part of his religion. Thus, they have a tendency to sanctifying everything because sanctification will make up for the pitfalls of their thinking and action. Chaudhuri puts it beautifully, "The Hindus discovered quite early in their existence in India that they could not preserve any delicate sensibility without making it a part of piety, nor could they keep up effort without making it a religious duty. To make things secular in this country is to make them weak, vulgar, and eroded" (208). Again within the realm of religion itself, the contradictions are likely to reach absurd extremities. Mr. Chaudhuri illustrates the extremity of the purity-mania with an example of a woman of his acquaintance who "used to wash the bed clothes, not sheets or pillow-cases, but quilts and mattresses—every morning even in winter" (213). The mystical indifference to filth and squalor is another religious value, which has damaged the Hindu sense of beauty and hygiene. Innumerable examples of this may be seen in the Hindu hagiographies (written or oral versions). Mr. Chaudhuri quotes from his own experience and reading to illustrate them. Eating faeces without the slightest sense of disgust is cited as part of the saintly achievement. One can easily see how this extreme sense of mystical indifference damages the Hindu sense of sanitation and hygiene. This accounts for the Hindu tolerance of the ubiquitous presence of excreta on the gutter sides and dark and deserted spots of Indian cities and villages. The Hindu obsession with the sub-rational and supra-rational thinking has incapacitated him of any kind of rational thinking and behaviour. Hence, his supreme belief in magic and supernaturalism. Mr. Chaudhuri is very frank in his remark, "Even today Hindu religious beliefs and practices retain a direct magical character, and are imbued with the spirit of animism, homoeopathic magic and spells" (218). Further he comments upon their irrationality, "In India Nature's relentless enmity to man has destroyed his self-confidence and completely undermined his faith in rational measures. Thus it happens that whenever he is in trouble and even when rational means exist and are applied, the Hindu will never remain satisfied with that, but calls in the supernatural, sometimes as an auxiliary and sometimes even as the principal ally" (218). Chaudhuri satirizes the Hindu emphasis on the negation of the world. He is perfectly right in his analysis of the Hindu character. The Hindu defiance and indifference to dirt, squalor and suffering are affected by the negative note of the Hindu philosophy, which makes him believe in the law of karma. Thus, ultimately the philosophy is twisted to the Hindu's convenience and rationalization. Says Chaudhuri, "As for the philosophical remedy, I have already said that it made itself unacceptable by its unrelieved nihilism. It preached the negation of the world without putting anything in its place, a mistake Christianity never committed" (220). Many Hindu zealots and patriots are not merely irritated but hurt by the Chaudhurian analysis. But Chaudhuri's question is—If the Hindu philosophy is optimistic and positive in its approach why is it that it has not enabled him to be on par with others in the modern world in the field of knowledge, i.e., science, technology, art, literature, architecture, etc.? Economic poverty alone is not responsible for the Hindu retrogression. Chaudhuri poses a rational question for which he wants a rational answer and not the supra-rational or mythological answer to be usually given by the Hindu proselytizers. Again contradictions are to be seen at every step in Hindu life. On the one hand, the Hindus preach and practise the principle of world-negation and on the contrary they fight for their communal rights and privileges. Caste-consciousness is an example of this. In spite of the constitutional declaration of India as a secular country, the Hindus still believe in the hierarchy of the *varna* system much to the chagrin of the downtrodden. It is because of this rampant caste-ism of the caste-Hindus that the *Sudras* are compelled to embrace Islam or Christianity. Again the religious conversions in India add to the socio-economic problems and psychological dilemmas. Taking the example of the conversion of the aboriginals to Christianity, Chaudhuri rightly points out the emergence of the new problems, "It was seen that, as soon as the aboriginal adapted Christianity, he became a different man. He lost his free spirit, and acquired the mental cast of a Hindu of the depressed classes. He began, on the one hand, to nurse grievances, on the other to depend more and more on his foreign Christian patron. He fell a prey to the inferiority complex, something which he had never done before with all the hostility of the Hindus arrayed against his" (88). Chaudhuri would have pointed out the recent agitation in Kerala by the caste Hindus against the conversion of the *Sudras* to Islam. The religious values and beliefs, however contradictory they may be, are bound to affect the general psychology and behaviour of the Hindu. The features commonly to be found in the modern Hindu, of course, form his national character. Chaudhuri not merely points out the weaknesses of the Hindu character like a true satirist but tries to account for them like an anthropologist. While he accuses the Hindu of being completely enervated, he also tries to explain it and attributes it to the rigour of the tropical climate of India. The enervation of the Hindu is ascribable as much to his philosophy of non-action as to the exacting climate of his country. It is because of the lack of energy that the Hindu has been incapable of achieving anything great and worthwhile in any field of life. This is especially so in the case of industrialization. Says Chaudhuri, "The Hindu order in its present state has neither the energy, physical and mental, nor the organizing capacity, nor perhaps the intelligence to carry through the type of industrialization which is now contemplated" (89). The physical and mental enervation paves the way for the moral enervation also. That is why Chaudhuri castigates the

Hindu's moral weakness. The Hindu lack of integrity is noticed especially by the foreigners, who expect great virtues in him. The British came to hate these qualities of Hindus. Says Chaudhuri, "Never did this exhibition of contempt and anger cease so long as British rule remained a live thing in India. 'Degraded, perverse, grotesque, contradictory'—were some of the milder adjectives used. The 'effeminate Hindu' was a stock phrase. The Hindus were regarded as untruthful, dishonest, and shifty and often described as such to their face" (94). Double-dealing, hypocrisy and fraud are the staple qualities of the Hindu personality. This accounts for Chaudhuri's anger in his satirization, which is very true though a little exaggerated. "From this follows a corollary that if you see a Hindu who appears to be pleased with himself and with the world around him, be on guard, for you are then facing a thorough rascal, all the more dangerous because of his bland plausibility. I think it was Plato who said that a rich man could never be a good man. I shall say that it is virtually impossible for an optimistic and self satisfied Hindu to be a good Hindu" (152). Chaudhuri's satire of Hindus is to be seen in the enumeration of the undesirables in Hindu culture and character. That India has been a land of irrationality is noticed by many people with a scientific bent of mind. Chaudhuri is certainly not new in repeating the observation. But his originality lies in the intensity of his experience and fine and clear-cut analysis of the phenomenon under his observation. He illustrates the element of irrationality with examples both ancient and modern. He shows how the irrational element is so blatant in Manu's *Dharmasastra*. A noble exposition of the Brahmanic way of life, the *Laws of Manu* has many irrational ideas. "It actually says that if a man steals silk he becomes a partridge, but by stealing dyed cloth he becomes not any kind of partridge but only a francolin partridge (black partridge). Some other threatened metempsychoses are—for stealing cotton cloth a man becomes a crane, but by stealing linen he becomes a frog" (103). One can easily see how the 'why' of such particular metempsychoses is not made known to the reader and therefore they remain unconvincing because of the irrational element in them.

Chaudhuri shows how even the modern politicians, professors and secularists pore over horoscopes in private life, though they pretend not to care for that in public life. Chaudhuri quotes the examples of the modern Hindu's conduct of a great *yajna* at Delhi, "the Brahmanic sacrifice to avert the destruction of the world at the beginning of February, the year being 1962" (104). The great irony of this *yajna* is that it is conducted by the spiritualistic Hindus with the help of the dollar of the materialistic Americans. Chaudhuri makes bold to say that there is no thinking proper among the Hindus. He says, "There is no such thing as thinking properly so called among the Hindus, for it is a faculty of the mind developed only in Greece, and exercised only by the heirs of the Greeks. A very large part of what is called Hindu thinking is wholly speculation or just mush" (174).

Contradictions loom large in Indian life both private and public. Chaudhuri's sharp intelligence is ever ready to detect them. The Hindu attitude towards sex is equivocal and contradictory. On the one hand, sex is looked upon as something ugly and a positive hindrance in the attainment of spiritual bliss, etc. This accounts for the high respect with which values like 'celibacy', 'virginity', 'chastity', were held. On the other hand, sex was frankly accepted as a means of procreation or sensuous gratification, which may at its highest lead to spiritual bliss, etc. Thus, sex-gratification and sexual abstinence have been found together in Hindu life. Chaudhuri exhausts his historical learning to illustrate these contradictions from the Vedic times to the modern time. He shows how "In India every ruling power has in past showed its particular taste in women. The Moguls, for instance, preferred Kashmiri beauties, the British, Muslim and Aboriginal girls, and the Hindus would rather have women of European descent, after they had outgrown their earlier taste for Muslim mistresses" (319). The paradox about 'sexual purity' in India is that it is confined only to the physical level. Most often it is nothing but sex-obsessed chastity. One may easily see how this kind of double standard breeds hypocrisy among the people.

The same kind of contradiction may be seen in the Hindu's day-to-day social behaviour. Quarrelsomeness is a common feature of the Hindu personality. Especially women are notorious for that. Quarrels take place in India between men and women, the old and the young, the kith and kin, neighbours and strangers. The reasons for such quarrels range from the serious issues like money, gold, property, woman or power to the silly ones like getting a seat in a bus or train. Chaudhuri has provided a number of such examples from his experience. What is most paradoxical and strange about these quarrels is that they do not last long. They do not make the quarrelling fellows permanent enemies. On the contrary, they make them close friends within five minutes after the quarrel is over. Chaudhuri evokes mild humour by illustrating the 'callous charity' of the querulous parties. The Hindus do not mind using the foulest possible language most of which is sex-centred. Says Chaudhuri, "Somehow an alkali is always present with the acid of Hindu life; it is a marvellous and boundless tolerance of bad language and blows, which is some sort of a conditioned reflex of forgiveness. The Hindus possess a faculty for callous charity. Two passengers in a railway compartment who have fought with shameless selfishness for seats, will, as soon as they have cooled off, offer betel, cigarettes, and even sweets to each other, and be friends for the rest of a long journey of, say, eight hundred miles. In the families the sun hardly ever rises on anger. After a brawl lasting till midnight not only peace but even harmony seems to be restored the next morning" (276). Quarrelsomeness and callous charity go on alternating in the Hindu's behaviour.

Another contradiction may be seen with regard to the Hindu view of violence. Probably, because of the great influence of Mahatma Gandhi on the Indian life, India has come to be known as the land of non-violence. But Chaudhuri points out how non-violence is a negative adjective implying the age-old practice of violence in India. He shows how violence was common in India from the epic age to the modern one. The paraphernalia of war like the warriors going to the battlefield, their murder there, the lamentation of wives, the rape and robbery and imprisonment have been discussed by Chaudhuri at great length which cannot be enumerated within this limited scope of this article. The war between Aryans and non-Aryans; Hindus and Muslims: Hindus and Hindus; Hindus and foreigners etc., have been cited by Chaudhuri. He especially draws our attention to the Gandhian principle, "In its application to the Indian nationalist movement, the Gandhian doctrine of non-violence led to some of the bloodiest riots, one of which compelled him in 1922 to call off the Non-cooperation movement" (130). Chaudhuri laughs at the way the Hindus justify their wars as *Dharma Yuddha* and even go to the extent of teaching the moral to the foreigners who have evolved the ultra-modern war-technology. The Hindus did not mind serving the non-vegetarian food to the foreign visitors in the Ashoka Hotel of Delhi named after an Apostle of Peace and non-violence. The bewildering contradictions of Indian life are attributed by Chaudhuri to the Hindu's psychological turbulence. He says, "Lifelong observation has convinced me that there is a streak of insanity in the Hindus and that nobody will arrive at a correct appraisement of Hindu private and public behaviour on the supposition that they have a normal personality" (132).

Thus, the Hindu character defies understanding and remains a puzzle to the rational observer. The contradictory nature of the Hindu culture accounts for the double-standard, hypocrisy, compromise and rationalizations which become inevitable. Chaudhuri employs the mythological metaphor to describe this phenomenon, "It is on account of the presence of such opposites that I have taken the Roman God Janus as the symbol of the Hindu character. But it does not present only two faces. It has a whole series of them, going in pairs. For this reason the Hindu personality might be called not even Janus Quadrifrons, but Janus Multifrons" (106). This is the way Chaudhuri has analyzed the Hindu culture and character, which are marked by contradictions, compromises, riddles and irrationalities, etc. The inevitability of these contradictory strands of the Hindu culture has been pointed out by Chaudhuri in a very subtle and able fashion. He concludes his satire by explicitly ascribing the puzzling nature of the Hindu to the evil effect of the demoness called Circe. The Hindus have come under the spell of the demoness and that explains their negative life and character. Chaudhuri employs metaphorical language to express his satirical vision. The Hindus are at the mercy of the evil Goddess. Says he, "They stood at the gate of the goddess with flowing tresses, and heard her. Circe, sweetly singing before her loom as she walked to and fro weaving an imperishable web, gorgeous and dazzling, such as only goddesses can make" (372). The Hindus seem to have lost their rationality, principles, heroism, piety and spirituality as they have been devitalized by the Goddess. Chaudhuri continues, "She lived on the island of Aeaea, and so she has in India. Men have stood at her gate, and called to be admitted, and to all she has opened her shining doors. She has taken them in, given them seats, and served food. But with the food she has also mixed the drug, which makes them forget their country. Then she has turned them into brute beasts" (372). Circe had cast her spell, on Chaudhuri quite early in his life. There is no doubt that every Hindu has come under Circe's spell. But is there no escape from that? There is. Chaudhuri says he found the answer for this question when in 1955 he visited the West, and realized that "We Hindus were Europeans enslaved by a tropical country" (373). The only way for Hindus to escape from Circe's spell is to recover at least our old European spirit" (374). He says that the 'Brown Colonialism' of the Anglicized Hindus will not help them completely. The best way to be happy is for Hindus to cease to think themselves as Orientals. Chaudhuri's satirical approach makes him compare the Hindus to beasts and even to Yahoos. Himself a beast of this kind, Chaudhuri warns his fellowmen. "Listen to a fellow-beast, who has been lucky enough to find freedom and wants you to be free" (374). Chaudhuri's concern and love for Hindus is quite evident here. He castigates the negative traits of this race because of his express desire to make them conscious of their true nature and overcome the difficulties. But the paradox is that the fellow-Hindus do not care for his words because of Circe's spell. "With a refinement of cruelty Circe has kept them in the human shape but in a form, which is even more repulsive than that of the Yahoos of Swift" (375). One difference between Swiftian Yahoos and Hindu Yahoos is that the former were not responsible for their ugliness, whereas the latter definitely are.

Even when he tries to awaken his fellow men, they do not bother to listen to him. That explains Chaudhuri's height of bitterness and anger. "I have recovered my Ariel's body from Sycorax, the terrible and malevolent hag, who stands behind Circe in India. So I can and should ignore the Yahoos. But I would save the fellow beasts. They do not however, listen to me. They honk, neigh, bellow, bleat, or grunt and scamper away to their scrub, stable, byre, pen and sty" (376). And Circe, the Sorceress is happy to see the completeness of her handiwork.

The Continent of Circe is an excellent satire ever written by an Indian English writer. It can compare with any successful satire in English literature. It stands on par with other works like *The Animal Farm, The Gulliver's Travels*, and *Erehwon,* etc. But a significant difference between *The Continent of Circe* and other satires cited above, is that whereas in those satires the technique of allegorization is followed throughout, in *The Continent of Circe* it is followed only partially. In other words, in *The Continent of Circe* the minute and elaborate treatment of the theme is realistic (i.e. historical, and anthropological, etc.), though the overall pattern of the work is one of allegory, the result of Chaudhuri's imagination. This is probably because of his personal intention. He calls it an 'essay,' as he wants to try to understand the nature of the peoples of India. Naturally then the discursive element of the essay is framed with the allegorical pattern. Chaudhuri's satire is an inevitable product of his essay. In other words, his aim is not to castigate so much as to understand the Indians. But in the process of understanding his countrymen Chaudhuri could not help satirizing them. Hence, the discursive allegory of *The Continent of Circe*. But unfortunately many Indian critics fail to understand Chaudhuri's satire because of their prejudices. Robert De Souza represents the unsympathetic Indian's point of view when he complains about Chaudhuri, "his criticism of the peoples of India may be welcome to certain extent and in due proportion, but will not serve a healthy purpose. He satirically criticizes the peoples of India, but does not suggest adequate means to remedy the situation. He seems to delight only in fault finding though he is apologetic here and there to disguise his cynical attitude."[4] It may be said that the aim of a satirist is to present a picture of life and consequently awaken the people concerned from their slumber. Again the so-called cynicism of a satirist is nothing but the observe side of his optimism and idealism. Paul Verghese makes the same mistake when he says, "*The Continent of Circe* is clearly not history; it is not a disinterested assessment of the Hindu character, it is not even a satire, but only bitterness."[5] Paul Verghese fails to read between the lines of the book and mistakes the spirit of Chaudhuri's argument. A minimum knowledge of the psychology of bitterness will help the critics like Paul Verghese to clear their misconceptions. A man will be angry and bitter with a people only when the latter fail to practise their high ideals. A man hates a people only when he sees a dichotomy between their philosophy and their actual way of life, which falls short of it. A man cannot exhaust his energy and scholarship in understanding and criticizing a people if he has nothing but contempt for them as Paul Verghese assumes. The bitterness and anger are the obverse side of Chaudhuri's love and concern for his countrymen. Satire implies an unwritten utopia. Paul Verghese cannot stomach Chaudhuri's castigating remarks because he belongs to the victims of Circe who, according to Chaudhuri's implication, cannot accept until it is sugarcoated.

Notes

1. K.R. Srinivasa, Iyengar. *Indian Writing in English*. Bombay: Asia Publishing House, 1973, p. 591.
2. Nirad C. Chaudhuri, *The Continent of Circe*. Bombay: Jaico Publishing House, 1974, p. 1 (All the subsequent references to the text are from this edition.)
3. Joseph T. Shiplay, *Dictionary of World Literary Terms*. London: George Allen and Unwin, 1970, p. 106.
4. De Souza Robert. *Goa and The Continent of Circe*. Bombay: Wilco Publishing House, 1973, p. 194.
5. C. Paul Verghese, *Nirad C. Chaudhuri*. New Delhi: Arnold Heinemann, 1973, p. 95.

Chapter 5

To Live or Not to Live: An Essay

No man with a keen sense of observation of life around him and a deliberate analysis of the observed phenomenon can escape the Hamletian dilemma which presupposes an awareness of the contradiction between appearance and reality, between the falsification of the traditionally sanctioned values and the simultaneous inevitability of a given phenomenon. A man who is caught in the strange context such as this cannot help responding to it in the Hamletian manner. Nirad C. Chaudhuri has the courage to see the problem in the face and try to understand and analyze it however ugly and insoluble, though it may be. There is a greater heroism in having the Hamletian knowledge of reality than in being satisfied with the ignorance of the same. As Aristotle says it is always desirable to have the knowledge of reality, although it is quite ugly and harsh. Chaudhuri who is known for his objective analysis of the Indian society is compelled to raise a Hamletian problem. *To Live or Not to Live* is an essay,[1] which shows Chaudhuri's attempt to understand and account for the peculiar problems of the Indian society, which make it difficult for a sensitive man to continue to live meaningfully in that society. Again the book need not be mistaken for a textbook of social psychology, as it is the embodiment of Chaudhuri's personal vision, which is the result of the lifelong observation and which may correspond to the impersonal vision of sociologists and psychologists. What makes his essay personal is the fact that his generalizations about the Indian society are based upon his personal experience with people, events and situations of the Indian society. His observations are *a posteriori* rather than *a priori* and hence assume an authenticity of individual vision as contrasted with that of scientific and hence universal vision. The ingredients of Chaudhuri's vision of life as embodied in *To Live or Not to Live* may be discussed in the following paragraphs.

Chaudhuri begins his 'informal' and 'discursive' work with a discussion of a basic question about living a meaningful life in India. Both the social and the family life fall within the large framework of human life. "That is why I have put these two aspects of living under a title which raises the general question of living soundly, living to some purpose—which alone is *living* to me, living unsoundly being in my view not *living* at all. In short, I would not deal with social and family life without raising the basic question: Do we live at all?" (7). Chaudhuri thus raises the fundamental and epistemological question about life because it is the epistemology which gives a sense of direction and vocation to all the aspects of life and makes it a matter of beauty and joy forever. Since Chaudhuri like many other sensitive men, has felt the presence of a great lacuna between the Indian ideals and the actual practice, he cannot but ask the basic question again and again. Life in India has become so paradoxical and farcical that one who wants to relate the actual values practised to the ideals professed, one is bound to have a Hamletian question as to whether to live or not to live in such a context of multiple contradictions. The Hamletian condition forced upon Chaudhuri is based upon his lifelong observation and a conscious analysis of the content of that observation. The details of his experience with Indian life could be enumerated as follows.

Life in India is not to be understood as a matter of intellectual awareness. On the contrary, it is one of intellectual blindness. Chaudhuri, therefore, describes the life in India as 'uncritical living'. "We live uncritically, without paying heed to Plato's famous dictum: The un-criticized (or un-examined) life is not worth living" (8). Life in India is marked by a general lack of ideals and is therefore characterized by negative qualities like eccentricity, stupid vanity, malice, spite and so on. The conspicuous gap between the tall ideals traditionally professed by the Indians and the stark materialism of their pragmatic life is bitterly noted and attacked by Chaudhuri in the manner in which the seventeenth-century England and the nineteenth-century England were attacked by Milton and Charles Dickens respectively. Chaudhuri's extraordinary sensitiveness to life around him is proportionately matched by, his courage to see the ugliness of life in the face and to withstand the shock that is caused by the minute analysis of reality. The overall impression of Chaudhuri about Indian life is that money plays an extraordinary role in the life of the major groups of society like the youths, the intellectuals and the politicians. Money thus becomes the keynote of the Indian society, of human relation, of enjoyment and of achievement. The Indians, according to Chaudhuri, can do anything and everything for money and are the potential sharks or swindlers.

The dominant feature of Indian life could be conspicuously noticed in the large cities of the country like Delhi, Calcutta, Bombay and Madras. These large cities in Chaudhuri's opinion exhibit the main ingredients of Indian character in a major key, whereas the minor cities or towns or villages do the same in a minor key. The difference between the Indian metropolis and the Indian village is one of degree rather than of kind. The great cities exhibit certain features and qualities of Indian character, which create an atmosphere of Indianness in all the fields of life. A great city is said to be a great desert where the individuality is lost in the mass life and the generalities of life look more conspicuous than the idiosyncrasies. Since there is uniformity among the great cities of India, the description or analysis of one city can as well represent that of other cities also. Chaudhuri, who is exigently compelled to stay in Delhi for a large part of his life, has obviously chosen to analyze the archetypal megalopolis of India. The first thing that strikes Chaudhuri's attention is the planning of the city of Delhi. In fact as noticed by him, there is no organization at all in the capital city, Delhi, which ought to be exemplary to other cities of India, is ironically enough, the most ill-organized city in the country. Chaudhuri rightly says that it is organized—if at all it is organized—only biologically and is like a go-getting machine. "...so far as Delhi is organized, it is so mechanically and biologically. It is a gigantic go-getting machine, as such it has the terrifying complexity of a modern computer with its logic elements, transistors, thermometers, capacitors, resisters and so on" (20-21). Obviously, Chaudhuri has implicitly shown the lack of artistry in the structure of Delhi. Even the American professor, who is interviewed by Chaudhuri, confesses his own puzzle about the city. Says he, "...I saw something today which I cannot understand. It was all disorganization and confusion and squalor" (21). The drabness and the absence of sophistication of Delhi are aptly described by Chaudhuri, who says that "...Delhi...was a crude descendant of Damascus, Baghdad or even the new Babylon of Nebuchadnezzar, through Pataliputra Ujjayini and Kanyakubja and of course, Muslim Delhi" (23).

After pointing out the structure of the city of Delhi, Chaudhuri captures the essential spirit and nature of the city. Delhi enjoys a special importance in the life of India on account of the role it plays in the lives of the Indians in different fields of life. Delhi, for example, is an industrial city with all the paraphernalia and is on par with other industrial cities like Bombay, Calcutta or Madras. But what distinguishes it from other cities is its political importance. Chaudhuri has highlighted two features of Delhi, which are of extraordinary importance. The bureaucratic government and the centralization of all the political administration are the striking features of the city of Delhi. It is this specialty that contradistinguishes it from the other great cities of India. Delhi, therefore, can be compared to the brain of the body of India. These two aspects are the manifestation of the great monster. Chaudhuri, as usual, employs the satirical language in describing this phenomenon. "The second force behind the growth of Delhi is a formidable Estatism, which might be called the advent of the Leviathan in this country—Ah! An incompetent Leviathan, not the Hobbsian. Socialism is only a euphemism for it or rather a cloak" (25). Then he points out the most striking features of these aspects of Delhi. The bureaucratic set up of India, of which Delhi is the seat, is represented by the clerical job for which every educated Indian generally hankers. Thus, the creation of clerical jobs was part of the expansion of the class interest of the urban land and moneyless middle-class. The worst feature of this bureaucratic system is the extraordinary and artificial importance given to the man whoever does the basic work and the consequent delay, check and dilution of the process of work. This principle holds water in all the bureaucratic units of Indian life. Chaudhuri, therefore, points out the conspicuous feature of this set up symbolized by the top-level administration of Delhi, "The most significant expansion has taken place at the top, in the more highly paid ranks. As a result for every clerk who does some original work there are about five stages of supervision by highly paid superiors. This also was bound to happen in the interest of the politicians. Most of them were members of the middle class who failed to get government jobs, and therefore, so far as worldly status is concerned, they regarded themselves as men who had been unfairly deprived of their legitimate inheritance. For this reason, after getting power, they do not show any disinclination to live wholly on the public revenues" (26). Thus, clericalism happens to be the keynote of the Indian administration as well as a means of livelihood for the middle-class people. Centralization, which is the second major aspect of Delhi, is again the conspicuous feature of Indian political administration. Chaudhuri's attribution of centralization to the four causes is a clear evidence of his historical sense and insight into the Indian psychology. The centralization is caused by (1) the unwillingness of the Indian to delegate power to the others; (2) the distrust by the central government of the provincial governments; (3) need for the formulation of a foreign policy paving the way for foreign help; and (4) the hang-over of the pan-Indian feeling. Chaudhuri depicts the Indian political behaviour in describing the capital city of Delhi. One can obviously see a combination of satire and description in his writing.

After providing a description of political aspects of Delhi, Chaudhuri proceeds to offer a visual picture of the great city, which testifies to his minute observation and keen perception. Like a philosopher he points out the contradictory nature of Delhi when he says that it is metropolitan as well as provincial. One can see the resident aliens, who come to India from foreign countries for political and non-political visits, as well as the provincials like Tamilians, Maharashtrians, Bengalis or Punjabis, who "never submerge their provincial identity in a pan-Indian identity, and very largely confine their social life to fellow-provincials" (37). Obviously, Chaudhuri's keen observation confirms the view that Delhi, like London, is a city of contradictions. Another peculiarity of this great city according to him is the pervading commercial and feminine atmosphere. "Due to this routine, the external impression of human life in Delhi is, in the first instance, all bazaar, and next all feminine. It is not the man-about-town but the woman-about-town, who sets the tone of urban life, and gives to it its movement, colour, and charm" (32). Another contradiction of Delhi, as pointed out by Chaudhuri, is the simultaneous presence of Islamic culture and superficial westernization. "Delhi is of the Islamic Middle East with a modern veneer. It is really Cairo of Tulunid, Mameluke, or Fatimid times, and Baghdad of Abbasid times, disguised by a superficial westernization" (33). Similarly, the splendour of Delhi is contrasted by the 'expanse of drabness'. Chaudhuri's description of Delhi provides us with an archetypal picture of a great city, which is, like life itself, full of contradictions of diverse types. His portrait of Delhi throws light as much about the life at Delhi as about the social and political behaviour of Indians.

He then turns his attention from Delhi to the social life in India. His observations again show his insight into human nature, his wide leading and his awareness of social psychology of Indians. "The Hindu Society," according to him, "is basically genetic in its outlook, and looks upon social life only as an extension of the family, clan or tribe. It is very difficult for us to get out of this mould of social life, which is really tribalism and to acquire genuinely social behaviour" (41). None who is acquainted with the Indian society can deny the truth of Chaudhuri's observation. He illustrates it by pointing out how the Indians in the streets address one another as *bhai,* or *bahn* or *baba.*

Marriages, illnesses and death anniversaries are very important occasions of the Indian social life. Far from being the celebrations of the events concerned, these occasions are turned by Indians, rather farcically, into those of pomp and show and prestige and what not. Chaudhuri therefore does not generally attend the wedding of his friends or relatives. "Rather than go through that experience I prefer to be a Diogenes" (44). Wedding ceremonies in India are occasions for showing off one's wealth and stature. Therefore, wedding invitations are sent even to strangers who happen to be big officers. Sometimes weddings serve as occasions for intimidating bride's or the bridegroom's side. Nowadays this habit has been "extended into a general attempt at intimidating neighbours, relations, and clients into a proper respect or fear of the host's wealth and positions" (46). Some of the wedding invitations contain special sentences like "some central Ministers are expected to attend," and the host's bureaucratic servility to his superiors and his arrogance towards his inferiors are comic and irritating simultaneously. Like marriages death anniversaries also are turned into occasions of pomp and show. Far from making people unhappy, deaths in some families act as good riddance and add to the happiness of the surviving members like sons, and daughters-in-law, etc. Sometimes the surviving relatives are very insensitive to the death of a person. Chaudhuri offers an instance of how the people behave comically and practically even at the funeral ceremony at the burning *ghats* at Delhi. Again, deaths have a serious impact on the sexual life of the surviving members, who are likely to indulge in sex in order to forget their sorrow of having lost somebody. Likewise illnesses are important events in Indian life in that whenever a person in a family is taken ill, it becomes mandatory on the part of the relatives and friends to go and see, and console and enhearten him and the members of his family. But even this is turned by Indians into a farce. "It is the traditional Indian habit of making illness, and more especially a serious illness, as frivolous a social gathering as a cocktail party in New Delhi" (52). The visitors, who flock to the house of illness, are quite likely to forget the sick man and indulge in their gossip and noise. This is how Mr. Chaudhuri shows the farcicality of the main events of Indian social life, which testifies, to his keen observation and sharp thinking. He is able to support his general observations of life with the examples of his own personal experiences.

Chaudhuri switches his attention on to the social behaviour of Indians. The first feature of the Indian behaviour is the ridiculous acceptance of his inferiority, which paradoxically enough, masquerades as superiority complex. Chaudhuri is never tired of repeating the fact that the Indian is notorious for his lack of perception, which is the result of the lack of social education. "The Hindu society never learned to value man as man, as an individual, as a personality, without reference to his worldly status" (59). It is basically because of this exaggerated importance attached to the economic status of man, that the Hindus cannot understand the total behaviour of man. Even their description of a man's character is so simple and elementary. Their poverty of perception could be seen in their description of a man's character in a word or two. "What I cannot explain about my people is their extraordinary insensitiveness to points of character. 'He is a good or a bad man' is the final summing up of a man's character with us, and I have hardly been able to get any idea of another man's personality from the talk I hear at secondhand about him" (59).

The economic poverty or wealth of the Indians plays a very significant role in deciding their behaviour. Whereas poverty makes them cherish the ideas of class-hatred, wealth instigates them to show it off on all the possible occasions such as large parties. This leads Mr. Chaudhuri to comment upon their behaviour. According to him, the Indians are not properly educated in the social behaviour. They can be very sociable in streets and bazaars but not in close gatherings as they lack the capacity for intelligent conversation. In India, there are, roughly speaking, two approaches to talking. According to one, they believe in the notion that the stature of a man consists in his being a taciturn. It may even be said that taciturnity is proportionate to his dignity. "To withhold *Kathamrita* or nectar of speech is recognized as a means of asserting one's importance" (63). By contrast, talking and talking incessantly is the mark of the undignified people. The Indian attitude towards talking may be said to be quite utilitarian, in that it is employed either for out and out pornographic purpose or for the profitarian purpose or for that of self-aggrandizement. The

Indians are generally very fond of talking smut, which provides a compensation for their sex-starvation. "In them, perhaps the most innocent and friendly thing is the ladling out of smut, which becomes more salacious among the 'England-returned' ones, who have been able to shed either their 'ingenuous shame' or Hindu prudery through their stay abroad" (63). Another typicality of the Indian indulgence in smut is that more often than not it is directed against the absent ones, and is therefore eloquent of the talker's malice. Otherwise talking is employed only for utilitarian purposes, like moneymaking, matchmaking, and disputations among pundits, homilies from holy men and altercations between doctrinaires or competitions. All these habits go to prove Mr. Chaudhuri's conclusion that the Indian social behaviour is marked by gregariousness rather than by genuine sociability.

Chaudhuri, then, jumps from the wider entity, i.e. society to the one of the most important components of that entity, i.e. woman. He has chosen to comment upon woman as she happens to form one half of the totality of life as much in India as anywhere else. But woman has been an object of special interest and concern in India because of the ambivalent approach of men towards her, which is again caused by the rigid puritanical background. In spite of the modern introduction of democracy into the Indian society, Mr. Chaudhuri is forced to say that "there is hardly any intercommunication between the sexes" (69). He is right when he points out the reverse method of improvement of relation between men and women in India. As it is, there is no social mingling between the two sexes, and the Indian authorities have wrongly taken a decision to solve the problem by putting the cart before the horse, i.e. by introducing co-education before paving the way for social mingling. This observation obviously holds a mirror to Mr. Chaudhuri's sociological imagination. There is indeed, no doubt that the Indians suffer from "an acute sex-consciousness" (70), which is easily attributable to their puritanical upbringing and atmosphere. That is why there is bound to be a perpetual tension between their natural instincts and their puritanical code of behaviour. Mr. Chaudhuri, therefore, remarks, "As things stand, any kind of natural and friendly intercourse between men and women has been made very difficult, if not impossible. The accepted code of conduct is to keep mum about women in public and talk smut in private" (71). Obviously talking smut in privacy is the natural result of the public restriction and disapproval of the exchange of views and feelings between men and women. It is because of the unusual social restriction about sex, that the Indians become sex-obsessed and therefore begin to read *Kamasutra* repeatedly. Mr. Chaudhuri's historical sense enables him to clarify the fact that *Kamasutra* was originally meant for the courtesans of India, but it is wrongly read by one and all in the modern days. In spite of the sexual taboos in India, paradoxically enough, sexual promiscuity could be seen on a large scale there. Mr. Chaudhuri offers one of his own experiences in Delhi office where a pretty-girl-steno-typist was the object of rivalry between his male colleagues. The popularity of the concepts like 'boyfriend', 'girlfriend', 'call girl' and 'dating', etc. is the sign of the promiscuity concealed or otherwise. Mr. Chaudhuri's keen observation cannot be rejected by anyone who has an awareness of the Indian society. He points out the shift of promiscuity from one area to the other. "What has really happened is that the area of the irregularity shifted. Thus, instead of being confined to family relationship, it has spilled out into social relationships, so that the liaisons are now with the friend's wife instead of being with the sister-in-law. In other words, it is a change in the veneer" (77). The puritanical restriction, which is responsible for the secret solutions sought for by men and women, should, according to Chaudhuri, be relaxed a little so that social mingling might be made possible. "We have driven the only alternative to arranged marriages of the traditional type, which is love-making, into the streets and parks, and made lovers literally street walkers. I would have unrestricted meeting between men and women for this purpose even at the risk of having some adultery" (78). Chaudhuri's observation about the Indian women is quite in keeping with his observation about the Indian life in general. Women's beauty, according to him, is not generally attended by the proportionate mental or spiritual beauty. There can, of course, be exceptions to this, but the general rule is quite unmistakable. The appearance of a woman in India can be quite deceptive and may be quite contrary to her inner nature. Chaudhuri offers a personal example. Once he saw an elegant woman clad in sepia and gold sari walking in a garden of Delhi and naturally thought her to be quite graceful and aesthetic minded as she carried a bunch of flowers with her. But as he went ahead for a while, he saw her stealing the flowers from a tree in the roadside compound. He was rather puzzled to see her chased by the shaggy mongrel and running away giggling. Chaudhuri has obviously shown the contradiction in that lady between her sweet appearance and her ugly behaviour. It is this dichotomy in character that is described by him as 'dimorphism'.

Chaudhuri's discussion of the joint family system of India is full of subtle observation and incisive remarks. "At its best the joint family is co-operative society based on the blood tie and a smaller and more closely knit replica of the village community" (100). The joint family system produces a particular type of behaviour in it. In fact, it is a mini world in itself. Family quarrels caused by women folk are quite common in it. The women, who take the initiative in the querulous adventures, seek the help of their husband-dogs. Most often it is the pent-up emotion caused by the cumulative quarrels that eventually creates divisions in the family. One of the aberrations of the Hindu society is the peculiar relation between the mother-in-law and the daughter-in-law. In fact, a wild kind of a law of vindictiveness is always operative in the Indian family where the daughter-in-law is ill-treated by the mother-in-law in the first half of their life and the mother-in-law is ill-treated by the daughter-in-law in the latter part of their life. Thus both of them have to undergo the two stages of serving and reigning in the reverse order. Chaudhuri's sociological imagination helps him to remark that the joint family has a tendency to erode and undermine the spirit of adventure and self-help in its members. The relationship between the different members of the joint family is governed by factors like sex status and age. For example, a son in the family will be more communicative with his wife and mother than with his brother's wife or his father or with the children. Chaudhuri's subtle observation shows that there is generally more intercommunication between women than between men. The mothers discuss anything and everything before their daughters but the fathers do not do so before their sons. One more peculiarity of the Indian joint family is that the grandchildren are generally closer with the grandparents than with the parents. Mr. Chaudhuri then discusses the problems and conditions of the working women in India. These women are rather forced by the circumstances to earn their livelihood and keep themselves and the members of their family away from the wolf. Sometimes their salary helps them to save some amount cumulatively until it grows big enough to be an attractive dowry for the highly-stationed grooms. Thus, employment of woman seems to be a stop-gap arrangement. Mr. Chaudhuri describes the condition of the working girl and the change of the locale very convincingly. "In my young days, when a girl was withdrawn from school or college in anticipation of marriage, we used to say that she was in the waiting room. At present a far larger number of girls are to be seen in the same waiting room, but it is now an office, and not the home. A bigger difference is that for many, the train does not arrive at all; formerly, at the worst, it was unpunctual" (138). Thus the feminine resort to a job is ultimately connected with the problem of marriage. India which is undergoing a transition from traditional to modern way of life, the educated woman who is neither purely traditional nor purely emancipated will have to lead a life of forced spinsterhood or to seek surreptitious satisfaction without losing her dignity in the society. Most of the time she will be waiting for something great to happen in her path of husband-hunting. Thus, late marriage of girls is invariably encouraged by the matrimonial Micawberism. Another reason for girls' attraction for jobs is the economic independence, which they enjoy, and the consequent love and obligation of the members of her family who depend upon her earning. "In a living society even the relatives of a girl do not feel embarrassed to be under financial obligation to her lover" (150). The married working women are more independent and arrogant than the jobless housewives. Mr. Chaudhuri shows how it is a Western imitation. "...the Indian phenomenon is really derivative. Its practical emergence is due substantially to the impact of Western influences, and its apologia is wholly imported. To cut the matter short, as in political ideas, economic organization, literature and art, or fashion, here too we are faced with a case of imitation, the working woman being only the economic counterpart of the woman in jeans" (146). Again the kinds of jobs preferred by the modern women are only desk-jobs and not the heavy ones like agricultural or industrial or military ones. Mr. Chaudhuri points out the three main interests of the married working woman in a priority order. "In the emotional life of our womenfolk three loves—for husband, for child, for saris—constitute a harmonic triad, in which the last love is the treble, the second middle register, and the first the bass note" (153). Whereas love of money is the characteristic quality of the working girl, love of clothes happens to be the dominant feature of the married working woman.

The marriage in Hindu society is attended by certain peculiar characteristics. It has typical antecedents and consequences in Hindu society. Whereas in ancient India marriage was basically meant for the procreation of children, in modern India it has come to mean a "means of enjoying the pleasure of sexual intercourse without the attendant risk of conception" (158). Mr. Chaudhuri has obviously shown how procreation, the primary goal of ancient marriage has become the secondary one in modern matrimonial world. This phenomenon shows the extra importance given to the sexual aspect of marriage. Mr. Chaudhuri says that the very origin of matrimonial attraction is sexual in nature. He uses his typical aesthetic vocabulary to describe this process. Love, which eventually paves the way for marriage, has a "geometrical basis" (159). Since more often than not love begins on the visual level, the sight of the feminine body plays a very important role in the amorous process. "The geometry of linear curves and of spheroids is, in a manner of speaking interwoven with love" (160). Since falling in love is caused and intensified by the curvilinearity of the pattern of the feminine body the inward beauty or grace or sublimity transcending the physical attractiveness are not at all cared for in India. Thus, love is rooted in the visualness of beauty and physicalness of attraction. It is this superficial attraction that sets a number of young men to daydreaming. Thus, physical or sexual attraction plays a very important role in love from the boys or girls' point of view. But when the same has to be referred to the family for sanction the economic consideration also creeps in. Mr. Chaudhuri rightly remarks, "The marriages are sordid scrambles for money" (170). In the matrimonial bargain, the bride's father pays an undue attention to the economic status of the groom's family and never cares for the groom's mental or moral achievements. Mr. Chaudhuri, therefore, says "In my young days some fathers and mothers talked about the character or talents of the young men, nowadays nobody pays any attention to these things" (171).

Having discussed the antecedents of marriage, Mr. Chaudhuri goes to analyze the consequences of marriage as seen in the routine life of the couple. Since most of the marriages are made possible only on account of mutual physical attraction, they are sure to crumble as the foundation of physical attraction wears into nothingness. Marriage at this stage remains only as a technical one, which is marked by the absence of true vitality. The husband and the wife cease to be so and begin to take a neighbourly interest in each other. Mr. Chaudhuri's presentation of this phenomenon is so clear that it needs no addition. "After the physical attraction has worn off most husbands and wives feel only a neighbourly interest in each other and sometimes also neighbourly animosity and hatred.... As married life advances, it ceases not only to be a marriage of true minds, but even of bodies. In many families the physical revulsion of old husbands and wives from one another shows itself painfully" (172). Another important feature of Indian society is the secretiveness of lust. The only difference is that whereas some people begin with it, some others end with it. The sex-starved young men and women and the sexually dissatisfied married couple will be always trying to have underground means of satisfaction without tarnishing their image in society. Mr. Chaudhuri rightly remarks that "In Hindu society, so long as appearances are saved, nothing is wrong" (177). In some aristocratic or snobbish families the couple will be practising prostitution with mutual connivance or understanding. That is why the slogans like, "Bourgeois marriage is legalized prostitution" written by the young-men on the walls of women's college are more a dream than a satire.

Mr. Chaudhuri's views, again, on the Indian unitary family are very insightful. He says that the dominant note of Indian family is staticity, which discourages all kinds of liveliness. "Most Indian homes are stagnant, stuffy, or even stifling in their psychological staticity and for this reason if a member of the family happens to possess a lively spirit he is driven out from the home to show it in places, which cannot be civilized, in its expression. The wet blanket is thrown about so relentlessly at home that few persons treat it as anything but a lair to sleep or an eating house, which supplies such bad food that good living has become identified with wish frequenting meretricious restaurants, where cuisine is never looked upon as the first attraction" (185). The absence of interests and boredom are the two important features of the Indian family. Sometimes the interests of the young men and women are curbed by the parents. "I have always been dismayed by the indifference to hobbies shown by my countrymen. Actually, many parents consider them to be moral delinquency in their children, and never allow them to have them when the children are obedient" (186). This kind of suppression of the interests of the young men and women is responsible for the cumulative frustration, which asserts itself at the earliest opportunity. "The revolt of the youth in India begins with the suppression of their interest in early childhood" (187). The things of the mind like literature, art, music, drama, etc. are not generally encouraged by the parents, who think that everything except an earning of livelihood is redundant and even a waste. Many times Indian family life involves soulless living together without a renewal of love and faith in the members. Thus, a sensitive man is likely to be terribly lonely in spite of being surrounded by his kith and kin. Mr. Chaudhuri offers a conjugal instance to illustrate the problem of maintenance of the family. "To send off a wife to her father's house, as it is customary to do in Hindu society, may be like sending a car for periodic overhaul to a garage, but to live with her calls for a different kind of attention, which, to continue the analogy of the car is like providing cooling and lubrication all the time the engine is running. Try to run it without these and it will not be long before it disintegrates" (192). The Indians have a remarkable talent for being unhappy and making others unhappy. Mr. Chaudhuri suggests that it is better to have a divorce than to endure constant nagging and bickering. He therefore says, "I would rather die of family cholera, which is divorce, than have its dyspepsia, which is bickering" (193).

The essay *To Live or Not to Live* is discursive, analytical, explicatory and elaborate in its style and helps the leader to understand the man-woman relationship from a liberal point of view. The clarity of views expressed in this essay is remarkable and speaks of Chaudhuri's sharp intelligence and stunning scholarship behind it.

Note

1. Nirad C. Chaudhuri. *To Live or Not to Live*, Delhi: Hind Pocket Books, 1970. (All the references to the text are from this edition.)

Chapter 6

The Intellectual in India: A Critique

Nirad C. Chaudhuri has put forth his ideas very frankly about the nature of the Indian intellectuals, their limitations and achievements etc.[1] Within the limited space of a monograph Mr. Chaudhuri has attempted to present an overall picture of the intellectual life of Indians in its historical and contemporary context. As usual Mr. Chaudhuri expresses his own distinct views about this issue, which are not mere imitation of others' ones. His views on this problem are strongly supported by his own knowledge of history of India in particular and of the world in general. Again his views are marked by an extraordinary freedom from inhibition and chauvinism that is typical of his personality. He has divided the monograph into seven chapters. Tracing the intellectual traditions in India at the beginning of the twentieth century, Mr. Chaudhuri points out the absence of purely intellectual pursuit in the country. He shows how the Hindus' concept of intellectual life consisted merely in the personal pursuit of philosophical or *Vedantic* knowledge which had no direct bearing on the day-to-day life. Thus knowledge, according to Mr. Chaudhuri, was inextricably connected with morality. Again knowledge, be it medical or philosophical, was presented in the hard integument of Sanskrit, which was not to be uncovered easily by the layman. Then Chaudhuri points out how the intellectual pursuit of the Hindu was never basically rationalistic, but more often than not supra-rational and at times sub-rational also. Thus the Hindu pursuit of knowledge consisted either in the supra-rational thinking or in textual explications, but never in purely rationalistic analysis. This approach, in Mr. Chaudhuri's opinion, is represented by Iswara Chandra Vidyasagar and Dayananda Saraswati both of whom continued their basically traditional intellectual movements in spite of their being influenced by the Western humanitarianism. They went back to the *Vedic* texts for fresh interpretations and empirical application of theoretical principles. Dayananda Saraswati's monotheistic philosophy and his establishment of the Arya Samaj are evidencing enough of traditional and moralistic approach.

The Muslim approach is not different from the Indian in its traditional and moralistic attitude to knowledge. Mr. Chaudhuri shows rightly how the Muslims, in spite of their Westernization and desire for a progressive ideology remained basically traditional and wanted a Muslim way of life. As compared with the Hindus, the Muslims were more rigid than the Hindus were. "In fact the perpetuation of the Islamic way of life was their aim, although they wanted it to become progressive, that is to say receptive of Western influence in certain matters" (6). Some of the very important Muslims like Sir Syed Ahmad Khan, Nawab Abdul Latif, Nawab Ali Ali, Sayed Amir Ali, Mohammed Ali Jinnah, and Iqbal are the embodiments of the Islamic traditionalism in India.

The third and modern tradition at the beginning of twentieth century in India is of the westernized Hindus. "It owed nothing at all to the older Hindu or Muslim traditions, and was one of the very rare instance to be found in history, of the wholesale transplantation of the modes of thinking evolved by one culture-complex to a society belonging to and inheriting quite a different one" (8). The Westernization of the Hindus was, of course, caused and expedited by the British rule in India. If the Hindus were influenced by the Western civilization the question would arise as to why they did not adopt the scientific outlook. Mr. Chaudhuri's sharp intelligence and subtle observation enable him to account for the problem. He rightly points out that "The missionaries did much more towards the spreading of European ideas, because they were interested in establishing Christianity, but they had no interest in preaching European rationalism" (9). The Hindus who were influenced by the European ideologies were more than willing to neglect or even reject the traditional Hindu values. It is because of this modernization which is synonymous with Westernization that there arose a great gap and alienation between the traditional pundits and the modern scholars. Raja Rammohun Roy is the supreme example of this spirit. In spite of his traditional background, "he was Western in outlook, and he adopted utilitarianism as his political and social philosophy" (10). As part of the modernization of the Hindu life, the acquisition of and the mastery over the English language became essential. This principle was operative in the field of letters also. "Prose was created for the first time in all the literary languages, which had so far embodied all their creation in poetry. Genres of European literature—fiction, short-story and novel, essays, literary criticism—were all introduced and acclimatized, and its readers gradually lost all taste for writings of the traditional type" (11). One of the striking features of the third phase of the Indian intellectualism is the entrance of politics into it. Thus, Mr. Chaudhuri points out how the three phases of Indian intellectuals were dominated by religion, (Western) literature and politics respectively.

The Indian renaissance, according to Mr. Chaudhuri is influenced by two phenomena: (1) the alien rule and (2) the impact of Western ideas and culture. This renaissance gave a new awareness to the Indians about their peculiar situation and consequently Indians began to ask new questions about their national self-respect and their adaptation to the Western culture, etc. Mr. Chaudhuri is quite objective and frank when he says that these Indians had been attracted towards the Western schools of thought because the old Hindu thought had come to be devoid of any creativity. Chaudhuri therefore says that the Indians began to cultivate the European ideologies like Liberalism and Conservatism. But the paradox of the Indian behaviour is soon pointed out when Chaudhuri shows the lack of clear difference between these ideologies. He shows how the most liberal Indian can be or turn out to be a conservative at heart or at critical moments of his life. Chaudhuri says, "The opposition between the Liberals and the Conservatives was much more over the range of innovation and the pace at which this was to be brought about, than over fundamentals. No Hindu conservative opposed the introduction of monotheism or disputed its superiority to image worship, he even advocated the adoption of Western science and some forms of knowledge relating to the external world, and he was for education in institutions of the Western type" (17). Mr. Chaudhuri points out another dominant obsession of the Indians in a very perceptive fashion. He shows how the Indians are always preoccupied with the 'mind' or 'psychological approach'. That is the reason why the Indians can never think of an Industrial Revolution, but on the contrary, believe in the "psychological approach to political question" (19). Mr. Chaudhuri cites Raja Rammohun Roy and Tagore as embodiments of this approach and shows how 'personality' and 'character' became ends in themselves. Since religion was the major preoccupation of the nineteenth-century Hindu, the leaders like Roy attributed a number of Indian social evils to the superstitions of Hindu religion and fought against them. The effect of this kind of thinking on the part of Indian reformers, according to Mr. Chaudhuri, was a gradual rejection of polytheism and acceptance of monotheism.

Next, Chaudhuri shows how the 'literary culture' came to have an important place in the Indian life. The 'cultured man' and the 'educated man' became synonymous phrases. The education of an Indian consisted in the imitation of the social, political and economic ideas of the Western world. The Western ideologies like Liberalism and Humanitarianism became very popular in India. The Indian thinkers like R.C. Dutt and Dadabhai Naoroji began to discuss the ideas of exploitation and industrialization, etc. Mr. Chaudhuri rightly deplores the fact that "even the negative ideology of Indian nationalism was imitative" (24). He further shows how the Indians borrowed their idea of Aryan superiority from the European Orientalists, and their idea of Dravidian ancestry from the European historians of India. Thus in all these details of the Indian literary culture the Indians show a strong tendency towards imitation rather than original thinking.

Another paradox of Indian society, according to Chaudhuri, is the fact that the minority of intellectuals in India forms part of the ruling class, whereas the uneducated masses "have been the eternal *Sudras*, and if they continue in this state, they will not play a significant part in any future conflict of cultures in India" (28). The 'majority of the dominant minority are to be found in the liberal professions and the higher ranks of civil service. Mr. Chaudhuri's keen observation enables him to remark that the women of India remained outside the current of the intellectual life. "As a rule, even in families whose men folk were actively carrying on the new intellectual activities the women led a traditional life" (30). After showing the disharmony between the middle class and the intelligentsia, Mr. Chaudhuri points out the qualitative limitations of the latter in a very frank manner. He says that most of the Indian intellectuals are interested in the so-called pursuit of knowledge for utilitarian reasons like earning a livelihood or wealth or power. Some of them do so for snobbish purposes. Mr. Chaudhuri shows how the social aspirants want to be seen carrying Darwin's *The Origin of Species* or Bergson's Creative *Evolution* with them. Even the great scientists of India cannot do without superstitious rites. Says Chaudhuri, "Even a professor of physics would not think that it was inconsistent with his vocation to wear an amulet. Highly Westernized barristers would utter spells before the image of Ganesa, the God of worldly success, and burn incense before it every morning so that his professional work might be successful" (32). Another feature that is associated with the Indian intellectuals, according to Chaudhuri, is the feeling of overstrain, because the intellectual activities are historically speaking, only of recent origin. The effects of this overstrain are to be seen in three ways: One, a cessation of all creative intellectual effort after a certain stage. Even the brilliant scholars give up their work as soon as they attain a secure position in their jobs. "Among Indian professors there are very few who produce new works after their first research thesis" (33). Two, the Indian intellectuals who have received Western education either at home or abroad maintain double standards. They, for example, apply very rigorous standards of analysis to Western works of history, philosophy or literature, etc. but begin to be chauvinistic and hortative in the case of Indian counterparts. Three, they revert to the traditional Hinduism. "There is a saying that to scratch the Russian is to find the Tarter, it could also be said that to scratch an elderly Indian intellectual was to discover the Hindu" (33).

The new type of intellectual work in India brought certain changes in the working conditions of people. Certain professions like law, medicine and teaching became more remunerative than they were in the past in India, although it must be remembered, they were not as remunerative as in the West. Another bane of the Indian education is frankly pointed out by Mr. Chaudhuri when he says that the intellectual height of a man in India is always measured in terms of the class or grade that he secures in the examination rather than the original work that he produces subsequently. The teacher never feels the necessity to do original writing and publication. Teaching in India is synonymous with transferring of established knowledge from books to students without any addition to it. Whatever may be the qualitative limitation of educated class in India, there is no doubt that it has contributed to the cultural stratification of India and has become one of so many other minorities.

Having given a broad outline of the Indian intellectual phenomenon, Mr. Chaudhuri examines the various reasons for this decay and attributes them to the 'general stagnancy'. "The general mood in India over the state of education is one of deep gloom" (39). Mr. Chaudhuri is absolutely right when he says that there is no outstanding intellectual in India below the age of fifty or sixty and that no original interpretation of Indian history or other aspects of India is offered in spite of the artificial spate of theses in the universities. One of the striking features of the Indian scholarship is its imitativeness. It is really a matter of paradox that the Indians always try in vain to adopt the Western ideas and make a mess of knowledge. But this phenomenon does not make Mr. Chaudhuri blind to the remarkable achievement of Indians in the field of mathematics and physics.

Another difference between the Western intellectual and the Indian pointed out by Mr. Chaudhuri shows his historical sense, subtle observation and psychological knowledge. He says that whereas the Western intellectual works against a tradition of scholarship started from the days of Charlemagne and the Carlovingian renaissance, the Indian intellectual works in a relative vacuum and his achievements are rather precocious and come to an early end. Mr. Chaudhuri observes rightly, "...such of them as took to the new activities showed an amazing precocity, but precocity is a risky thing, because it often brings untimely decay in its train in personal as well as national development. The Indian intellectuals create what might be called a mental *tour de force,* an achievement comparable to those of the Indian magicians who plant a mango tree and make it grow fruit before the spectators. Such a growth brings in exhaustion and contributes to rapid decay" (43). After making this historical observation Mr. Chaudhuri examines the details of the Indian intellectual phenomenon. The Indian intellectuals are unable to do any sustained work because of a variety of reasons. For example, the food that the Indian middle-class intellectuals take is entirely unsuited to give then the vigour that is required for hard work. Then, they have no privacy at home because of the overcrowded nature of their joint family. Since they are compelled by family responsibility and poverty to earn money all the time, they have no rest at all. Likewise he finds no stimulating atmosphere in the universities also. Thus, Mr. Chaudhuri relates the intellectual poverty of Indians to their economic poverty. "Thus the intellectual insolvency and the economic insolvency of the middle class have been running along parallel course during the last thirty years, each keeping pace with the other and helping each other" (46).

In spite of the little intellectual work that is going on in India because of the Western impact, there is no growth of the rationalistic intellectualism in India because Mr. Chaudhuri rightly says, "It is the authoritarian and intuitionist leanings of the Hindu mind which makes it unintellectual and sometimes positively anti-intellectual" (46). The Hindu mind follows either sub-rational or supra-rational method in the understanding of the truth of life. That is the reason why the seeking of knowledge is always connected with a sense of secrecy, esoterism, grotesqueness, authoritarianism and intuitionism represented in the Hindu's knowledge of the *Veda*. The common man in India always preferred a man of occult powers to a man well versed in the *Veda*. Such intuitionist and occultist tendencies of the

Hindu mind naturally curbed the exercise of objective and pure kind of rationalism.

Even the influence of the Western science on the Hindu knowledge is confined only to the field of technology. Far from adapting the scientific spirit, the Hindus pursue only the Western technology and the popular culture of the West in the form of Western recreations like cinema, and sport. The influence of films has been very adverse on the Indian life. Mr. Chaudhuri, therefore, says that "On the whole, the cinema, both through foreign and Indian films, has been the greatest instrument of the degradation of every kind of cultural activity in this country" (51). Likewise, the pre-Gandhian and the Gandhian nationalisms did much to undermine the intellectual approach. Whereas the pre-Gandhian nationalism made the intellectuals partisan in spirit, the Gandhian nationalism lowered the intellectual life of Indians by leading them back to the naive intuitionism.

In the next chapter, Mr. Chaudhuri shows with facts and figures, how it is not possible for an intellectual to earn his livelihood purely on his intellectual achievements, and how this problem becomes more acute in an 'anti-intellectual' country like India. He points out how the bureaucracy or the film industry positively harms the intellectual side of a man's personality. Finally, he shows that in spite of the anti-intellectual atmosphere in India one can pursue his intellectual ideals and one of the best examples of this possibility is Mr. Chaudhuri himself who started his publication at the age of 54 or so.

Mr. Chaudhuri points out the stagnant atmosphere of the Indian intellectual world. The Indian universities, which are supposed to provide the highest kind of intellectual training or orientation, have miserably failed in the task. "They are intellectually stagnant. The Indian academic world is laden with a deep somnolence without the justification of deep positions: it is mental vacuum, and not vintage port, which produces the abstracted air on the faces of the professors" (64). The same kind of stagnancy and lifelessness is to be seen in the Indian journalism. Bureaucracy, of course, worsens the situation. All relationship between the employer and the employee is marked by the monster of malevolence manifesting itself in envy and authoritarianism, which mar the spirit of free thinking in people, especially in the young intellectuals. Mr. Chaudhuri offers his own official life in the Delhi AIR as an example of suffering the consequences of envy and revenge by his colleagues and superiors. Another hindrance in the life of the Indian intellectual is the peculiar nature of his wife. According to Mr. Chaudhuri, there are two kinds of wives in India: one, the harpy, "who looks upon any activity in the husband other than earning money and ever more money as a sin against marriage vow" (71); two, the empty-headed and frivolous gad-about "who regards quiet home-life and quiet work as the same sin" (71). The Indian intellectual has to be a Prometheus if at all he has to achieve anything in his life in spite of his wife.

In the next chapter Mr. Chaudhuri offers certain suggestions to the young Indians, who aspire to write in English. He asks them not to have 'an egregious snobbery or xenolatry,' but try to be native both in theme and in style. He points out how the foreign publishers are not sure of the sales of books on India even in India. Mr. Chaudhuri enheartens the Indian writer to continue his writing and to have a lot of patience. He asks the writer to find a publisher suitable to the theme of his book. He suggests that young Indian writers should try to write in natural English and not affect the artificial one. He warns that "... the self-conscious, showy, and ultra-fashionable English which many young writers of English in India affect will fall completely flat" (78). The style of the book should express the personality behind it. This is possible, according to Chaudhuri, only when the writer has achieved a technical mastery over the English language including the natural rhythms of the language. To be able to attract the attention of the Western readers, the Indian must write not only with competence but also with distinction and should have sufficient sincerity in his accomplishment.

Note

1. Nirad C. Chaudhuri, *The Intellectual in India*. New Delhi: Associated Publishing House, 1967. (All the references to the text are from this edition.)

Chapter 7

Scholar Extraordinary[1]: An Epical Biography of Max Muller

Biography is an important genre, which tries to depict the life of an important or interesting person thereby providing some material to help the reader understand the person better. It is said to be "An account of the life of a person. The modern biography, which is based on careful research and which is relatively dispassionate in attitude, is a comparatively recent form. Classical and medieval biographers were generally written to illustrate a thesis. In the typical saint's life, for example, the subject was reduced to an illustration of the qualities of a Christian saint. The Renaissance and the Reformation, however, produced a new emphasis on the individual, and by the time Boswell wrote the life of Dr. Johnson, the development of the modern biography was substantially complete. The subjectivity of the Romantics, later reinforced by Freudian theory, has produced the biography which attempts to recreate the inner life of its subject. Recently, the techniques of the novel have begun to influence the writing of biography, as in the work of Andre Maurois."[2]

In Indian English Literature, biography happens to be very poor when compared to fiction for a variety of reasons. One reason might be that no creative writer considers this genre as creative as fiction, poetry or drama. Another reason might be that the biographee or the man on whom a biography has to be written has to be so great as to attract the public attention and be generous enough to lend his private diaries, letters or other documents to the biographer to help him reconstruct the former's life as realistically and reliably as possible. Similarly, no biographer in the Indian context would volunteer to write a biography on a person until and unless he is an ardent admirer of the latter on some solid ground—say commercial, professional or ideological. Nowadays commercial biographies are commissioned by rich people, Industrialists, sportsmen and politicians as part of self-aggrandizement. But strangely enough, film actors and actresses do not come forward to get their biographies written as they desire to keep the reading public in the dark about the dark side of their life.

Indians are notorious for their inhibitions and do not generally wish to show or confess their private thoughts, criminal and sinful deeds, secret compromises, which often run counter to the public image projected by them. Even if some daring biographer writes about such people, especially about unsavoury aspects of their life, the former has to face the risk of being beaten up, harassed by the goons, or imprisonment and even being murdered. Indians generally wish to project only idealistic and positive aspects of their life and cannot tolerate the biographers who may be interested in portraying a balanced picture of their life including the negative and the positive aspects.

Another reason might be the Indians' lack of a sense of history. They do not bother to maintain diaries or to preserve the letters that they receive from others. They are utterly indifferent to the extraordinary importance of documentation.

Nirad C. Chaudhuri's biography, *The Scholar Extraordinary: The Life of Friedrich Max Muller* (1974, which won the Sahitya Akademi Award in 1975) happens to be a very significant contribution to this genre. It is a happy coincidence that one serious scholar has written on another serious scholar, although temperamentally they are almost diametrically opposed to each other. As M.K. Naik rightly says, "Chaudhuri's first attempt at biography, is a curious work, because there is obviously a yawning gap between the biographer's and the biographee's attitude to Hindu culture. It is indeed ironical that Chaudhuri, the inveterate Hindu hater should write the life of a European, who once Sanskritized his name as 'Moksha-mulara'. The upshot is a strange ambivalence which ultimately makes the biography rather colourless."[3]

The importance of Chaudhuri's biography on Max Muller becomes clear to us when we compare it with Max Muller's autobiography published in.... A conspicuous difference between autobiography and a biography (on the autobiographer) is that whereas autobiography offers a subjective picture of the self and the external world, biography offers an objective picture of the person concerned and that too from multiple points of view. Whereas autobiography is characterized by self-examination and self-expression, biography is characterized by the world's understanding and evaluation of the biographee. In fact, both kinds of picture supplement and complement each other.

Another important thing about the two is the sequence of their publication. By and large the later work may be better than the earlier one in so far as it may fill in the lacunae of the earlier work. For example, the autobiographer might highlight some aspects of his personality neglected by a biography published earlier. Similarly a biography might highlight some aspects of its protagonist's life neglected by the latter's autobiography. Chaudhuri's biography of Max Muller is published long after Max Muller's *Autobiography* is published. One may say without any hesitation that Chaudhuri's biography on Max Muller is definitely more comprehensive and research-oriented than Max Muller's autobiography, which is rather brief and selective.

The distinctiveness of Chaudhuri's biography on Max Muller may be seen in the technique of his writing. Chaudhuri does not follow the exclusively chronological narration of Max Muller's life, but offers a classified depiction of the life of his protagonist like his early life, his professional pursuit of Sanskrit scholarship, his wife Georgina, his contribution to philology, his days in Oxford, the political and scholarly polemics about him and his views on Indian culture and people. Being a brilliant student of history, Chaudhuri not only depicts the events of Max Muller's life but also relates them to the broader social, political and cultural aspects of England and Germany and critically comments on them authoritatively thereby placing his protagonist in a wider perspective and accentuating the characteristic features of Max Muller's personality in a very convincing manner.

As Chaudhuri makes it clear in his Introduction, "This book is a biography, that is to say, an account of the life of a man, who was a scholar and a thinker; it not except incidentally a discussion or evaluation of his work in the fields of knowledge with which his scholarship was concerned" (1). Chaudhuri points out how Max Muller enhanced the prestige of Germans as the sympathetic and profound interpreter of Hindu civilization and spirituality. He deplores that "Indians hardly remember that if Max Muller was a German, he was equally an Englishman" (1). Highlighting the wide popularity of Max Muller, Chaudhuri quotes the telegraphic messages sent by very important persons like Queen Victoria, Edward VII, the Empress Frederick, Princess Christina, Kaiser William II, the Queen of Romania and the Indian social reformer Malabari to Mrs. Max Muller. In India distinguished scholars like R.G. Bhandarkar, R.C. Dutt, and Swami Vivekananda paid rich tribute to the late Max Muller. Similarly, his friends and acquaintances in England like Macaulay, Tennyson, Thackeray, Ruskin, Browning, Matthew Arnold and political figures like Gladstone and Lord Curzon and Archbishop Trait paid great tributes to the late Max Muller. Chaudhuri rightly remarks, "His fame spread out from the scholarly field to the lay world like that of Darwin or Einstein, but with a stronger and wider impingement, which bore political results in some countries" (7).

Max Muller believed that he was not a man of action like Carlyle or Emerson. As rightly remarked by Chaudhuri, he was a scholar-thinker and had the capacity for experiencing the emotion of scholarship and is comparable to Karl Marx in the possession of deep faith or conviction. Max Muller is known for his provisional explanations of some of the deepest facts of life like religion, mythology and language. Chaudhuri wants to bring out the grandeur and misery of a *savante*. He advises the reader as to how to understand the significance of life, "Significance of life must be found in the grains after sifting the immense amount of chaff of insignificance, which covers it. The really unintelligent reaction is to be clever and blasé, and not to be excited by the grain and saddened by the chaff" (10).

***

Chaudhuri begins the biography of Max Muller quite traditionally with the date and place of his birth, "Friedrich Max Muller was born on December 6, 1823, in the town of Dessau, now in Eastern Germany, but then the capital of a sovereign state, though a very small one" (13). This principality was ruled by Duke Friedrich Leopold, during Max Muller's time. Max Muller had pious feelings towards his native state in spite of his critical view of it.

Chaudhuri, being primarily a student of history, takes keen interest in offering the historical background of the principality, its ruler and his dynasty. He briefly mentions Duke Franz's love for his subjects, his ideals and his encounter with Napoleon. Likewise he mentions Duke Leopold's virtues, culture and his feudal love of hunting.

Chaudhuri shows the connection between the ducal family and Max Muller, "Max Muller's relationship with the ducal family was closer than that of others. For one thing, his father was the Duke's librarian, and was held in great esteem and affection by him. Secondly, his grandfather on his mother's side was the Duke's chief minister or President of the Duchy" (19).

Chaudhuri refers to the beautiful landscape of the Duchy including the river Elbe and its tributary, the Mulde; the forests of oaks as well as of firs. The city was walled in. The houses generally had only one story and had a mirror fastened outside the main window. The population was divided into two classes, i.e. the educated and the uneducated. Trade was almost wholly a Jewish monopoly. The Jews, who lived in their ghettos, were only a tolerated community.

After offering a brief geographical, physical, social and economic picture of Max Muller's place of birth, he gives an inner and cultural picture of the people when he says that in the world in which Max Muller lived, mental status was more valued than wealth; that the horizon of this world was narrow but stable; and that gossip ruled supreme in the town. But in spite of being a small town, it did not impose its limitations on mental growth. Chaudhuri rightly infers that the reading of the works of Goethe, Jean Paul, Shakespeare, Dante and Calderon in Max Muller's maternal grandfather's house and parents' house must have impressed him deeply. Max Muller's father Wilhelm (1794-1827) besides being the Duke's librarian was a classical scholar in Greek and wrote a book on Homer. This information, obviously, helps us to know how scholarship ran in the blood of his family. His mother, Adelheid Basedow was very beautiful and highly cultured and knew English, French and Italian perfectly. But unfortunately his father, who was a most devoted father, died at the age of only 33, on October 1, 1827 when Max Muller was only a boy of four years.

The unexpected death of his father left his mother aged only 28, inconsolable. Though she lived for fifty-six years as a widow, she never married again. Max Muller developed a lifelong love for acacia trees as he saw them planted in the cemetery of his father's grave. Chaudhuri points out, "Although Max Muller from his early childhood grew up in the shadow of death, he came on both sides from a stock which possessed great vitality and as a small boy he was full of fun and mischief" (23).

Muller's mother began a life of great hardship. Although the Duke sympathized with her and granted her a pension of 150 thalers (15 Pounds) a year, it was not adequate for their sustenance. In winter, they had no sufficient clothes. For breakfast they had only coffee and a roll. The hard life made Muller suffer from headaches throughout his early life.

After briefly referring to the unexpected loss of father and economic tragedy of the family, Chaudhuri highlights the religious atmosphere of the family, "Naturally, religion was an important element in his early life" (24). Muller used to listen to religious songs sung by his mother. He was deeply influenced by the music sung in the church. "Music was the greatest enjoyment of his life at that age" (25). Muller grew up in the general musical atmosphere and accompanied his mother when she sang. His formal musical education began very early and secretly at the hands of Schneider and later Kahle was appointed as his music teacher. Chaudhuri has pointed out two important elements in Muller's early life, religion and music, which played an important role in his later life. While Muller was at school, he was advised by a young teacher to be worthy of his father. Max, therefore, developed a feeling of piety about his father.

Chaudhuri opines that there is a slight difference between the English Orientalists and German Orientalists. Whereas the English Orientalists were interested in Eastern and Indological knowledge for the practical purpose of colonial administration of India (and other countries), the German interest in India was more idealistic and part of the Romantic Movement. He also states rightly that the English Orientalists distrusted the German Orientalists as the latter had no firsthand experience of India, but had developed a bookish 'myth' of spiritual India.

Chaudhuri mentions that Max Muller was not interested in philology or literature, but was mainly interested in the evolution of religion and philosophical thought, although he did a great deal of work in philology also. That is why Max Muller began his scholarly career with a translation of *Hitopadesa*. Max Muller discovered India through his Sanskrit scholarship. In his letter to Gladstone Max Muller says that his discovery of India is greater than Vasco da Gama's. He is justified in saying so. Whereas Vasco da Gama discovered the geographical India, he discovered the spiritual India.

Thus, Max Muller began his odyssey of Sanskrit scholarship and a life of total dedication to it. In his early years, he was advised by an old scholar in Paris, Burnoff to concentrate on the *Rig Veda* and publish Sayanacarya's commentary on it. Max Muller obviously took his advice seriously and worked on it very hard until he could publish it in London. When Muller started publishing the *Rig Veda* in London, Burnoff admired him wholeheartedly.

After some hard work Muller felt overburdened with the editing of the *Rig Veda*. He was advised by Bunsen to appoint an assistant. He, therefore, engaged an assistant Dr. Aufrecht (who came from Oxford from Berlin) to help him. His hard work culminated in the publication of the *Rig Veda* (607 pages) on August 3, 1859, the day of his wedding. It was a great success. All the copies of the first edition were sold out in just five months. It was favourably reviewed in learned journals as well as newspapers. Muller had a sense of fulfillment. As human life is characterized by happiness and sorrow alternating each other, Muller was rather disappointed to get the Boden Professorship of Sanskrit at Oxford at the end of 1860. But in spite of this disappointment, he continued to work on the text and translation of the *Rig Veda*.

***

In the second chapter of his biography Nirad Chaudhuri highlights Max Muller's love and marriage with Beata Georgina. He shows how Max Muller had to suffer a sort of humiliation in his love affair with Georgina on account of his economic instability. Chaudhuri offers all the important details of Muller's meeting with Georgina and his attempt to marry her. Muller met Georgina Granfell in 1854, but he was rejected by her family, especially her father, due to his poverty and lack of high position. Muller held a quasi-religious view of love and had an equal devotion to the *Rig Veda* and to Georgina. Georgina knew that although Max Muller was poor economically, he was very rich in his scholarship and mental accomplishment. His income per year was only 500 pounds as a Fellow of Oxford College plus 250 pounds from his writings, thus totaling up to 750 pounds only. Therefore, Georgina's father was rather hesitant to allow his daughter to marry Max Muller.

Another reason was that Georgina's family was generally very religious and believed in God, but a friend of Max Muller had maligned him by reporting to Georgina's family that Muller was an agnostic. Muller, therefore, struggled hard to remove this misconception about his so-called agnosticism. Due to these two reasons Georgina went on worrying about whether to marry Max Muller or not. In fact she had other suitors also. Chaudhuri quotes many letters and diary entries to show Georgina pining for Max and authenticates his biography with proper documentation. One day Georgina's love for Max Muller climaxed in her fainting. It was only after the doctor warned her father that the latter gave his consent to their marriage. Then both Georgina and Muller lived in a delirium of joy for a few days until their wedding took place on August 3, 1859 at Bray Church. Max Muller's disappointment in love before marrying Georgina enabled him to write a short story, "German Love", published anonymously in 1856, which became very popular in Europe and America and went into several editions.

★★★

In the third chapter Nirad Chaudhuri highlights Max Muller's preoccupation with the study of language or philology and his enormous contribution to this field, which helped the imperialist Government of Britain to understand India properly from the Orientalist perspective. Chaudhuri offers abundant details to show Max Muller's dedication to the study of language, which later paved the way for the linguistic research in Europe. The study of the Rig Veda kept Max Muller occupied for thirty years. Chaudhuri rightly remarks that Muller's mind was speculative and metaphysical and hence he had a natural inclination towards generalization. He mentions Madam de Wagner's comparison between Darwin and Max Muller. According to her Darwin studied the origin of species, whereas Max Muller studied the development of human reason. Muller's main interest was in Comparative Philology and his definition of language is very interesting. He says that "Language is the autobiography of the human mind" (179). For him language is closely connected with the race and culture. He delivered many special lectures in Oxford and other places on Aryan culture, which became very popular in Europe. Max Muller may be said to be the founder of the Oriental Studies in Britain and Europe. He rightly pleaded for the necessity of Oriental studies for the ICS officers and administrators from Britain so that they could rule the country with real understanding. He insisted on the establishment of the Schools of Oriental Studies in England for political reasons, for ruling over the east. Edward's Said's ideas on Orientalism may be seen in Max Muller's crusade and mission.

Chaudhuri offers a contrastive picture of Max Muller and Macaulay. Whereas Macaulay was notorious for his dislike of Indian knowledge-systems Max Muller was known for his ardent love for India and Sanskrit. Hence there could not be any agreement between the two as far as their attitudes to India were concerned. Max Muller's lectures on language were so interesting and impressive that even Queen Victoria attended his lectures. His lectures were known for his highlighting of the stratification of language and his extraordinary clarity of thought and style.

According to him the science of language was one of the physical sciences and has three stages of study: one, the empirical stage of data collection; two, the classificatory stage, and three, theoretical or metaphysical stage. Muller believed that the problem of language could not be solved historically. He refused to apply the Darwinian theory of evolution to language. Language, according to him, is a special faculty of man denied to animals and the origin of language and the origin of thought are coeval. Language and thought are inseparable but not identical. Language has growth, but not a history. Growth of language involves dialectal regeneration and phonetic decay. The real growth of languages is to be found only in dialects. The growth stops when the dialects were written down and became artificial. Literary dialects are like stagnant reservoirs. Language involves continuous break-up and new formation. According to Max Muller the science of thought involves four stages of sensations, percepts, concepts and names. Language and thought are inseparable.

Max Muller believed that the knowledge of Sanskrit is compulsory for a comparative philologist. He established the concept of an Indo-European family of languages more firmly and spread the idea of a common Aryan family and culture. He continued the age of wonder of linguistics for himself and his readers.

Nirad Chaudhuri has very intelligently collected the data regarding Max Muller's contribution to philology and presented it coherently. The reader can easily understand the enormous contribution of Max Muller to the science of language in general and the Oriental Studies in particular. According to Max Muller the science of language has to follow three stages of study like (1) the empirical stage of data-collection, (2) the classificatory stage, and (3) the theoretical or metaphysical stage. Max Muller believes that the problem of language cannot be solved historically. He refuses to accept the Darwinian theory of evolution as applicable to the language, which is a special faculty of man denied to animals. According to him the origin of language and the origin of thought were coeval. Hence language and thought are inseparable, but not identical. Language has growth, but not history. The growth of language involves dialectal regeneration and phonetic decay. The real growth of languages is to be found only in the dialects. The growth stops when the languages are written down and become artificial. Literary dialects are like stagnant reservoirs. Language involves a continuous break-up and new formation. Thus Max Muller has offered his hard won insights into the science of language.

Max Muller believed in the view that the knowledge of Sanskrit was compulsory for a comparative philologist. He established the concept of an Indo-European family of languages more firmly. He spread the idea of a common Aryan family and culture. Thus he continued the age of wonder of linguistics for himself and his readers.

In this chapter Nirad Chaudhuri has offered a very perceptive picture of Max Muller's contribution to the science of language or philology and highlighted his achievements. One may easily see the enormous importance of Max Muller's foundational work in the field of language, which paved the way for later researches in the study of linguistics all over the world.

***

In the fourth chapter Nirad Chaudhuri depicts the life of Max Muller at Oxford by connecting Muller's scholarly life to Oxford and Oxford University. As a typical historian, who is generally interested in broad social or cultural or political movements, and temporal fluctuations, Chaudhuri offers a broad picture of the life at Oxford and its University including the positive and the negative aspects and placing Max Muller in the right perspective. For example he begins the chapter by giving a brief history of the Oxford University from the beginning. He says that the Oxford University was transformed from an educational monastery run by a clerical oligarchy into a secular body i.e., an advanced public school and that by the end of the 19th century, it had transferred its allegiance from God to Caesar. He observes further that the imperialistic reorientation of Oxford University brought in a new awareness among the students and teachers.

Then Chaudhuri digresses a little to comment upon the Indian students, who go to Oxford to study there and makes his incisive remarks about the Indians duality of experiences. For example he says that the Indians, who go to Oxford, pick up English manners, and are better informed, but they cannot have real friendship with the British students. He further comments upon the Indians, who return to India after completing their education at Oxford, behave very arrogantly with their own countrymen and yet feel guilty about serving a foreign government.

Chaudhuri offers Max Muller's views on India, which are very important and hold good for Indians even today. According to Max Muller, India can never be anglicized totally, but it can be reinvigorated and their own national literature be re-studied and their pride and self-respect reawakened.

Notes

1. Nirad C. Chaudhuri, *Scholar Extraordinary,* New Delhi: Orient Paperbacks, 1974. (All the page references are to this edition.)
2. Karl Beckson and Ganz Arthur, *A Reader's Guide to Literary Terms*, London: Thames and Hudson, 1972, p. 25.
3. M.K. Naik, *A History of Indian English Literature*, New Delhi: Sahitya Akademi, 1982, p. 268.

Chapter 8

Chaudhuri's Sartorial Vision in *Culture in the Vanity Bag*

Perhaps no Indian writer has thought so seriously about the Indian clothes and the philosophy underlying them as Nirad Chaudhuri has. He is such a keen observer of life around him and such a minute scholar that he is amply qualified to relate his observation to his wide and historical scholarship and evolve a very interesting sartorial philosophy about Indians. One might easily say that *Culture in the Vanity Bag*[1] is an Indian parallel to Carlyle's *Sartor Resortus*. Whereas Chaudhuri's book is historical in perspective and analytical in method and realistic in style, Carlyle's is romantic and synthetical in its overall approach to the problem. Chaudhuri's analysis is as usual, tinged with satire and intellectual humour. The sophistry that he brings to bear on his analysis and the perspectivization of the whole problem is indeed very admirable. But M.K. Naik is critical about Chaudhuri's *Culture in the Vanity Bag* when he says, "The book, an application of Chaudhuri's favourite thesis on Indian history to sartorial fashions, shows that both his Anglophilia and his Hindu-baiting continue unabated."[2] In spite of critical controversies about Chaudhuri's writings, it is interesting to study his insightful views on the Indian life and culture. The highlights of his arguments may be seen in the following paragraphs.

Chaudhuri, who has observed the Indian life very keenly, is able to show the connection between the Indian clothing and the Indian history. Clothes are, obviously, the external manifestations of the innermost cultural habits of men adapting themselves to the peculiar geographical, social, religious and even political phenomena around them. That is why Chaudhuri says, "The evolution of clothing in India has been only a part of the historical evolution of the peoples of India, possessing similar features, following similar lines and producing similar results" (xi). Although the present India is a 'museum of warehouse of cultures' exhibiting a motley of clothing, having a group or individual autonomy, their origin and development could be traced to the historical movements, which swept India from the earliest times to the present.

Chaudhuri offers a taxonomical break-up of the evolutionary history of clothing in India. The first category of these, according to him, is the Mongoloid clothing, which consists of two pieces of 'loom-woven clothes', "one of which is thrown around the shoulders and the other, the main piece, wrapped round the waist" (14). This type of clothing is used mainly by the Mongoloid peoples in the Himalayan regions.

The second category, according to Chaudhuri, is the aboriginal one, which consists of one piece of cotton cloth "anything between eight to fifteen feet in length and thirty to forty-five inches in width. With a slight difference in the design of the borders, it is worn by both men and women. Men wrap its middle section round the waist, pass the left half section between the legs and tuck it behind, while the right-hand portion is sometimes tied round the waist and sometimes folded and hung in front" (15). The women wear the same with a slight variation. This is the simplest and most basic costume worn by all the aboriginal peoples of the Central Indian plateau and the Deccan.

The Aryan costume, which forms the third category, is an elaborate form of the aboriginal costume. It consists of a long piece of cloth worn as the main garment by both men and women. It is known as dhoti, when worn by men and as sari when used by women. "The dhoti is worn roughly in the same fashion as the cloth of the aboriginal man, but it is longer and wider, and is worn with so many folds, gathers, and tucks that it gives the impression of much fuller draping. More especially, the gathers and folds in front are heavier and hang lower" (16). Similarly, the sari is an elaboration of the aboriginal woman's cloth. "A section of about four feet of its length is gathered in front and tucked in at the middle point of the front waist line, and this constitutes the main feature of the Hindu manner of wearing the sari. All over northern India women wrap it over the lower limbs like a skirt but in South India Brahmin women tuck the left end at the back like their men folk, though modern women are giving it up" (16).

Sometimes an odd combination of the aboriginal and the Aryan costume is formed and worn by the labouring population. It is called 'decency clout' and is used by these people due to poverty and for convenience of work.

The nomadic costume forms the fourth category of clothes. It is "the first and earliest of any sewn costumes worn by a particular ethnic group permanently settled in India" (18). Further, it is "a harmonious whole from head to foot" (18), which is made up of a full shirt with deep and ample gathers; a closely fitted bodice, a waistcoat. "The ensemble has a linear unity and rhythm of surprising beauty and dynamism" (18), and because of the addition of bright colours and bold designs, gives an impression of a very strong individuality. This costume is worn mainly by the people of Rajaputana from Kathiawar to the west to Delhi to the east.

The Muslim clothing of the fifth century consists of *sherwani* or *achkan* and *kurta* or *kamiz* for men and stalwart-*kamiz-dupatta* ensemble for women. These costumes are worn by the Muslims of India, by the Hindus of Punjab, the Sikhs and also the Islamized Hindus of Hindustan.

The European clothing, which forms the sixth category, consists of the standard garments of men and women like suit (pants, shirt, coat, hat and tie) and skirt respectively. These clothes are adapted by a large number of Indians, who once used to it never go back to the Indian costumes.

After offering a taxonomical picture of Indian costumes in general, Chaudhuri enumerates the chief components of the typical Hindu costumes. He rightly says, "...the correct Hindu dress must be unsewn. Next, it must have two essential garments. A Hindu must be, whether male or female, a person of *two* garments. These are the *dhoti* or *sari* for the lower limbs, and a scarf or shawl for the upper part of the body. In Sanskrit the two pieces are called *vastra* and *uttariya* respectively" (22). Chaudhuri also discusses the mode of wearing the *vastra*. He says, "...being *dvivastra*, a man of two garments, a Hindu must also be *trikachcha*, a man of three tucks, and the places at which these are to be put are the back on the alignment of the spine, navel and the left side of the waist" (23). After showing the relation between the Hindu garments and the sacred prescriptions, Chaudhuri makes certain observations about the purpose of the Hindu's wearing of certain types of garments in certain styles, which testify to his sharpness of perception, boldness of judgment and freedom from inhibition. He, for example, takes up the traditional Hindu prescription that a man should take off the back-tuck while urinating. But Chaudhuri asks a simple, straightforward and uninhibited question as to why a Hindu should take off the back-tuck when he can perform his nature call without taking it off and that too when the back-tuck is the most unnecessary to take off. Then Chaudhuri explains in his typical fashion that this habit or rather prescription is founded upon the usual Hindu habit of non-thinking.

The dropping of the back-tuck by the Aryans is attributed by Chaudhuri to the aboriginals of India. The back-tuck, for example, is not used by the unmarried Brahmins and non-Brahmins. This habit of wearing the *dhoti* without the back-tuck perhaps suggests the defective status of unmarried Brahmins and all Hindus of non-Brahmin castes.

After offering a taxonomical picture of the basic Indian costumes, Chaudhuri examines the philosophy of clothing in India in general. Clothing in India, especially among the Hindus had not only a utilitarian role but also an aesthetic role to play. Clothing is used not merely to cover the body from the climate, but also as a means of self-assertion and self-protection. It is used in India to show off one's superiority over the enemies. "There is no doubt that in the true and honest Hindu tradition of display, women's clothing is aposematic" (32). That explains the Hindu woman's habit of over-dressing without feeling the slightest sense of embarrassment. In this respect clothing has an asexual rather than inter-sexual significance. Even in matrimonial bonds, for example, clothing plays a role subordinate to that of physical attraction. Chaudhuri, therefore, points out that "in wedlock the access to the body is so untrammeled that artificial attractions are wholly superfluous" (32).

The urban and the so-called civilized (or cultured) people of India attached a lot of importance to the aesthetic role of clothing. The extra attention shown by women to clothes is more often than not motivated by the sexual desire to attract the male attention. Sophisticated habits of clothing are, therefore, associated with courtesans and brothels among Hindus. But the Muslim did not bother much about the 'sublimation of the brothel', as he "could have any blend of sensuality and refinement in the harem itself" (34). The extraordinary sexual importance attached by the urban Hindu to clothing sometimes leads him to draw wrong judgment about woman's character. Chaudhuri, as usual, supports his observations with illustrations from his personal experience. Once, in Delhi, Chaudhuri saw "two gorgeously dressed Punjabi young women" (35), who were described by a passer-by as '*Randi hogi*'—'Must be whores' (35). On another occasion one of Chaudhuri's senior servants asked the sweeper woman to change into cleaner dresses, the husband of the latter is said to have remarked that only the whores among sweepers put on finery. Sometimes the sexual significance attached to clothes in India is intensified by the accompaniment of feminine coquetry. Thus, gorgeous or sophisticated dressing earns the label of a *demi-mondaine* for a lady whether she wants it or not.

Chaudhuri rightly points out the connection between jewellery and clothes. He is also quite correct when he attributes the Hindu sartorial surplus to their numbness of sensibility caused by the Indian hot climate. "For one thing, the Hindu sense organs are so enfeebled by too much glare, heat and noise that they cannot take in at best more than half of the sense phenomena presented to them, and so there must always be, if there is to be any effect at all, an overdose" (36). He further points out how ostentation was not considered by the Hindu *monde* as morally wrong. That is why there is a good deal of sartorial magnificence even in their routine life. "At cocktail parties in New Delhi, for instance, I often observe Western women looking at the magnificent Indian ladies with a puzzled expression, as if they were wondering whether they were not seeing a mirage of the ranks of duchesses, marchesses and countesses at a coronation ceremony in Westminster Abbey" (36-37).

The element of Hindu excess could be seen both in jewellery and in clothes. Chaudhuri exhibits his capacity for minute observation and intelligent connection of things and features of life when he says that gold is the most important metal used for ornaments by the Hindus. Gold is preferred by Hindus because of a variety of reasons. First, the Hindu ornament was on the gold standards, i.e. economic status of the metal. Second, it had a sacred status. Third, it offered the best security for the people at the time of crisis in their life. It is because of the sacrosanctity of gold that it was meant only for the upper parts of the body and was forbidden for the lower parts, which deserved only silver ones. Because of its economic status, it offered them an unfailing security. "So their ornaments were often they only resource, a sort of marriage settlement, and never knowing what the next turn of the wheel of fortune might bring, they clung to their gold as if it was their life-belt" (38). It was also because of its intrinsic worth that gold could be the cause for creation of contradictory responses in the Hindu women. It "always raised the women to a higher level of mental life" (39). That is why these women "would give the gold to a husband, son, or even relative in trouble, to be sold or mortgaged, and never say a word or take credit" (39). On the other hand, they could be so possessive of gold that they could be totally callous to their near and dear ones. "The love of gold would drive out the love of husband and child from their heart, make the mere idea of a lover a dirty smear, and turn them into chryselephantine statues with a demoniac soul" (39).

Chaudhuri rightly equates the Hindu woman's attachment for gold to her madness for saris, "The motive of self-assertion and acquiring worldly importance explains the extraordinary craze our women now have for saris. They go on buying them regularly even when they cannot and do not wear a fraction of their stock. They are the hoarders of clothes, corresponding to the male hoarders of money" (42). It is on account of this madness for sari that the Hindu women make it a point of reference and comparison in their familial and social life. They also make it a means of endearment between friends and relatives; a test of husband's preferential love and also a means of social estrangement and matrimonial derangement. Thus jewellery and clothes, as aptly described by Chaudhuri provide the best chance of expression for the Hindu feminine moods, which blow hot and cold alternately if not simultaneously.

It is very difficult to have an affirmative answer to the question whether we have an Indian dress in India. Chaudhuri, therefore, says in his typically categorical fashion that "just as there is no *Indian nation,* there is no Indian dress" (49). He further shows that India "became a museum of diverse cultures fairly early in its history" (49). Since India had been conquered by foreign races there was bound to be a battle between the Hindu and the non-Hindu clothes as also other things of culture. The first battle was naturally to be between the Hindu clothes and the Muslim ones. Whereas the Hindus believed in non-sewn garments, the Muslims believed in sewn garments. Because of the exclusiveness of the Hindu culture, it never encourages either the proselytization of the Hindu clothes or the adoption of the Muslim clothes. But the Muslim culture, because of its at least one-way traffic of proselytizing encouraged the adoption of its clothes by the Hindus. As a religious policy the Hindus did not like the use of Muslim clothes at all except by way of self-denigration or contamination. Chaudhuri is perceptive enough to show the evolution of the sartorial battle between the Hindu and the Muslim culture. He shows how in spite of the initial Hindu hatred of the Muslim clothes, the Hindus—some of them at least—adopted it for the purpose of pleasing the Muslim leaders and authorities in social life. Chaudhuri rightly relates this habit of the Hindus to their national character when he says, "Hinduism forgives every transgression of Hindu standards out of opportunism, but no adherence to any non-Hindu value from conviction. So if a Hindu showed signs, either through his opinion or his behaviour, that he was acquiring new loyalties or even remaining Hindu, widening his personal life by adding non-Hindu qualities, mental or external, he was without any compunction thrown outside the pale whoever he might be, and no less a Hindu than Raja Rammohun Roy was excommunicated in this manner, though he is rightly looked upon as the creator of the modern Indian mind" (55). The religious conflict between Hindus and Muslims was reflected in their sartorial conflict also. The ambivalence in the former is repeated in the latter also.

With the British conquest of India, the sartorial battle between Hindus and the British repeated the pattern of the older battle between Hindus and Muslims, of course, with slight variations. The Hindus, in spite of their religious rigidities, jumped at the opportunity of imitating the British (or Western in a broader sense) clothes for the purposes of fashion, snobbery and worldly success, although the British did not like the Hindu imitation of their clothes, as they thought it to be tantamount to the contamination of the superior British culture by the inferior Hindu culture. But the Hindus did not bother about the British superiority complex at all. Consequently the Hindus went on adopting the British clothes like suit, tie and hat for their social life if not for their private religious or sectarian life. The boldest of the Hindus were the Anglicized or 'England-returned' ones, who affected the British clothes and maintained costly wardrobes with real style and gusto. Thus imitation of British clothes was a virtue allied to other habits like, for example, speaking and writing English, quoting Shakespeare and Milton; "airing rationalism and contempt for Hindu image worship; eating beef; and drinking until dead" (59). One might easily say that imitation of the British clothes was the strongest aspect of the Westernization of Hindus.

Among the many effects of the British clothes on Hindus was the growing Hindu tendency towards covering the body, "...with the coming of British rule, the practice of covering the body became more general; in fact, to remain bare-bodied except when being comfortable in summer in private, became more or less rare.... In addition, the women have made the petticoat an integral part of their dress" (61).

In India, there is no strict connection between clothes and morals. "In other words, the moral connection is a secondary relationship, a matter of association of ideas" (72). After categorically showing the absence of moral connection with clothes, Chaudhuri shows how the pattern of clothes of a particular culture, though originally decided by the immediate climatic conditions, are not likely to be changed to the new climatic conditions into which the people concerned are thrown. Thus, for example, the British refused to change over from their suit to anything Indian in spite of the horrid climate of India. Similarly, the Muslims were unwilling to give up the *salwar* and *kamiz* in spite of their being inconvenient in the Indian climate. Thus each culture believing in the validity and sanctity of its own clothes refuses to respect those of the other, except for utilitarian purposes.

Chaudhuri offers a contrasting picture of the Muslim clothes and the Hindu. The Muslim clothes had "combination of magnificence, purity and strength" at least until the time of Aurangzeb's sons in India. But the Hindu approach to clothes was governed by a dual idea that "personal adornment through clothing ought to be a combination of the highest and the most refined beauty of the nude with that of clothing and ornaments. It fused what are regarded as incompatibles and it did so with glorious success" (81). The dual aesthetics of the Hindu clothing, according to Chaudhuri, suffers from two handicaps: one, its effect depends "as much on the body of the wearer as on the quality of raiment and not all men and women could boast of perfect figures" (81); two, it tends itself to misjudgments on moral counts, although at the other extreme it attains an unearthly purity.

The battle of clothes in India, says Chaudhuri, does not have any dignity or elevation about it, though it has been fought perpetually all through the Indian history. It has, therefore, become a mere squabble. Chaudhuri puts forth his views very frankly, "...the battle of clothing in its current phase is of a low quality. Just as the governance of the country by the present Indian ruling order, which I call brown colonialism, is a caricature of British imperialism, the conflict of clothes is also nothing better than degenerate aping, without any ideal or principle behind it" (87).

The Hindus had been so slavish in their imitation of the European clothes that they easily tolerated the public conveniences including interminable railway compartments being earmarked for "Europeans only," Chaudhuri points out the height of paradox when he says that the governmentally owned Asoka Hotel of Delhi would not be able to admit the Buddha himself if he were to come now in his usual garments as represented in Gandhara art. That the Hindu piece of cloth, i.e. *dhoti* should be forbidden in the hotel owned by the Hindu government is indeed beyond all sense and logic. Too much dependence by the Hindus upon the white mythology is obviously satirized severely by Chaudhuri when he says, "that above every fluttering national flag in India today I see its idea in the Platonic sense—a transcendental union jack" (91).

Then Chaudhuri shows how even the great Indians like Rajendra Prasad, Jawaharlal Nehru and Indira Gandhi had taken to the Muslim and European garments respectively. Jawaharlal Nehru, who was brought up in the Islamic garments, changed over to the European clothes when he was at Harrow and Cambridge for his education; took to dhoti for the utilitarian purpose of participating in the Indian independence movement and switched over to pajama and shirt, which are still popular as 'Nehru pajama' and 'Nehru shirt'. Likewise Mrs. Indira Gandhi had taken to frock and hat when in England for her education; then she changed over to sari in India although she kept head bare, but after her assumption of the status of Prime Minister ship of India, she began to cover her head with the end of her sari in the true Hindu fashion.

Like everything else in India, clothing has also been reduced to the ugly minimum. Chaudhuri never tires of stating and illustrating this very Indian truth. He shows the Gandhi-cap and the Jawahar waist-coat are no better than their old counterparts. The adoption of Gandhi-cap by the 'miserly Congress Party' is an evidence of the extraordinary poverty of aesthetics betrayed by the Congresswallas. Similarly, the adoption of Jawahar-coat, which is an adaptation of a Muslim garment, makes it very difficult for the 'Westerners to distinguish between Indian diplomats and butlers'. These instances are a proof of the lack of any sound aesthetic basis for the sartorial habits of Indians. Even in their imitation of the Western clothes, the Hindus are so poor that they easily make a farce of it. They neither use the standard material for their garments nor stick to the original shape of the Western pattern, nor are able to maintain them properly. In spite of the Indian compromise with sartorial predicament, they continue to indulge in their arrogance and snobbery.

The beauty of clothes has, of course, got to be supported by the beauty of the human body. Chaudhuri shows how the Hindus have failed to achieve the necessary concordance between the body and the clothing. The linear beauty of a woman when seen from a lateral angle depends a lot upon the poetic cascade of long hair, but as Chaudhuri deplores, the Hindu woman, nowadays has begun to spoil it by cutting her hair thus playing the sedulous ape to the Western woman. He also shows the folly of the Hindu woman, who, instead of achieving a 'glossy finish' for her hair by oiling it, turns it into 'horse hair' thereby spoiling the crinal beauty. Similarly, the Hindu woman's habit of powdering her face takes away the ivory look from her and turns her skin into 'suede leather'. The habit of painting the lips with red does not always produce the happy effect. The contrast between the red colour on the lips and the dark face of the Hindu lady will be so sharp that it creates a meretricious look. The growing habit of 'mammary and even mamillary ostentation' and 'the exhibition of the posterior' by the Hindu lady are deplorably ridiculous, sensual, ugly, provocative and shameless. Obviously all these recent habits of the Indian-Hindu woman are shown by Chaudhuri to be anachronistic and incongruous in the Indian contest and produce a look of cheapness and vulgarity.

Sometimes, the sartorial fashions become so unhealthy from the Indian point of view that they become matters necessitating police control. Chaudhuri says, "The fashions have even become a police matter, because they are being connected with a scandal, which is growing in all the big Indian cities" (133). The rowdyism, eve-teasing and molestation of girls and women, which have been increasing in the streets and on the University campuses in India, are all directly or indirectly caused by the 'provocative' and 'glamorous' methods of feminine dressing or clothing, which have a touch of sensuality. Chaudhuri is very correct when he shows the connection between the cheapening of clothes and the vulgarity of the Indian film world. "...our cinema has reached a level, whose degradation is not approached even by the lowest films from Hollywood" (139). Then Chaudhuri shows how the Indian politician also has a large share in contributing to the sartorial ugliness of the people.

Culture in the Vanity Bag shows Chaudhuri's serious approach to the sartorial habits of Indians. He analyzes the philosophy of clothing in a very sophisticated manner armed with the historical sense. He has shown how the Hindus are casual and mindless in their imitation of the Muslim or the British clothes and how they are not bothered about contradictions in their sartorial habits. The book is historical, analytical and satirical at the same time and holds mirror to Chaudhuri's microscopic intelligence and incisive analysis.

Notes

1. Nirad C. Chaudhuri, *Culture in the Vanity Bag*, Bombay: Jaico Publishing House, 1876. (All the references are to this edition.)
2. M.K. Naik, *A History of Indian English Literature*, New Delhi: Sahitya Akademi, 1982. p. 268.

Chapter 9

Clive of India: A Political Biography

Nirad Chaudhuri states in his Preface that he was asked by Christopher MacLahose to write a biography of Clive for Barrie & Jenkins, and that he did not know that 1974 was the year of 200th anniversary of Clive's death and 1975, the 250th anniversary of his birth. Being a diligent student of history, especially interested in the colonial period of India, Chaudhuri undertook the onerous task of writing a biography of Lord Clive. A biography is "an account of the life of a person. The modern biography, which is based on careful research and which is relatively dispassionate in attitude, is a comparatively recent form."[1] Chaudhuri's *Clive of India*, undoubtedly belongs to this category of seriously researched biography. In the *Introduction* he confesses honestly, "This book is not a work of fresh research. That is to say, it is not the product of a re-examination of the manuscript sources already drawn upon by previous biographers or of a study of a new material not available before. It offers only a re-interpretation of the personality and achievements of Clive on the basis of the printed documents and secondary works."[2] He acknowledges the presence of earlier biographies on Clive by authors like Forrest, Malcolm, Macaulay, Gleig and Malleson and highlights the fact that Macaulay's account of Lord Clive remains the 'standard portrait'. Justifying the necessity of re-interpretation of historical data, Chaudhuri says rightly, "Nonetheless, a new biography of Clive may be justified on grounds other than new information. To my thinking, the inadequacy of the existing biographies of Clive is to be faced not in the incomplete utilization of the sources, but in the unsatisfactory interpretation of the sources, but in the unsatisfactory interpretation of well-known facts.

This, however, is not the fault of any particular biographer, but has been found virtually forced on them by a preconditioned approach" (2). Chaudhuri rightly says that neither Clive nor the East India Company has been properly historiographed due to the polemical approach of the people and scholars. The polemical approach was created by the unexpected birth of the British Empire in the form of the East India Company. "The polemical approach was created by the very manner in which the Empire came into existence. The British people were not prepared for it either intellectually or morally. So, when they saw it emerging they not only failed to understand what was happening, but took up a hostile attitude. Chronologically British imperialism was in being before the appearance of the Empire. The great French historian and political thinker Alex de Tocqueville...said that an empire two thirds the size of that of Alexander the Great was founded against the formal orders of the authorities at home. According to him more singular was the failure of the deliberate attempts made by the East India Company, the British government of the day, and even British public opinion to arrest the growth of the Empire. Although, he said, the birth and growth of the Empire of India appeared to the world as an unexplained puzzle, almost as a miracle. This bewilderment lingered even as late as the middle of the nineteenth century" (3). The time had come to dispel the clouds of incomprehension, of hostility and moralizing, of false glorification, false contrition and false romanticizing. But these clouds have not been dispelled.

Although James Mill in his *History of British India* condemned the actions and the methods of the British Empire, later it became a matter of pride for the British. For example, Macaulay was very proud of the British Empire. "...he chided Englishmen for knowing less about their own Empire in India than about the Spanish Empire in America" (7). The history of the Empire is determined by officers like Clive and Warren Hastings, who influenced the historiography of British India. Chaudhuri observes rightly, "The men as microcosms determined the treatment of the macrocosm—the Empire. The moral issues raised by these two men in the sphere of practical politics were carried into the biographies and from the biographies into the histories, so that it may be said that Clive and Warren Hastings cast their shadows on the entire historiography of British India. Moral criticism and appraisement became the main purpose of both history and biography" (7).

Nirad Chaudhuri is interested in historical truth and wants to write about it with a sense of detachment. Says he, "In this book I have been very scrupulous in distinguishing between what is fact and what is only inference, or merely supposition" (11). He tries to correct certain misconceptions of historians by stating his point of view very clearly. "It is not readily admitted even by those, who write history that there can be neither a Marxist interpretation of history nor a Christian, neither an imperialistic interpretation nor another that is anti-imperialistic—the only legitimate interpretation is the historical one. In respect of both Clive and the rise of the British Empire in India I have tried to give that" (14).

In the first part of the biography Chaudhuri traces the gradual rise of Clive between 1725 and 1755 by offering a background picture of the political life in India. At the very outset he points out the unexpected birth of the Indian Empire through an image of maternity, "The Indian Empire was born like the child of an inexperienced unmarried girl, that is to say, without any design to found it, or even awareness that it could come into existence, or any admission of its legitimacy" (17). The British involvement in India was often the outcome of chance and unpredictable circumstances.

The rise of the British rule in India was accelerated by the decline of the Mughal Empire. It was not an organized Empire. It was more a mosaic than a monolithic power supported by an ensemble of scattered military colonies founded by the Persian, Afghan or Pathan soldiers of fortune. Even at the height of its power i.e. during the combined reigns of Akbar, Jahangir, Shah Jahan and Aurangzeb (1556-1707) it had only a relative stability. Since dynastic succession was its main agenda, there used to be frequent and ferocious in-fights and murders.

As the Mughal Empire, like all Islamic kingdoms, was an autocratic monarchy, its fall was the result of the decline of the energy, power and position of a dynasty. The Muslim rulers tried to become independent of one another rather than being united. Then the rise of the Maratha power led by Sivaji acted as a threat to the Muslim rule in south India.

Clive came to India at this juncture in June 1744. The English East India Company had become a very prosperous trading concern. It had three separate centers of operation in India called presidencies: Bombay on the western coast, Madras in the eastern coast of peninsular India and Calcutta in Bengal. "The three so called presidencies were wholly independent of one another, and in direct relationship with the Company in London. Each was under a governor assisted by a council. The governor was the president of the council—hence the name presidency" (45). The English servants of the Company in India were divided into four classes: writers, factors, junior merchants and senior merchants. They had been granted the right to private trade, which they carried on with great energy and some rapacity. "As a rule, after a relatively short stay in India they could return to England as rich parvenus and objects of envy to their neighbours" (45). But there was no means of attracting them to do the Company's work in India other than by offering monetary incentives. "Life in India was risky, drab and irritating. There was no attractive society, and though the native women might assuage the *rage de la culotte*, as Dupleix himself described the elemental necessity, they were at best palliatives, at worst dangerous. Dour pursuit of money by any means was the only counterbalancing attraction" (46).

The Company permitted its servants to pursue private trade in India, as it did not diminish the possible gains for the Company. The native Indians were employed by the English. "Even for the Company's trade in cotton fabrics, its English servant was at five removes from the weaver. He had, first to have his native secretary called the *banias*, who in his turn hired brokers called *gomasthas* and there were several others after them. Ignorance of the language and manners of the people of the country compelled the English servants of the Company to employ these intermediaries" (46). Consequently the natives employed by the English in their trade later became the moneyed aristocracy and powerful agents for the establishment of British power in India.

The servants of the East India Company sought permission of the Mughal Emperor like Aurangzeb and put pressure upon the Muslim kings like Murshid Quli Khan (Nawab of Bengal), Nizam-ul-Mulk (Viceroy of the Deccan) to elicit their permission for trading in their respective areas.

Like the English East India Company, there was also another trading company called the French Company working in India at the same time. As in the English East India Company, so in the French, trade was divided into two parts: the public and the private. At that time Dupleix was the governor of Pondicherry, with authority over all the French settlements in India. Naturally there was a kind of rivalry between the English and the French East India Companies for trading privileges and profit. The local kings and chiefs were also divided in their loyalty and connection with these foreign companies.

Clive's arrival in India at this juncture is of historical significance. His biography is naturally intertwined with the history of East India Company as well as that of India. His role in the strengthening of the Company was of great importance. Nirad Chaudhuri begins the biography of Clive at the time of his arrival into India. He makes a remark of philosophical insight about Clive, "The Hindus call their upper castes as well as brides, twice born. Clive was twice born—physically in England, and again, in the only significant sense, in India" (65). Just as Clive needed a *karmabhumi* for the actualization of his potential, perhaps India also needed a dynamic officer like Clive to bring some order into the political chaos prevalent at that point of time. That is why Nirad Chaudhuri rightly remarks, "Clive could become the founder of the British Empire in India only because that country was at this point disintegrating politically. So he became Clive of India, not of England" (62).

Chaudhuri gives an insightful view about Clive by comparing him with Napoleon and others. Whereas Napoleon, Hoche and Mareau were accomplished students of war and trained soldiers, Clive had no such training in the early part of his life. "He had no mental training, even. He went out to India as an unskilled and callow youth, and learned his job by doing it—and went on discovering himself" (63).

Chaudhuri explores the romantic myths about Clive's early childhood and states the plain truth, "In actual fact, apart from these apocryphal stories, Clive's early life was very humdrum and uneventful" (65). He, then, mentions the biographical details about Clive, like his birth on September 29, 1725, in the hamlet of Moreton Say near Market Drayton in Shropshire, his baptism on October 2 in the parish church; the ancient lineage of his family; his father Richard Clive's legal profession and his mother's deep influence on him.

Chaudhuri mentions that as a child, Clive was delicate, but when he was seven years old, he had developed a fierce temper and readiness to fight. He was trained in a private school in childhood, then transferred to a grammar school at Market Drayton and again transferred to a private school at Hemet Hampstead in Hertfordshire.

"When he was seventeen the decision was taken to send him to India as a writer in the service of the East India Company" (66). He was accepted by the Court of Directors. Consequently he sailed for India on March 10, 1743 and reached Madras on June 1, 1744.

Very little information is available about Clive until he was nineteen. But the three letters that he wrote to his father, uncle and cousin show him as a typical product of the impoverished English middle class, with all their obsessions about money and economy. Within three months after reaching Madras, Clive showed his loyalty to family and clan in the letters that he wrote to his parents. Like almost all the servants of the Company, he had come to India mainly to make money.

But after staying in India for some months, he naturally began to suffer from homesickness and depression. In order to overcome these feelings, he began to write letters to his home and felt heartbroken when he did not get replies. In one of his letters he wrote, "The Intemperance of the climate together with the excessive heat of the Sun are very obnoxious to our

Health, and I really think that the Advantages, which accrue to us here, are greatly overbalanced by the Sacrifices we make of our Constitutions" (71). Comparing Clive's early experience in India and his later growth Chaudhuri shows the conspicuous contrast between the two, "Yet this young man was to develop into the man, who was denounced at the end of his life as a monster of high-handedness, greed and perfidy. That, simply, is the measure of the transition he was to make in India" (73).

After being taken prisoner with the rest of the English, by the French in September 1746 (after the capture of Madras), Clive escaped in the guise of a *dubash* and suffered due to lack of employment and money. It was during his twenty-second year of age that Clive formally entered the military service. He, then, participated in the siege of Pondicherry and later Anglo-French conflict and emerged as a bold military leader. That he had the making of a good regimental officer in him was noticed by Stringer Lawrence, a professional soldier, who had taken over the command of the troops at Fort St. David.

In the next four years Clive made a name for himself in India and England as an able and dashing military commander. "The operations that gave him this position were part of a very strange war in the Carnatic" (77). What may be gathered from the abundant information offered by Nirad Chaudhuri is the fact that initially neither the English nor the French Company was interested in establishing its imperial power in India. They were solely interested in trade and profit and not really interested in interfering with the rule of native kings. But historical contingencies arose in India in favour of these two rival companies. Whenever a local king was in trouble (like loss of power through treachery or due to other reasons) he appealed either to the French Company or to the English Company for help. The authorities of either of these companies would help the native king with their military power and in return demand some city with a fort and land with good revenue. Thus a sort of competition and rivalry started between the English Company and the French Company for profit. For example, Nirad Chaudhuri offers a detailed picture of how the English Company (Charles Floyer) supported the Raja of

Tanjore whereas the French Company (Dupleix) supported Chanda Sahib. Nirad Chaudhuri points out how the birth of the British Empire was rather unexpected and accidental. The war between the English and the French as the auxiliaries of the native princes had its periods of inaction and hesitancy and the doldrums were as characteristic as the trade winds. Nirad Chaudhuri makes an insightful comment on the birth of the British Empire, "For all that it has been regarded as the first act of the great drama—the founding of the British Empire in India—which itself show how unedifying were its beginnings. There is a French saying: 'If faut fumer les meilleurs champs.' Which is capped by a Bengali one: 'Lotus blooms on the dung-heap'. The British Empire in India was to rise out of a very evil smelling process of decomposition, and the compost for its later rank growth was not rotten enough to lose its stench even when Warren Hastings took over the task of extending it" (83).

Clive's quiet and tedious life came to an end when he was appointed as a lieutenant of foot in the Company's service and took part in the Tanjore's expedition. With the end of Tanjore expedition Clive's military career was interrupted again. He took up a civilian (and also quasi-military) post of a steward for supplying the stations and became famous at the age of thirty-six when he fought in the siege of Arcot and was victorious. Then after some time, he captured Covelong and Chinglepet. "It was through the operations from Arcot to Covelong and above all his defence of Arcot, that Clive established his reputation as a military leader" (99). Clive never shrank from personal danger and that made a great contribution to his reputation as a leader.

Clive sailed for England on March 23, 1753 after achieving his reputation as a military leader in India. Chaudhuri offers a contrastive picture of Clive's image in India and England, "In position he was second only to Lawrence in India, his military ability was regarded as outstanding and his achievements indisputable: he had become rich, and he had also got married. Henceforth his life was to be divided between acts in India and *entractes* in England, and the alternating stages were to exhibit a curious contrast, for the English phases were as commonplace as the Indian were out of the ordinary" (107). Chaudhuri continues to say, "Clive tried to make use of his exceptional career in India to live or rise socially in the most conventional manner in England. The conventionality was different in the successive stages, and could be seen in a rising scale. This meant that whenever he returned to England there was also a relapse in him from the extraordinary to the ordinary" (107). What is admirable in Clive was that, according to Chaudhuri, he showed unquestioning loyalty to his family and his old friends, although he added a touch of flamboyancy and some grandeur to his lifestyle.

But there was a clash, at first latent, but increasingly manifest, between the two lives he was to have. Chaudhuri makes a beautiful observation about Clive's duality of experience, "This became more and more clear as his outlook generated by his Indian career, was brought to bear on his life at home. A stable and static English society tried to digest the Englishman re-made in India, and had Clive remained the normal East Indian nabob it would have absolved him. But with each period of activity in India his achievements became more grandiose, his outlook more exotic, and his idea of what was due to him more over pitched. On the one hand, he threw his Indian weight about, and on the other, English society found him too big, too strange, and too intractable for reclamation. He would live among his countrymen only on his terms, and so, finally, England profited by his ability and achievements but destroyed him personally" (108).

Chaudhuri mentions the occasional fits from which Clive suffered. Then he refers to Clive's marriage with Margaret Maskelyne at Fort St George (Madras) on February 18, 1753. He rightly comments that Clive's wife remained a shadowy figure. Chaudhuri remarks insightfully about the Anglo-Indian pattern of life, "In those days English girls, especially those, who did not have money, came to India to seek husbands, among the young men, who were making money there. In England it was the young men, who looked about for money and in India the young women hoped to find it along with their husbands. As money was plentiful among the men, and women were scarce, falling in love was predetermined" (110). Chaudhuri points out how the pursuit of money was at the back of all human relationships and professional adventures in the life of the servants of the East India Company. Both men and women were motivated by the desire for money. Chaudhuri says, "There was nothing uncommon in the fact of Clive's money-making in India" (111). The Nawab of Carnatic had made a present of ₹ 40,000 to Clive. The English authorities did not grudge against Clive's amassing of wealth as they admired his merit and professional efficiency. That is why when Clive returned to England in 1753, the Committee of Correspondence recommended that a sword set with diamonds to the value of 500 Pounds be presented to him. Money was very important for Clive especially as he had come from a poor family. He wanted to rehabilitate his family's position, "Clive's early outlook on life had been formed by the relative poverty of his family, and after acquiring money it was natural for him to exhibit the generous side of that outlook" (115). Chaudhuri points out how money-making is a striving after security or pursuit of power. Clive earned money not to hoard but to spend in order to live in style. Stories were told later of Clive's extravagance and ostentation during this period. Clive bought a house in Queen Square near St James's Park. Then he became a Member of Parliament.

Although Clive had improved his economic and material conditions in England with the money he had earned in India, he suffered from a sense of alienation in his own country, as the British people did not accept him as their own man. But on the contrary, India was the real *karmabhumi* for him to realize his potentiality and have a sense of achievement. Chaudhuri offers a very insightful contrastive picture of Clive's life in the two countries, i.e. native and alien, "For one thing he had exercised power in India, which he could never do here. Personally, far from being able to dominate those among whom he wanted to live, he would not even have been adopted by them as one of his own. Most important of all, he had discovered himself in the adventures, dangers and exceptional situations of his Indian career. That self could not survive in England" (118). That is why Clive never cut himself off from the East India Company. He was eager to go to India again he could get a chance once again. In March 1755, he was offered a post in India as a member of the Council with seniority next to the Governor and as deputy at Fort St David. He sailed to India in April 1755. Thus a new chapter began in Clive's life.

The French people could not build an Empire in India, as their interest in India was only commercial. Dupleix could not get any support from the French Government to extend the imperial rule in India. He was recalled from India by the French Government. The lack of imperial ambition of the French in India naturally intensified the imperial ambition of the English in India. But the circumstances and method of the English Company were different. "In giving all credit to Dupleix for being the forerunner and teacher of the English in certain matters, it should not be forgotten that British rule in India was established by a wholly different method and in different circumstances. It did not grow out of the process set going by Dupleix" (147).

The main reason why the British succeeded in founding the Empire in India was their military superiority and success, although they had recourse to other nefarious means like intrigues, trickery, cunning, bribery, etc. "The very first thing that has to be said about the foundation of the British Empire in India is that it was established by means of military power and military success..." (154). After emphasizing the military superiority of the British, Chaudhuri summarizes Alexis de Tocqueville's views about how the lack of unity among Indians was very advantageous to the British adventurers, "...what the English did was nothing new—the Arabs, Afghans and Moguls had done it before them, as had the Portuguese and the French, it is always an advantage for a conqueror to come after others; India had always been a country most prepared for conquest and servitude; the conquerors never encountered a great but a multitude of small groups insufficiently united; it was not courage that was lacking in the Indian people, but the will to apply their courage to resist foreign invasion and tyranny; the natives were accustomed through the ages to see rulers of other races and religions dominating them, for the greater part the English did not have to fight any great nation in India, but only a foreign aristocracy" (155). Chaudhuri endorses Tocqueville's opinion that conquering India by the British (as also by Alexander the Great in the past) was not a matter of merit and that the British armies were commanded by officers of just ordinary merit, Chaudhuri rightly observes that the Indian kings, Muslims or Hindus, were given to superstitions and consulted astrologers or wanted for good omens before launching a battle; and that the Indian soldiers were habituated to eat a large meal at night and sleep so heavily at night that they would not attack at night and could also be easily surprised by a night attack.

Initially the English had no idea of establishing their Empire in India, "Their only object was to oppose the designs of Dupleix and make the French innocuous in India. For this purpose they were as ready to help an Indian prince as to oppose one, according to circumstances" (159). London was worried about the continuation of the war with the French.

Since Colonel Lawrence, the most senior officer in India was suffering from asthma; Clive was appointed by the Council to command the Company's land forces in order to re-take Calcutta from Sirajuddaula (an eastern imitation of Caligula and Nero). Finally they succeeded in re-occupying Calcutta on January 2, 1757. After a futile struggle with the British, Sirajuddaula had to sign a treaty of peace on February 9, 1757. But on June 23, the battle of Plassey was fought. In that battle Siraj was overthrown and killed. Clive installed Jafar as *Nawab*. Clive was not yet thirty-two, but he became more ambitious and wrote to his father about his wish to be appointed the Governor-General of India.

Then Clive attacked Chandranagore and captured it. The capture of Chandranagore eliminated the French as a possible source of trouble for the English in their dealings with Siraj. There was a conspiracy in the English Company to get rid of Siraj. Clive was the principal in this drama. Omichand had demanded a huge sum of money (i.e. 5% of all the *Nawab's* treasures) from the English Company. But Clive was so clever that he made two versions of the treaty, one real and the other fictitious and decided to deceive Omichand systematically. Clive never felt any qualms about this deceptive transaction. Chaudhuri points out that the British Empire in India came into existence after the battle of Plassey was won, "The exact point reached both politically and psychologically in the creation of the British Empire in India when the battle of Plassey was won should be obvious to anybody, who reads the contemporary records of the doings, thoughts and feelings of those, who were concerned with it" (278). The initial solution of a commercial problem in July 1757 paved the way for the Imperial rule hundred years later, i.e. 1857. Chaudhuri comments on the teleology in history insightfully, "There is indeed teleology in history, but it is only perceptible in retrospect, and is never controlled by free will. There can be no doubt that after the battle of Plassey the course was set for the Proclamation of Queen Victoria in 1858" (278).

Clive became very unpopular both in India and in England for having deceived Omichand. "Thus Omichand faded away in India, only to acquire a great name in England among English moralists as a martyr to the villainy of Clive..." (283).

Chaudhuri highlights an important aspect of Clive's life, i.e. his greed for money. Clive and other officers of the Company used to receive large sums of money as gifts from the native princes of Bengal. "The acceptance of these gifts was not contrary to the regulations then in force for the King's Army and Navy nor were they forbidden by any rule laid down by the Company" (284). Clive never felt guilty or ashamed of receiving presents from the princes. On the contrary he tried to justify it. Clive became notorious when he became an owner of a *jagir*. In exchange for the help that Clive had rendered to Mir Jafar, the latter recommended a *mansab* for Clive in 1757. "This was granted to Clive formally by an order of the Emperor of Delhi, which said that Colonel Clive, an European, be favoured with a Mansab of the rank of 6000 and 5000 horse, and the titles of Zabdat ul Mulk, Nasir ud Daulah Colonel Clive Sabat Jang Bahadur" (297). A British man becoming a *Jagirdar* or *Mansabdar* in India was very strange, but it was a reality. His acquisition of a *Jagir* stirred the jealousy of other English officers at met with disapproval from England.

Chaudhuri offers a brief account of how Clive and other officers like Watson succeeded in eliminating the French and the Dutch from India. He admires Clive's ability and tactics. Clive acted as a virtual dictator in Bengal. In 1758 he became the president of the Calcutta Council. In 1769, he returned to England for the second time.

That Clive worked energetically and consequently fell ill repeatedly in India due to the tropical climate. But his ambition of making money propelled him to go ahead with the exegetical challenges. Chaudhuri points out the paradoxical element in Clive's life insightfully, "This dichotomy sprang from his aspiration to reap in England the exotic crop he had raised in India...which in its turn stemmed from his incapacity to forget England and live away from his country, and the still greater incapacity to break with the lower middle class antecedents of his life. Even his body and India did not agree. After every bout of demoniac energy and spectacular achievement he felt seriously ill and seemed to say to his real vocation: 'The spirit is willing, but the flesh is weak.' So he has to go back to his country to regain his health. But to do was also to fall into the clutches of the ambition derived from his social origins, which was to live the life of an opulent English gentleman. This would not have been impossible, but unfortunately the ambition had become inflated to the scale of his achievements in India. So magnified, given the social and political conditions in England of that age, it could never be satisfied" (317).

The professional achievement of Clive in India had awakened his ambition and given him grand ideas. Mir Jafar's generosity had helped Clive to live luxuriously in England. His ambition was revealed in his letter to his father, "If I can get into Parliament I shall be very glad, but no more struggles against the Ministry; I choose to be with them" (318). Clive dreamt of becoming a Member of Parliament because of the prestige attached to the post. Chaudhuri remarks rightly, "But in the England of that period, and for a long time afterwards, the social ambitions of a man could never exclude Parliament, because it was not simply a political body, still less a mere legislature, but the grand club of all Englishmen of any significance" (320). His ambition was determined by his social origins. The poor boy and the son of a petty attorney wanted to show in England the prizes he had won in India, as any school boy does" (323).

In England Clive was initially treated as the prize boy. His reputation had preceded him. He was considered as 'our East Indian hero' on account of his victories. Clive began to get some recognition in his motherland. Towards the end of 1761, he got his title, which was an Irish one. He chose the name of Baron Clive of Plassey, County Clare in the Kingdom of Ireland. The Plassey in Ireland was his estate of Bally Kitty, which he renamed for the title, yielding 2000 Pounds. Macaulay also opined that honours and rewards awaited Clive at home for his achievements in India. Thus Clive became a legend in his native country.

Clive earned a lot of money both by his professional adventures and by the gifts from the eastern ruler, Mir Jafar. Chaudhuri says that even Clive's money, which was the most concrete of his possessions, became a legend, and was a subject of general conversation and speculation. Chaudhuri quotes from the Annual Register for 1760, edited by Burke to show the earnings of Clive, "'It is supposed that the General can realize 1,200,000 Pounds in cash, bills, and jewels; that his lady has a casket of jewels, which are estimated at least at 200,000 Pounds so that he may with propriety be said to be the richest subject in the three kingdoms.' Actually Clive's fortune yielded him an income of about 13,000 Pounds a year, and if the 27,000 Pounds or so from the quitrent of his *jagir* was added he had approximately 40,000 Pounds a year—not an exceptional sum even for a merchant" (327).

Having earned the huge amount of money by the Indian standards, Clive spent his money liberally instead of living like a miser. He "spent it in a manner not thought decorous in a parvenu. He gave away 50,000 Pounds in gifts to friends and relations; settled an annuity of 500 Pounds on his father, the same amount to his old Commander, Lawrence, 150 Pounds a year on his aunts, and so on. He took a house a Berkeley Square, and not satisfied with repairing Styche, his old home, acquired

Walcott Park at the inflated price of 92,000 Pounds and had a house built there" (328).

The material success that Clive had achieved in his life created a sort of envy for him in the British society. There grew some kind of alienation between him and the popular mind. His enemies unscrupulously spread calumnies about him because they considered him as an upstart from the lower middle-class. After the accession of George III in England, Clive was disrespected by the public as a selfish man pursuing his own private interests in a public role. In the election to the Court of Directors of the East India Company, Sullivan was elected as Chairman and Clive lost. Sullivan became an enemy of Clive. "Clive had come to England in search of health and recuperation. But he was the last man to enjoy rest. Such men must be active or they fret" (340). Clive had some minor frustrations in connection with his friends and colleagues. This was a period of doldrums for him. Chaudhuri rightly points out that Clive was not a self-sufficient man, but a man for whom others have to provide opportunities. In England Clive suffered indifference by his own countrymen and had no opportunity to realize his ambition. "Clive's stay in England was characterized by self-interest and seeming hypocrisy. Any comparison between Clive's activities in India and in England shows that "India raised and England lowered him.... Clive's moral tone, like a snake's temperature, varied with the environment in which he had to act" (345). Chaudhuri repeatedly reminds the reader that Clive's personality had no elevated moral element in it. There is a blatant contrast between Clive's life in India and in England. Clive was more like Macbeth than like Hamlet. He was a man of action rather than a theorizer. This aspect of his personality is insightfully highlighted by Chaudhuri, "Clive had no interest in the theories of political ethics. He was a man of action, interested in thought as a means for action. He always thought correctly when some political course of action had to be determined. Thus, how he would show himself depended wholly on the situation he was in. That is to say, the environment governed his behaviour. The Indian environment of his life was stark, elemental and challenging and India always raised the level of his capacity. The English environment of his life was petty, and it always degraded him..." (346).

In England, there was a quarrel between Clive and Sullivan over obtaining control of the central direction of the Company in London. There were two functions fighting for power. Many parliamentarians felt that the Company should not be made a fighting instead of a trading concern, thereby giving its servants motives of avarice and ambition and the natives a knowledge of war and exposing Englishmen to cruel incidents. Meanwhile the political rivalry between Clive and Sullivan continued.

In February 1762, Clive was alarmed by the objections of his own countrymen about his ownership of a *jagir* in India. Clive felt a bit insecure and tried to falsify it on the Indian side. In 1763 Clive was defeated in the election to the board of directors of the Company by Sullivan. Then the Sullivan faction took their revenge within two weeks by writing to Calcutta ordering the stoppage of all money to Clive from his *jagir*. This ended the cordiality between Clive and Sullivan.

Chaudhuri points out that the English people were not aware of the concept of a British Empire in India. "In that age English political thinking was not able to deal with the embryonic Empire at all" (378).

Chaudhuri has offered a detailed biographical picture of Clive's political life, but has very little to say about his private life. He confesses, "Nothing substantial can be written on Clive's private life...the reason is simple—insufficiency of material" (379). The little information that we have on Clive's personal life shows that he was a man with a very great capacity for affection and loyalty in his personal relations. He used to write letters to his wife in his leisure time. He was happy when Lady Clive was delivered of a boy (i.e. Edward, the future second Baron). He had a fancy for rare animals and birds and he sent some of them to Lady Clive and (to the King of England). Similarly he sent precious stones like topazes, amethysts and casks of Constantra wine to his wife.

Clive reached the height of his glory when he was made the Governor of Bengal for the second time, during his third visit to

India. Macaulay praised, "His name stands high on the roll of conquerors" (383). When Clive was called upon to save what he had conquered, he accomplished it with extraordinary insight and energy. He enjoyed absolute authority to act. "He had an aura of personal power, which made others obey him—either from trust or from fear" (385). His character, behaviour and luck, all in their turn, played a part in building him up.

This time Clive was not in favour of any addition to the Company's conquests and possessions. But he was alert in keeping the Muslim princes under check as he saw the possibility of continuous ill will on their part. Now he was not interested in acquiring more wealth. As he gave an assurance for himself, "I propose no advantage to myself.... I am determined to return to England, without having acquired one farthing addition to my fortune. Surely then I cannot possibly design anything but public good" (391).

During this period Clive became acutely aware of the rampant corruption among the servants of the Company. They could earn wealth from the private trade they were allowed to carry on and the precious gifts that they received from the native kings. Besides they fought for fat remuneration for their services from the Company and double remuneration from the native kings. Sometimes the Company officers mutinied for higher wages.

Clive was over conscious of his money making in India. There was nothing secretive about it. But he worked hard to deserve it. Chaudhuri offers details of his monetary gains from three sources: from his regular allowances as governor, which amounted to only 841 Pounds in round figures; from the amount received from his share in the salt trade, which he capitalized by selling the profits to five of his colleagues for 30,857 Pounds; from the commission, at 1.5%, on the revenues of the *diwani*, which was officially sanctioned, amounting to 30,866 Pounds. The total was 62,564 Pounds over a period of one year and ten months" (418). Clive's acquisition of money created jealousy in some of his countrymen.

Immediately after October 1766, Clive's health failed completely and the worst part of his illness was a severe nervous breakdown, which was of a very different nature from the one he had in England. "Ingham told him afterwards that for two days he was out of his senses and his lower jaw was immobile. On one day he had to be given fifteen grams of opium. This, however, was only a palliative. He was cured by a bark, which had a surprisingly creative effect on his nervous disorders" (423-24).

Clive left Bengal on January 29, 1767 for his motherland. Chaudhuri states clearly that Clive was the founder of British power in India and not of the British Empire in India. But the authority and prestige enjoyed by Clive was not possessed even by Warren Hastings.

While traveling to England, Clive wrote a few letters to his wife. He wanted to offer her the gifts of diamonds, rubies and gold *mohurs* given to him by the native kings of India. He complimented her for bearing the pain of separation from him and concentrating her attention on the growing family.

Clive wanted to lead a contented life in England along with his wife and son. But he could not be happy totally because of his mistake. Chaudhuri points it out clearly, "Auld Lang Syne was regained with the happiness of personal life. But it was also to bring public persecution. Clive was not Byron, and could not shake the dust of England off his feet. This was his basic mistake" (433).

After reaching London on July 14, 1767, Clive distributed some presents to the King and the Queen. Horace Walpole wrote to his friend Mann, "Lord Clive is arrived, has brought a million for himself, two diamond drops worth twelve thousand pounds for the Queen, a scimitar, dagger and other matters covered with brilliants for the King, and worth twenty four thousand more. These *baubles* are presents from the deposed and imprisoned Mogul, whose poverty can still afford to give such bribes. Lord Clive refused some over plus (surplus), and gave it some widows of officers: it amounted to ninety thousand pounds" (435).

Clive was unhappy to learn that his *Jagir* was extended for a period of ten more years after the expiry of the current term, and that it was not to be his permanent possession. He did not like the way the Company took the decision without taking him into confidence. He, therefore, quarrelled with the Directors of the Company.

In August 1767 he fell seriously ill. His illness aggravated his irritability. He had to go to Bath for recuperation. Then in February 1768, he went to France along with his wife, brother-in-law, Strachey and Ingham. There he enjoyed better health and returned to England in September 1768.

After his return from France, Clive began to lose interest in public life. "...in regard to India he was getting into a mood of despair, which made him think of giving up public life altogether" (439). He was disillusioned with his own nation. He wrote to Sir Robert Barker, "To tell you the truth, after the next general election, I find myself very disposed to withdraw myself from all public concerns whatever. My own happiness and that of my family is the only object I have in view, and that can only be attained by retirement from the bustle and noise of a busy, debauched and half-ruined nation" (440). After the death of his close political friend, George Grenville, Clive grew more indifferent to home politics.

On the other hand the Company's position was also becoming shaky. There was near collapse of the Company's financial position in the course of which East India stocks declined sharply. By 1772 the Company found itself unable to give money and even had to ask the government for a large loan in order to escape bankruptcy. The Company's financial deterioration resulted finally in the taking over the government of India in 1858 by the Crown. The transfer of power from the Company to the British Queen's Government was due to four major reasons. Chaudhuri classifies them clearly and insightfully, "The Company had, however, had provided good reason for the Government's intervention. After Clive's departure from Bengal in 1767, there was a relapse into the conditions seen after 1760, though there were no new conflicts with the country's powers. The reason for the confusion and inefficiency was the same as before: weakness in the management in Calcutta. Clive attributed the deterioration to four causes: a relaxation of government under his successors; great neglect on the part of the administration; notorious misconduct on the part of the directors; and the violent and outrageous proceedings of the General Courts, of which contested election were the main cause" (444). Though Burke opposed the transfer of power from the Company to the British Government, he appreciated the Company for enriching the government. "Finally, he said that it was enough to provide good government for the future, and not discredit the Company, which had added an empire to the possessions of Britain" (449).

Although India made Clive a conquistador, Clive could not keep up that image in England, as the English people did not approve of his illegal earnings, insolence and pride, tyranny and rapine. They disliked the upstarts like Clive and the vulgarity and garishness of their lies. They were especially unhappy about Clive's ownership of an Indian *Jagir*. A playwright called Foote wrote a comedy, "The *Nabob*" parodying the Englishmen amassing a large wealth from India. Thus the British people vented out their righteous indignation and satirical humour at the officers of the East India Company like Clive. They talked of him as a 'fiend incarnate'. "It would seem that popular imagination raised Clive to the dubious status of a man, who had sold his soul to the devil for money" (458). Throughout these troubles Clive maintained an unapologetic and defiant attitude and never felt guilty about his illegal wealth. Though the Company thought of punishing Clive for his misuse of power for making money in India, it finally decided not to punish him in the light of the great services rendered by him to the State.

Offering a comparative picture of Clive and others, Chaudhuri rightly remarks, "In his political actions, too, Clive never showed the high-handedness of Warren Hastings, Wellesley or Dalhousie" (472). Similarly Chaudhuri appreciates Clive's honesty and transparency in money-making, "In respect of money-making, Clive never did anything that was not done openly and avowed openly. He never acquired money by dishonesty, by the disregard of any existing moral obligation or by oppression. Both in his public and private transactions, he never resorted to extortion" (473).

Now the old age problems started in the life of Clive. He was both tired and ailing. His recurring stomach ailment was accompanied by gout and kidney trouble. According to his secretary Henry Strachey, Clive had a very powerful form of dyspepsia accompanied by vertigo. But the real complaint was never diagnosed. Besides Clive was by nature melancholic and given to brooding, especially when without active employment. He suffered from depression.

Finally Clive died on November 22, 1774. There are different versions about the manner of his death. The generally accepted view is that he committed suicide. But this view has been contested and it has been maintained that he died of an overdose of opium. As Horace Walpole wrote to the Countess of Upper Ossory on November 23, "Lord Hertford has just been here, and he told me the *manner* of Lord Clive's death. Whatever had happened, it had flung him into convulsions, to which he was subject. Dr. Fothergill gave him one dose of laudanum, but he wanted another, upon which the doctor said that a second dose would result in death. Even so he took it and with fatal effects" (477-78). Lady Mary Coke erroneously wrote that Clive had committed suicide by slitting his throat with a little instrument like a knife. Chaudhuri questions such opinions. He even complains that Dr. Johnson was also prejudiced against Clive and did not know anything about the personal characteristics of Clive.

Anyway, the Englishmen of the eighteenth century saw "in Clive's death the end of a great beast" (483). But Chaudhuri laments the Englishmen's inability to understand Clive through a simile of hunting, "A fine poet has described the death of a wolf. Riddled by bullets, and with daggers of the hunters plunged to their hilts in his ribs, the beast gets up, licks his blood, glares at the gun barrels, still pointed at him, lies down again and closes his eyes without uttering a cry. But at least the hunters understood the wolf's death, whereas the contemporaries of Clive did not understand his" (484).

On the whole, it may be said that Chaudhuri's *Clive of India* is an excellent political biography of Lord Clive, which is inextricably connected with the history of East India Company.

By contrast, it may be said that it is not a literary biography like Boswell's *Life of Johnson* or Chaudhuri's own *The Scholar Extraordinary*, which is an excellent biography of Max Muller. A serious student of history, Nirad Chaudhuri has placed Clive in the larger perspective of Indian history and shown the interrelation between Clive and the East India Company on the one hand and the native Indian kings on the other and their fluctuating friendship and enmity. Chaudhuri's elaborate documentation and minutia of detail will be of enormous importance to any student of Indian history. But a student of literature is likely to be bored with the tedious details of historical facts and figures and epistolary evidences. In spite of the abundance of historical and political details, a student of literature may glean the biographical details of Clive's personal life—like his ambition, adventurous spirit, political alertness, military strategies, his desire for money-making, and professional success etc. and construct a cohesive picture of his personality. One may say that Clive's biography is ingrained in the political history of the East India Company. A student of literature has to wade through the jungle of details, to collect the rare flowers of biography. The picture of Clive that emerges in this biography is that an adventurous and ambitious young man, who realized his full potentiality in India rather than in England. Hence the title *Clive of India* is fully justified. Nirad Chaudhuri has provided rich source material to the students of history, political science and literature simultaneously. As M.K. Naik rightly says, "Chaudhuri is naturally on far surer ground in *Clive of India*... which is perhaps the most objective of this author's works, though Chaudhuri's admiration for Clive's spectacular rise and his commiseration for the sad last days and sudden death of his hero are evident enough."[3] Similarly K.R. Basavaraj rightly opines, "This biography should put at rest the controversy about Clive's conduct still lingering in serious histories. The author has been most judicious in his views about the Black Hole tragedy and the troublesome Jagir. The appendices which serve as excellent notes on the issue, the chronological table of Clive's life, the Glossary, the Select Bibliography of the works consulted to write this biography and the Index further enhance the worth of this book. Certainly, the author is justified when he maintains that no previous biographer has assembled facts of Clive's career and near miraculous achievement in an objective manner free of didactic assumptions. In this volume the author presents Clive as he was and his age, too, as it was."[4]

Notes

1. Karl Beckson and Arthur Ganz, *A Reader's Guide to Literary Terms*, London: Thames and Hudson, Reprint 1972. p. 25.
2. Nirad C. Chaudhuri, *Clive of India*: Bombay: Jaico Press Pvt Ltd. 1977. p. ix. (All the subsequent page references are to this edition.)
3. M.K. Naik, *A History of Indian English Literature*, New Delhi: Sahitya Academy, 1982. p. 269.
4. K.R. Basavaraj, *The Karnatak University Journal: Humanities.* Vol. XX. Dharwad. 1976. p. 337.

Chapter 10

Hinduism: A Religion to Live By: A Historical and Panoramic View

Nirad Chaudhuri's *Hinduism: A Religion to Live By*[1] is conspicuously different from his other books in the sense that it happens to be a discursive and objective book on the historical evolution of Hindu religion over the centuries. It is quite different from the other philosophical books on Hinduism written by other scholars like Radhakrishnan, M. Hiriyanna, P.T. Raju, Das Gupta, Swami Vivekananda, who have written patriotically and romantically about the major doctrinal issues and philosophical schools, as though everything was in a final shape all of a sudden. But Chaudhuri, being a serious student of history, takes the rather difficult path of tracing the evolution of this religion in its various manifestations of gods, goddesses, temples, rituals, cults and doctrines, etc. A conspicuous difference between Chaudhuri's book on Hinduism and others' (especially the philosophical scholars) books on Hinduism is that whereas Chaudhuri's is a diachronic approach that of others is synchronic. Many Indologists write about Hinduism from an essentialist's point of view or from thematic and doctrinal points of view. But they are not interested in knowing how the present form of Hinduism evolved gradually over the centuries by absorbing the foreign influences and elements and transforming them according to the requirements of the people. Chaudhuri clarifies it in his 'Preface' to the book as follows:

> This book attempts to give a description and interpretation of the religion of the Hindus as practiced and experienced by them. It is not a summary of their mythology, dogmas and rituals as found in the texts....

> The emphasis is throughout on the religious psychology and behaviour of the Hindus....
>
> The book is addressed to those, who, either in India or in the outside world take an intellectual interest in Hinduism in all its greatness and strangeness as the product of a particular kind of mind in a particular environment.... (xi)

Being a diligent student of history, Nirad Chaudhuri writes about the gradual development of Hinduism in terms of its gods and goddesses, ritualism and priest craft etc., and how they attained the present form. He offers a scientific survey of religion rather than a subjective and sentimental description of it. His study of Hinduism may be easily contrasted with those by patriots and zealots like Swami Vivekananda and Radhakrishnan and so on. Chaudhuri's impersonal views on Hinduism are likely to shock and hurt the staunch believes and fanatical Hindus. That is because truth is generally bitter and therefore hurts people.

In his 'Introduction' Chaudhuri makes a few general remarks about Hinduism, which are very perceptive. For example, he says that Hinduism is a human phenomenon of immense magnitude and bewildering diversity. Then he amends it and says that Hinduism is not one religion but a conglomerate of many religions. He states further that Hinduism is one whole, despite its all-too-obvious inconsistencies and that it is a special kind of religion, which has to be met on its own terms.

Chaudhuri clarifies at the outset that Hinduism does not lend itself to the Western definition of religion as a bond of piety between man and the Divinity. The Western people began to have regular communication with India from the 15th century onwards and tried to understand Hinduism as a religion full of esoteric wisdom, spirituality, *yoga*, *tantra,* etc. but ultimately failed to understand it correctly and wholly.

Although Hinduism repeatedly refers to salvation and the otherworld, its main concern is with this world. Hence it is not a religion of world negation. The Hindus believe in the superiority of Hindu culture over the European due to the intermingling of religion and worldly life in it. In other words, the secular and the religious are inseparable in Hinduism. The abstract dharma denotes righteousness and connotes religious consciousness. In Hinduism the natural world and the supernatural world are inseparable. Far from being irreligious, the Hindus sanctified the worldly prosperity in a very striking way. The worldly life is sanctified through the cults of gods, though the gods have no sanctity by themselves. All the gods in Hindu theogony are all human beings on a heroic scale, with all the human failings in godly measure and also power, but no virtue. Chaudhuri highlights the elemental character of Hinduism beautifully, "Hinduism in its fundamental aspect is a civilized amplification of the primitive man's way of living in the world by accepting the conditions which he believes are inexorably laid down by the supernatural spirits who really own and govern it.... In modern times, the collaboration between man and the supernatural spirits might be called religious feudalism based on the principles of fealty, service and protection" (22).

Another fundamental aspect of Hinduism is created by the geographical environment and historical evolution of the Indo-Aryans. Chaudhuri rightly points out that "...the environment was wholly hostile, because in India nature in all its aspects was in arms against man. Therefore to win the battle against nature they had to seek the help of the supernatural in everything" (23). Historically the great achievement of the Hindu religion is that "it has enabled Hindu society and culture to survive through vicissitudes, which have destroyed other societies and cultures contemporaneous with it" (24).

In the first chapter Chaudhuri recounts the difficulty of writing a history of Hinduism and opines that one can give only a speculative reconstruction of it, which tends to be fragmentary. He comments that the Hindu's chronology of Hindu stages is fantastic and it has confused and confounded even the Western Orientalists. The exact time or dates of historical phases of Hindu writers, texts and events cannot be ascertained exactly. That is why Chaudhuri wants to draw on dependable historical evidence like: (1) inscriptions, (2) art-objects, (3) religious buildings, (4) accounts of foreign travelers, and (5) works of secular Sanskrit literature.

Referring to the epigraphic data, Chaudhuri opines that the cult of Vishnu (or Krishna and his consort Laxmi) and of Siva (and his consort Parvati) and the Sakti (Mother) worship are found in those epigraphs. Similarly references to Dakinis (female evil spirits), the sun-god and a temple for the sun-god are also found in the inscriptions. About gods and goddesses, Chaudhuri states clearly as follows:

> Gods and goddesses for whom there were no major cults, but whose names are familiar from mythology, are mentioned in the inscriptions. Among them are Varuna, Indra, Sachi, Yama, Kuvera, Kartikeya, Kama, Rati, Chandra and others. Even the monkey god Hanuman is mentioned. The attributes and associations given to them in the inscriptions are identical with those given in the Puranas. (48)

Chaudhuri states further that even the Asvamedha (or horse-sacrifice) is mentioned in the inscriptions.

Then he points out that the representation of the deities in art supplements the data from the inscriptions bearing on the development of all Hindu cults. But the expression of Hinduism in art is very much later than that of Buddhism. The legends of Buddha began to be illustrated in sculpture at least from the second century B.C. In contrast, the Hindu gods and goddesses like Siva, Vishnu and Sakti (or Durga) do not appear in art on any noticeable scale before the fifth century A.D.

Chaudhuri draws our attention to the fact that the earliest representations of these gods and goddesses are not in sculpture, but on small objects like seals and coins. The representation of Gaja-Laxmi, Siva, Vishnu and Durga, Kartikeya and Ganga were found on the coins of the second to fourth centuries. "Clearly, by the end of the fifth century the gods of Hindu mythology and cults had received their well-known iconographical forms" (50).

In the next phase the representations of the major gods and of mythological themes are to be seen on the walls of the caves of Udayagiri near Bhopal. Vishnu with four arms and in his boar incarnation, Siva and *linga* and the cult of Durga were to be seen on them. One thing to be specially noticed is that these gods were illustrations of mythology and not images meant for worship in temples.

***

The information available in the travelogues of foreigners is scanty. The Greek and the Chinese travelers and the great Muslim scholar Alberuni have left some accounts about Hindus, but they are very scanty. The Greek scholars, who accompanied Alexander the Great (327-325 B.C.) in his expedition to India and Megasthenes (who met Chandragupta Maurya) offer adequate information about Hindu religion. But Strabo and Assian (who wrote on the authority of Megasthenes) give an idea that in the mountainous regions the people were votaries of Dionysios, whereas on the plains they honoured Heracles. Chaudhuri sows the correspondence between these Greek names and Hindu gods, "In any case, the existence of the mythology of Siva and Krishna seemed to be suggested, and also the later connection of Siva with the Himalayas and of Krishna with Mathura" (54). Most of them refer to Brahmins and Gymnosophists or naked philosophers and ascetics.

The Chinese travelers like Fa-Hien visited the religious centres of both Hindus and Buddhists. Yuan Chwang refers to Hindu temples, Buddhist *stupas* and gods like Surya and Siva and to the holy River Ganga where sin and guilt are extinguished.

***

The information available on the secular literature about Hinduism is inexact and uncertain. The Puranas, the two great epics (the *Ramayana* and the *Mahabharata*) and the later plays present one coherent body of mythology as against Vedic mythology. But these two epics mention Vedic type of religious rites, but none of them refer to temples or image worship.

Commenting on the connection between inscriptions and secular classical Sanskrit literature, Chaudhuri opines that inscriptions, in form are "the epigraphic counterparts of poetry in the books" (60). Chaudhuri's conclusion about the fixity and change of Hinduism may be seen in his own words as follows:

> Hinduism from that age down to the present shows the continuation of rituals derived from the Vedic traditions with worship according to the later cults, which have always been its basic feature. The infrastructure of the religion...has not been affected by any subsequent change. The cults of the three supreme deities, Siva, Vishnu-Krishna and Sakti (the Mother Goddess) have flourished side by side as they are still doing. The only new development is the transformation of the cult of Vishnu-Krishna into the cult of Radha and Krishna, which is as puzzling doctrinally as it is historically. Otherwise, Hinduism has remained the same despite an immense proliferation of variations and offshoot. What can be said of trees is also true of the religion; new branches or twigs and the falling and coming of leaves do not make a new tree. (61)

But the Hinduism of the present day is not an ancient religion. As a fully developed religion, Hinduism does not belong to any time before the fifth century A.D. It is not an old civilization, but contemporaneous with the late Roman and Byzantine and thus Hindu civilization and historic Hinduism are coeval. Chaudhuri states clearly that the early Hinduism was an archaic one embodied in the Vedas, but the doctrines and rites of the later cults are left to option.

***

In the third chapter Chaudhuri highlights the Indo-European core of Hinduism by pointing out the fact that all the languages of northern India, both ancient and modern belong to the Indo-European family and that the Dravidian languages are not a separate body but that they belong to the Aryan-Brahmanic culture.

Quoting the authority of Emile Benveniste he states that there is a common vocabulary of Indo-European institutions relating to economy, family, social life, power, law and religion. Similarly, invocating the authority of Georges Dumezil, he states that there is a common religious heritage of the Indo-European peoples.

He points out that there are many common words in respect of liturgy and ritual among the Celtic and Italic groups on the one hand and the Indo-Iranian on the other. Worship of light and worship of fire are the two important expressions of the Hindu religious consciousness, which must have come from some cold region, especially from the assumed habitat of the people, who spoke the Indo-European languages i.e. the European plain from Danube to the Volga. Chaudhuri points out that an "ecstatic attitude to light is the most striking feature of the most rarefied religious sentiment of the Hindus" (68). For them light is identified with Atman or Oversoul. Chaudhuri opines that the whole idea of refulgence as a source of joy would be foreign to India. Then he expresses his views boldly and authoritatively, "I put forward the theory that the Indo-Aryans had formulated their association between light and religion from what they saw on the snow-covered plains of their original home, probably in south Russia, and took it with them to India, where it was an intrusion" (71).

The Hindu worship of fire also denotes the original area of cold climate from which it migrated to India. Agni is a personified and deified fire, to whom Hindus offer great reverence, because fire is useful for many of his day-to-day activities like cooking, etc. Chaudhuri states very clearly, "The old religious attitude of the Hindus to fire is akin to that of the Romans and Persians. In all of them this must have come from a common habitat" (74).

Then Chaudhuri observes that the elaborate rituals of the Vedic religion testify to their Indo-European character. He shows the close connection between the Romans and the Indians in their rituals, which shows their common origin in a prehistoric past. The parallelisms are very striking, especially in the rite of sacrifice. The *yajna* is the major rite in Hinduism, so is *sacrificium* in Roman religion. The purpose of sacrifice among both the peoples was the same i.e. to obtain and secure worldly welfare of every kind.

Next Chaudhuri moves from rituals to the higher i.e. conceptual level of Hinduism and their mythological expression. At this juncture the whole content of comparative mythology is combined with comparative religion. "The most primitive

Indo-European notion of a divine order is perhaps the idea of the bright sky as a non-anthropomorphic deity. The Greek Zeus Pater, the Latin Jupiter and the Sanskrit Dyus Pitr, all embody it" (79). The most striking oneness of all the Indo-European pantheons is to be found in the structure and organization of the society and hierarchy of the gods and goddesses, especially the tripartite organization (like the sovereign gods, the warrior gods and the economic gods). "In the pantheon of even a late age these three classes of gods were grouped into classes known as the Adityas, Rudras and Vasus" (83).

In the fourth chapter Chaudhuri sketches the evolution of the Hindu religious experience. He says that the Vedic corpus shows a good deal of stratification and great heterogeneity. It is a canonical embodiment of beliefs and practices, which had developed over a fairly long period of time. It underwent a drastic change over the time.

According to Chaudhuri, the first change that the Indo-European form of Hinduism underwent since its unknown origins was the shift from a non-anthropomorphic concept of the supreme deity to an anthropomorphic concept. Unlike the Greeks and the Persians, the Hindus did not abandon the pre-anthropomorphic deity at all, but put him in a parallel channel of their religious life with their anthropomorphic polytheism. "This is the famous Way of Knowledge or Gnosis (*Jnana Marga*), in which a formless, attribute-less, eternal and infinite deity is the object of mystical contemplation. In other words, the notion of Brahman or Atman was the continuation of the old non-anthropomorphic idea, and so far as the Way of Knowledge survives among the Hindus it has remained non-anthropomorphic" (86). Then the concept of the Atman came to an end in religious life and passed into philosophy.

Chaudhuri makes a very perceptive observation when he says that the Vedic ritualism and the Vedic mysticism seem to have continued side by side until a new type of cult with Siva and Vishnu-Krishna as alternative deities emerged in the first century B.C. The two Hindu gods were more like the monotheistic God of the historic religions and had some of their attributes. Instead of one, there were two gods of the monotheistic type, either one of which could be chosen by a votary as his personal god. Besides, there was no obligation on any Hindu to worship any one of them. He was free to choose any one of these two gods and become the worshipper of a monotheistic god, in a very special sense. "I would call this cult polymorphous monotheism, a very special form of monotheism created by the Hindus" (88). Chaudhuri clarifies further that in this polymorphous monotheism, the cult of Siva or Saivism emerged first, and the Vishnu-Krishna cult or Vaishnavism came afterwards as an imitation and duplication.

The cult of the Mother-Goddess was added to those of Siva and Vishnu-Krishna. These cults, says Chaudhuri, took a few centuries to become fully developed, but by the beginning of the Christian era the first two had taken root. "With this also came the greatest revolution in the history of Hinduism—the introduction of image worship in temples, which the religion had not known before. To the outside world and even to non-Hindus in India, Hinduism is identified now with idolatry and temples. Yet the religion had existed without them for one thousand years at least" (90). Then Chaudhuri points out that the worship of the images in temples is wholly optional. He observes further that the idol worship, which was an expression of anthropomorphism of Indo-European religions, found practical expression among the Greeks, and deeply influenced the Hindu culture after the invasion of India by Alexander the Great. "There can be no doubt that temples and images were taken over by the Hindus from the Greeks, who had settled in what is now Punjab and Afghanistan. This would be perfectly consistent with the general development of architecture and sculpture in ancient India" (95).

After the adoption of temples and images, the next great change in the Hindu religion is seen in the introduction of a wholly new feeling for the monotheistic gods, which is the famous Way of Love (*Bhakti Marga*).

Next Chaudhuri points out that the Hindu religion was not influenced by the aboriginals or untouchables, as was believed by the romantic German scholars, who attributed everything base and dishonourable to the non-Aryans or aboriginals.

Commenting on the role of the South, Chaudhuri says that from the ninth century onwards new religious speculation, exegesis and movements originated in the South. There was a shift from the philosophy of the Vedanta, but also a new religious feeling manifested both in Saivism and Vaishnavism. Another interesting aspect of the geographical shift is that in contrast with the north, where all the religious and philosophical texts had fictitious or eponymous authors, mostly the legendary sages, in the south these were composed by definite historical persons. The anonymity of Hinduism came to an end" (99).

***

In the second part of the book Chaudhuri offers a descriptive picture of Hinduism. He avers, "To give a description of Hinduism is not as difficult as to reconstruct its history" (103). But even this has a problem. A scholar has to wade through superabundant mass of information on mythology, doctrines and rituals contained in the texts and show Hinduism not only in its fully developed state, but also at its most typical.

Chaudhuri observes that Hinduism has undergone some kind of erosion in the twentieth century due to the cultural impact of the West and the economic changes in life. The cultural elite of India are superstitious and the villagers practice a simple kind of Hindu religion. He rightly opines that the picture of Hinduism does not become clear until about the seventeenth century when the Europeans began to write about it. These European writers were all Christian priests or missionaries. The first book was written by an English clergyman, Henry Lord and published in London in 1630. Chaudhuri summarizes some of his observations about Hindus like the effeminate and maidenly look of the *baniyas* (or Vaishyas) and the shyness and reticence of Brahmins.

Then Chaudhuri mentions the second description of Hindus by a Dutch priest, Abraham Roger. Administrative necessity also gave rise to a genuine scientific interest in Hinduism. The foundation of the Asiatic society of Bengal marks the beginning of serious studies. H.T. Colebrooke, a civil servant of the East India Company was the first scholar to provide a reliable account of Vedic literature and to describe the current aspects of Hinduism. The second official to contribute to the knowledge of Hinduism was Horace Hayman Wilson, a leading English Sanskrit scholar of the age. Gradually the religious interest among the administrators widened into the ethnographic and sociological as well. Most of these Oriental scholars wrote about Hinduism in order to understand the Hindus and convert them into Christians.

Apart from serious books on Hinduism, there were also popular books written by Westerners, who described and laughed at the Hindu things and events like the car of Juggernaut, the suttee, the bloody sacrifices, the lechery of Krishna and of his worshippers, hook-swinging and mothers throwing their babies into the River Ganga, etc. Unfortunately such accounts became more popular than the serious books.

Chaudhuri values the missionary writings on Hindus and Hinduism in the nineteenth century for their historical importance, although the missionary motives were ulterior. He sees two trends in their writings, one, polemical and the other, objective. But Chaudhuri deplores the modern Hindus' condemnation of even the objectivity of the missionaries. Even the realistic approach of the missionaries has not been liked by the Hindus. For example Abbe Dubois' famous *Hindu Manners, Customs and Ceremonies* (pub. 1897) is very valuable for the immense amount of information it gives about the state of Hindu society and religion in South India. There is no book like that for any other part of India. But the only point that may be made against this book is that he, like other missionaries, ignores the higher religious sentiment and thought, which can be found in the doctrinal texts, especially *Upanishads*.

The Hindu writing about Hinduism becomes complementary to what the European missionaries and British administrators have written about it. But Chaudhuri points out that the Hindus' formal presentation of it is either polemical or apologetic. The first Hindu to produce this kind of apology was the reformer Rammohun Roy (1772-1833). Commenting upon these Hindu apologetics Chaudhuri rightly remarks, "What they attempted to do was to make Hinduism consistent with the European thought of the age, especially with the conclusions of comparative religion and even anthropology" (112).

Chaudhuri observes that the foreign travelers like Alberuni and scholars like (the Frenchman) Abbe Dubois faced great difficulties in eliciting full information about Hinduism, especially Brahmins, who were notorious for their unwillingness to communicate with *Mlechchas*, purity mania, superiority complex, secretiveness and hauteur. But the foreign travelers and scholars tried their best to overcome these difficulties and presented their observations on Hindus precisely and honestly.

Chaudhuri quotes the opinions of European scholars about the decadence and corruption of Hinduism. The Orientalist scholars like Max Muller, and Sir Monier-Williams thought that Hinduism was decaying slowly and on its way to death. But Chaudhuri strikes a balance by quoting a passage from Sir Alfred Lyall, who strongly opined that Hinduism would not die at all, and that it was a living religion.

Chaudhuri points out the paradoxical nature of Hinduism when he says, "Of Hinduism it was said to that the more it changes the more it remains the same thing. So it creates the impression of staticity and perhaps even of stagnancy" (120). He points out further that Hinduism cannot die as it has a great psychological hold on the people and exercises its intangible authority over them. Chaudhuri adds in his typical satirical tone that "Hinduism has shown that anarchy can be as authoritarian as any totalitarian state" (121).

In the second chapter Chaudhuri comments on the regional and social diversity of Hinduism. Because of the bewildering diversity, Hinduism appears like a conglomeration of religions. Chaudhuri compliments the Europeans for giving accurate descriptions of Hindu religious practices, rites and customs of a particular part of India. And he deplores the ignorance of native Hindus of the practices of other Hindus of other parts of India.

One important general observation that Chaudhuri makes is that although India was a land of temples, only south India is conspicuous for them now. That is because most of the temples in north India were destroyed by the Muslim rulers. "Over seven centuries from the eleventh to the end of the seventeenth all the great cities of northern India dating from Hindu times were sacked by the Muslim invaders and conquerors of India. All the temples there and in all other centres of Hinduism were systematically destroyed. None were left standing at Ujjain, Ajmere, Delhi, Mathura, Brindaban, Kanauj, Prayag, or Benares—which were the centres of the political, cultural and religious life of the Hindus. In most of these places masques were built on the sites of the temples, and in some with pillars taken from them. This religious vandalism also worked its fury on the Buddhist centres.... For most of the period of Muslim rule, there was a ban on building new temples and rebuilding the old in the regions the Muslims controlled" (126). Hence, Chaudhuri points out, it is impossible to ascertain what Hindu temple architecture was like in its homeland in the greatest age of Hindu civilization. Due to the Muslim rule, north India became Islamized, but south India was relatively safe from this danger. That is why Chaudhuri says, "It must not be forgotten that the most famous commentator of the Vedas, Sayana, and the greatest exponent of philosophic Brahmanism, Samkara, came from the south" (129).

Chaudhuri points out that the cult of the Mother-Goddess is virtually absent in the Gangetic basin, but is found in Rajputana, Nepal and Bengal; and that the Krishna cult in the sub-Himalayan regions of the north-west is the same as in Bengal. Chaudhuri points out how the Hinduism of the aboriginals of central India signifies vaguely a conglomeration of sects, tribes, races, hereditary professions etc., and looks like a heterogeneous confusion.

Highlighting the significance of the geographical diversities Chaudhuri says that whereas the Muslims go to the place of origin of Islam, Mecca, the Hindus have no fixed place, but go to the farthest places of their religion. "In contrast, the Hindu seeks to do so by visiting the farthest places his religion has reached in the course of his religious life unless he has made his pilgrimage to Amarnath, Badrinath, or Pashupatinath in the Himalayan fastnesses; Somnath on the Arabian Sea; Puri on the Bay of Bengal; Rameshwaram or Kanyakumari on the

Indian Ocean; Jwalamukhi in the Punjab hills; or Kamrup in Assam" (135-36).

Chaudhuri observes rightly that the Hindus have a uniform and coherent outlook on religion. "While Hindu religious beliefs and practices are multiform, the Hindu religious outlook is very unitary.... It is more a particular religious outlook than a particular religion" (136). The existence of this unity is all the more marvelous because it has not been created by propaganda or intercommunication. According to Chaudhuri, this unity has been maintained by the priestly class, the Brahmins, whose mode of life all over India remains the least affected by social changes; by the prevalence of the Sanskrit language, which has maintained the unity of ideology in the Hindu order; and by the corpus of standard religious texts collectively known as the Sastras.

Chaudhuri shows how Hinduism is the product of social stratifications in Hindu society—like the priestly class, the landed aristocracy and the commercial class. The Brahmin priests were well-versed in the sacred texts, liturgical practices and aggressive dogmatic and held the conscience of all lay Hindus. The commercial class consisted of the Vaishyas. The landed aristocracy and kings extended financial support for the priestly class. "They were in a figurative sense the owners of the religion, which the Brahmins were not" (139).

The mass expression of Hinduism could be seen in a folk-religious culture. Its nomadic expression could be seen in the lives of holy men or saints living as hermits in forests or mountains or places of pilgrimage.

In the third chapter Chaudhuri comments on the intrinsic diversity of Hinduism, which is bewildering, especially to the European scholars. That it is often compared to a banyan tree in which roots and branches cannot be distinguished clearly. It is also compared to an elephant as understood by a group of blind men.

Then Chaudhuri points out that Hinduism has no fixed doctrine and that a Hindu has an unlimited capacity for faith and therefore reconcile and unite a number of inconsistent dogmas.

Referring to the trinity of gods like Brahma, Vishnu and Siva Chaudhuri says, "...all three are thought of worshipped exactly as a monotheistic divinity would be, but a Hindu can choose any of these three as his particular monotheistic deity, without denying his allegiance to the two others. At some unknown time these distinct gods of the old Hindu polytheism appear to have undergone a process of conceptual syncretism, which made their particularity irrelevant to devotion, without doing away with that in liturgy and iconography. To this monotheism I would give the name of polymorphous monotheism, because in it one God has three forms" (151).

Chaudhuri points out that the enormous number of 33 gods of the *Vedas* slowly receded to the background. By the end of the 18th century, a large number of them were no longer worshipped. Some minor gods survived. The most important of the polytheistic deities who survived, were the following three: Laxmi, the goddess of wealth and prosperity; Ganesa, the god of worldly and especially commercial success; and Saraswati, the goddess of learning. Certain gods remained locally important, like the war god Kartikeya worshipped in the south and in Ceylon by the Tamils settled there and Hanuman, the monkey god, worshipped in the Gangetic plain.

All the major religions of the world believe in some coherent theory of human destiny after death. Chaudhuri points out that the Vedic religion believes in the view that the departed spirits live in a shadowy world called *Pitri-loka* (world of the ancestors) or the *Preta-loka* (world of the spirits) comparable to the abode of Hades of the Greeks or that of Pluto of the Romans, and Sheol of the Jews. Chaudhuri summarizes the Hindu belief in the after-life, which looks rather inconsistent and contradictory:

> But this early concept of after-life remained throughout ritualistic, and never intruded into the living beliefs about the dead. There were the following: (1) the dead if very virtuous obtained *moksha* or salvation, which was liberation from earthy existence and absorption

> in the Oversoul; (2) they were reborn in the world; (3) they ascended to heaven or descended to hell; (4) they existed as ghosts. Of these, it may be repeated, the notion of salvation was wholly unreal, or matter merely of theorizing. The view of after-life to which the Hindus clung with the greatest fervour was of rebirth in another household. (153)

Then Chaudhuri highlights the importance of the obligatory rites for the twice-born, the *Gayatri* mantra, Gurus, vows (*Vritas*) by women, the optional duty of visiting the places of pilgrimage especially those by the sides of rivers; fairs and festivals.

In the fourth chapter Chaudhuri makes his observations about the priesthood and sects. In India, all priests are Brahmins, but all Brahmins are not priests. But there were and are distinctions of status within the profession. At the top of the Brahmins were the spiritual directors, teachers of Hindu philosophy and consultants on points of sacred law. After them came those who performed the seasonal worship for fees. Lowest in the hierarchy were the salaried priests, who performed the daily rites in the houses of the wealthy. The professional priests always had a working knowledge of Sanskrit.

Chaudhuri observes that the general evolution of the religion by means of which all Hindu beliefs and practices became separated and were reduced to three major cults i.e. those of Vishnu, Siva and Sakti; that special sects were created by the religious innovators, reformers and popular prophets. These may be called the dissident or non-conformist sects of Hinduism; that the sects were also related to the position of a group in Hindu society—like the laity i.e. the Hindus, who are in the world and the renunciants like ascetics, hermits and mendicants. Besides the sects, the Hindus have a close connection with the caste-system.

In the fifth chapter Chaudhuri writes about the religious control of Hindu life. According to him, the Hindu religion exercised a rigorous control over their lives in every aspect and in every activity. The Hindus have to observe these taboos very strictly, otherwise they would be excommunicated. The punishment of excommunication is very severe psychologically and worse than death.

These taboos became more stringent by the end of the eighteenth century because of Muslim domination. As foreign colonists in India, the Aryans found their way of life threatened from the first by a native population, i.e. non-Aryan aboriginals. Then there came the threat from the external non-Aryan barbarians, who invaded India from the first century B.C. to the third century A.D. and again in the fifth century. The last horde of invaders, the Huns created as great a terror in India as they did in Europe. Their invasion must have fixed the notion of *Mlechcha*, unclean foreigners.

In the next phase of foreign invasion, the Muslims created a great threat to Hinduism. At the next stage the English created a new threat. That is the Hindus had to preserve their purity by avoiding any contamination from the *Mlechchas*, both Muslims and the English or Westerners.

Chaudhuri mentions how the daily life of Hindus was controlled by these taboos. For example, Brahmins were generally vegetarians, but meat eating was allowed to warrior castes and lower castes. But beef is the supreme taboo for all the Hindus. This is an extension of the worship of the cow and abstention from cow-killing, which was the most common reason behind Hindu-Muslim riots before politics entered the feud.

Commenting on the taboos regarding clothing and adornment, Chaudhuri says that the first requirement in all Hindu clothing was that it could not be sewn. The Hindu could wear only unsewn clothing, which had to be draped round the body. Normally, both for men and women, there had to be two pieces of cloth, one worn round the waist to cover the lower limbs, and the other thrown round the torso. Tucks were a quasi-religious feature of Hindu clothing. Another important restriction was that no clothes made from cotton could be worn for any religious ceremony. The participants had to be dressed in silk.

As to the ornaments, most of them were of solid gold and precious stones were not very highly regarded. But gold, being a noble metal, could not be worn below the belt. So the ankle and toe ornaments were in silver. Widows could not wear any ornaments. A widow, who wore ornaments, was regarded as loose. Similarly the widows could not wear saris with a coloured border, but only a white sheet.

Commenting on guilt and atonement, Chaudhuri says that the Hindu notion of sin covers almost everything that can befall a householder, or be done by him, e.g. the accidental death of a cow, being bitten by a dog, or sexual intercourse during the day. "All conceivable transgressions from the murder of a brahmin, incest, or robbery to those referred to are classified in order of gravity, with due regard to justice and the degree of responsibility. In doing so the treatises on sacred law (*Dharma Sastras* or *Smriti*) display that relentless logic, which makes all Hindu reasoning the height of irrationality" (198). Chaudhuri shows how the Hindu law classifies offences as *Ati-pataka* (sins beyond classification), *Maha-pataka* (great sins) *Anu-pataka* (minor sins, which are equivalent to mortal sins) and *Upa-pataka* (venial sins) and prescribes very rigorous atonement for them. Then he mentions that at some unknown date sea-voyages had become taboo for the Hindus.

Chaudhuri points out how Hindus firmly believe in the view that everything in their mundane life is determined and controlled by the planets and stars. Hence they consult the Brahmin priests, who are also astrologers, and who forecast the future events with the help of the almanac. Marriage, career, dangers to life, auspicious and inauspicious hours, dates of journeys, eclipses etc., are all understood with the help of these astrologers.

Chaudhuri observes that a Hindu's concept of life was dominated by the notion of impurity. All material things, including the human body, could become horribly impure, and some were intrinsically and irredeemably impure. "This idea was as obsessive as the idea of the innate sinfulness of man has been to many Christians.... The purification was the Hindu counterpart of Christian regeneration. But while the Christian could become regenerate only through the grace of God, a Hindu could always employ a rational and material means of purification, for example, water or cow-dung. The latter was obligatory to purify the cooking oven" (205). Then Chaudhuri offers several examples of impurity like days of solar and lunar eclipses, roads, the shadow of an untouchable, death of any animal or human being, childbirth, kissing and menstruation etc.

★★★

In the first chapter of the third part, Chaudhuri comments upon some special features of Hinduism. He shows his typical candour when he says that Hinduism has been the victim of both moral and intellectual diversity and hypocrisy. His first attack is on the ambiguity of meaning denoted by Sanskrit words. He opines that ancient Sanskrit lexicography was never good and modern is also very unsatisfactory. He ascribes the next difficulty to the verse form of the texts. He opines that the Sanskrit rhetoric and poetics were as pretentious as they were arid; that the writings in Sanskrit were known for their mere artificial prettiness and far-fetched conceits.

Commenting on mythology, cults and devotion, Chaudhuri offers his very frank opinion, which may shock the orthodox Hindus. "Even at the risk of being considered paradoxical and even eccentric, I must say that Hindu mythology has been the most serious obstacle in the way of understanding Hinduism as a religion" (220-21). He attacks the modern Hindus for equating their mythology with their religion. "Hindu mythology is even worse than the Greek and Roman in respect of the morals of the gods and goddesses..." (221). That is the reason why, Chaudhuri points out, the critics say that a religion, which prescribes the worship of such gods, must be much degraded.

Chaudhuri clearly points out that Hindu mythology and Hindu religion are essentially different things. He even goes a step ahead and says that "The relationship between Hindu mythology, cults and devotion is extremely complex. At times they seem to coincide, but most often they do not, and remain independent of one another. That is to say, the cults do not follow mythology, and the devotion disregards both mythology and cult" (221). In keeping mythology and religion separate, the Hindus were keeping company with the Greeks and the Romans.

Chaudhuri draws out attention to the contradictory elements in the play (the *Sakuntala*) and the epic poem (the *Raghuvamsa*) wherein religious and erotic sentiments are absurdly combined. Referring to the sexual enjoyment of Siva and Parvati, Chaudhuri remarks, "Kalidasa makes a staggering *volte face*, and in the eighth canto of the poem describes their sexual enjoyments with a frankness and gusto, which is not surpassed even by Cassanova. If one has to understand Hinduism such acrobatics of mind have to be faced squarely" (224). The Siva of devotion described in the invocation does not harmonize with the Siva of mythology (i.e. Eros) described in the later part of the epic poem.

Then Chaudhuri illustrates the separation between cult and devotion so far as it exists in the worship of Siva. Iconographically this is a phallic cult, for the god is now worshipped almost universally in his *linga* (representation of the penis) and not in anthropomorphic images. He points out further how the *linga* standing on a platform, which is a stylized representation of the vulva, happens to be a misrepresentation. This combination is unnatural, for it shows the penis coming out of the vagina.

Chaudhuri points out the absurdity of the combination of erotic sentiment and religious sentiment in the temple sculptures. The recent interest in it is rather pornographic, but the people do not acknowledge it openly because of their intellectual dishonesty. He offers a number of examples from sculptures, literature and mythology to illustrate the element of absurdity in the combination of contradictions.

★★★

In the second chapter, Chaudhuri makes a very scholarly, perceptive and comparative study of the cults of Siva and Durga-Kali. He rightly remarks that the cult of Krishna originated and reached its full development in India in the historic period, but the origins and early history of the cults of Siva and Durga-Kali are very obscure.

Then Chaudhuri offers a very valuable and interesting comparative picture of the gods and goddesses of Asia Minor and those of India. "Certainly the prototypes of Siva and Parvati are to be seen in this Hittite divine couple. The most decisive argument in favour of this conclusion is the identity between the mounts of the Hittite god and goddess and those of Siva and Durga. Teshub stands on bulls and Hepat on a lioness, as do Siva and Durga. It is impossible that it can be mere chance coincidence that two supreme deities of two pantheons should be both husband and wife and stand on the same animals in Asia Minor and India. Besides this there are two other analogies. The Hittite deities are connected like Siva and Parvati with mountains, and Teshub stands on some minor gods of mountains. Next, the couple have a son named Sharruma, who is shown standing behind his mother on a lion and is apparently a god of war like Kartikeya. These figures date from the thirteenth century B.C., when the Mitannians were still in upper Mesopotamia. It would not be unreasonable, therefore, to suppose that the Hittite divine couple traveled from Mesopotamia to India with the Aryans in their eastward migration, and then became Siva and Durga. But how that happened is wholly unknown" (238-39). Chaudhuri says further that Rudra of the Vedic pantheon bears resemblance to the Hittite Storm God. An important observation that he makes about the later mythology is really noteworthy, "But later mythology has as one of its main themes the story of a cyclical war between the Asuras or Danavas and the Devas, which can only be a mythological transformation of a historic conflict" (239).

Referring to the Mother-Goddess, Chaudhuri says that "She is not a Mother-Goddess of the Sanskrit type worshipped in Western Asia. Her character is wholly different. As the Hindu Mother-Goddess, she is not a hieratic divinity, but a goddess of rulers and warriors. Re-created in Hindu mythology out of the original Hittite goddess on account of the Indo-Iranian conflict, she remained the goddess of war throughout" (242). The worship of Durga with its accompanying animal sacrifices

Oxford and Sterling although he had never studied in those temples of learning.

As a writer he has extended the frontiers of the genres of Indian autobiography, biography, satire, and travelogue and enriched the field of cultural criticism. Like Joseph Conrad, who mastered the English language and excelled the English writers themselves, Nirad Chaudhuri has shown to the world that he can write and excel the British writers themselves in spite of learning it as a second language. It is indeed an adventurous task which requires hard struggle and deep dedication.

Negative Remarks

So far we have enumerated the positive qualities of Chaudhuri as a writer, thinker and a stylist. But he has attracted a number of detractors and enemies by his provocative and even hurting remarks. Many sensitive readers are touched to the quick by his remarks and observations which are brutally frank and ruthless and expose the hypocrisy and cunning of the people in their thought and behavior. Such people comment upon him harshly rather vindictively. For example, they accuse him to be a prophet of doom notorious for his eccentric and pervert and even foolish views. They accuse him that he has neglected the economic history of India and the British brutality practiced in India.

They complain that he works along the line of Western Orientalists like William Jones and others because of his own hard-boiled westernization and anglophilia. They comment that he is a man with a mission to defend the British rule in India and singles out Hindus for their double-dealing and hypocrisy, although such qualities are common to the people of all religions of the world. They accuse him that he defends the Indian caste-system and is unsympathetic to Muslims of India and highlights the incompatibility of Hindus and Muslims in India.

They further complain that his opinion about the decadence in India, England and America is rather arbitrary and journalistic and that he has not read or noticed the achievements of modern science like the discovery of DNA tests, anti-biotics and medicines against leprosy and inventions of computers and the cultural life of India.

They further complain that all his examples from literature are from extant literature; that he is out of step with modern literature and sensibility and that he invariably depends upon the authority of Western scholars for writing about India and never refers to Indian writers. They also club him with V.S. Naipaul and dub both of them as India-bashers.

Finally, it may be pointed out that Nirad Chaudhuri has his weaknesses like any other man or scholar and that he is not a God Almighty to be perfect in everything that he writes about. But what is remarkable and astounding is that being born in a small village of Kishorgunj in Bengal, and not being educated in a foreign University or taught in the English medium schools and colleges, and having battled with humiliating poverty, he has achieved something great in the world of letters and attracted the attention of the sensitive and sensible scholars all over the world. Like Goldsmith's school teacher his small head contains a large wealth of ideas and notions which are inspiring and provocative at the same time. He has made India proud though he lived away from India.

***

Select Bibliography

Primary Sources

Chaudhuri, Nirad C. *The Autobiography of Unknown Indian*, New Delhi: Jaico Publishing Company, 1972.

———. *A Passage to England*, Delhi: Hind Pocket Books, 1974.

———. *The Continent of Circe*, Bombay: Jaico Publishing House, Fifth Impression, 1974.

———. *The Intellectual in India,* New Delhi: Associated Publishing House, 1967.

———. *To Live or Not to Live,* Delhi: Hind Pocket Books, 1970.

———. *Culture in the Vanity Bag*, Bombay: Jaico Publishing House, 1976.

———. *Clive of India,* Bombay: Jaico Press Pvt. Ltd., 1977.

———. *The Scholar Extraordinary,* New Delhi: Orient Paperbacks, 1974.

———. *Hinduism: A Religion to Live By*, Oxford: Oxford University Press, 1979.

———. *Thy Hand, Great Anarch!* London: Chatto & Windus, 1987.

———. *Three Horsemen of the Apocalypse*, Delhi: Oxford University Press, 1997.

———. *Why I Mourn for England*, Ed. Dhruva N. Chaudhuri. Calcutta: Mitra & Ghosh Publishers, Pvt. Ltd., 1998.

———. *From the Archives of a Centenarian,* Ed. Dhruva N. Chaudhuri. Calcutta: Mitra & Ghosh Publishers, Pvt. Ltd., 1997.

———. *The East is East and the West is West,* Ed. Dhruva N. Chaudhuri. Calcutta: Mitra & Ghosh Publishers, Pvt. Ltd., 1996.

Secondary Sources

Almond, Ian, *The Thought of Nirad C. Chaudhuri (Islam, Empire and Loss)*, Cambridge: Cambridge University Press, 2015.

De Souza, Robert, *Goa and The Continent of Circe*, Bombay: Wilco Publishing House, 1973.

Dhawan. R.K. *Nirad C. Chaudhuri: The Scholar Extraordinary*, New Delhi: Prestige, 2000.

Iyengar, K.R. Srinivasa, *Indian Writing in English*, Bombay: Asia Publishing House. Second Edition 1973.

Karnani, Chetan, *Nirad C. Chaudhuri*, New York: Twayne Books, 1973.

Kaul, R.K. *Nirad C. Chaudhuri: The Renaissance Man*. Jaipur: Rawat Publications, 1998.

Naik, M.K. *A History of Indian English Literature*, New Delhi: Sahitya Akademi, 1982.

Naikar, Basavaraj, *Critical Articles on Nirad C. Chaudhuri*, Dharwad: Sivaranjani Publications, 1985.

Sinha, Tara, *Nirad C. Chaudhuri (A Sociological and Stylistic Study),* Patna: Janaki Prakashan, 1981.

Verghese, Paul, *Nirad C. Chaudhuri*, New Delhi: Arnold Heinemann, 1973.

has survived only in those parts of India, where Hindu rulers and the Hindu aristocracy have also survived, especially in Rajputana, Nepal and Bengal.

Chaudhuri points out that the cult of Krishna is connected with the Way of Devotion (*Bhakti Marga*). But he distinguishes the images of Krishna as given in the *Bhagavad Gita*, the *Harivamsa* and the *Bhagavata Purana*. In the *Gita* Krishna speaks as God in his own person, as Allah does in the *Quran* or Jesus in the *Bible*. The *Bhagavata Purana* shows the illicit character of the relations of the *gopis* with Krishna. "Adultery is both the doctrinal and the practical expression of the cult of *bhakti* in this book, and adultery itself is committed collectively and promiscuously. The whole concept of religious devotion in it based on adultery, which is given a spiritual value" (270).

Chaudhuri points out that Radha entered late into the Krishna legend, but how and why she came into it cannot be explained. Then Chaudhuri traces the theme of Krishna as depicted in *Brahmavaivarta Purana*, Jayadeva's *Gita-Govinda* and manifested in Chaitanya's Vaishnavism.

⁂

Chaudhuri remarks that the Hindus got all the opportunities for asserting power on the one hand and on the other, protection and a sense of security from their adherence to their religion. He offers a very valuable psychological interpretation of the effect of religion on Hindus. "In the first instances, this was due to the weakening of the will to live brought about by the decadence of all cultures, but also by the exposure over centuries to the enfeebling climate. The two in combination undermined confidence in dealing with the problems of life rationally and created a sense of inadequacy of human effort. Thus the Hindus came to feel that without help and succour from the gods their life and welfare would always be in peril" (295). Fear of the enemies haunts Hindu life. All relatives, neighbours, acquaintances, even wives and sons were regarded as potential enemies.

Chaudhuri points that Hindus fall back on religion in their sorrows and disappointments. Hindu philosophers declared that philosophy was intended to deliver them from sorrow, but the ordinary Hindus thought that the medicine was worse than the disease. Hence they derived consolation in sorrow. Otherwise they went to experience the joy of life by way of escaping from the daily grind and by enjoying the regular festivals around the year, like Durga Puja, Dussera, Dipavali and Janmasthami etc. The public entertainment, display, music, dancing, plays and banqueting was all provided by religion and not by social intercourse. Chaudhuri observes that Hindus are gregarious by nature and gather in big number in religious festivals and derive *tamasha* of all kinds. "Religion among the Hindus was never separated from their general life, and so they saw nothing wrong if provision for sensual enjoyment was made at the fairs and festivals" (299). Prostitution is also part of the religious fairs and festivals.

Chaudhuri is right when he says that modern Hindus have no eye for flowers except for worship, for which they are indispensable. There is no secular gardening. But stealing flowers from another man's garden for the sake of worship has become almost legalized by custom.

According to Chaudhuri the 'Commons of Hinduism' have a psychological desire for support or protection, which is satisfied by a religious Guru chosen individually by a particular person. By contrast the 'Lords of Hinduism' have a strong desire to possess power and to have freedom. Their desire for religious power is parallel to political power. They may be endowed with occult powers and work miracles and command respect and obedience by the masses. Their religious power extends to places beyond the reach of political power. That is why the holy men of India are invariably addressed as Maharaj or Great King. Chaudhuri is right when he opines that the psychological power of such holy men exercised on women, especially young, is very great. Many of them will be seen to be ministering to his bodily comfort by massaging his feet or fanning him. "There can be no doubt that there is a para-erotic streak in this homage, and at times the relationship goes very much further, and if the holy men choose to be sensual the women do not scruple to surrender their honour and chastity to them" (305).

Chaudhuri points out that an alternative to religious power is only political power. But everybody is not endowed with a political aptitude. Then he enumerates the details of freedom desired by the *sadhus* or holy men like freedom of speech and expression, freedom of worship, freedom from want, freedom from fear, freedom from the compulsion to work for food, freedom from the bondage to soil, freedom to wander, freedom from the compulsion to find houses, wear clothing and freedom from social ties and obligations.

***

Chaudhuri reminds us that there is no Sanskrit word for spirituality, but the Hindus have wrongly adopted the word *adhyatmic* as its equivalent, but it really means 'concerning the self'. Comparing the Christian spirituality to the Hindu spirituality, he opines that "The Hindu spirituality is a pursuit, not of beatitude, but of power" (315). He points out the paradoxical togetherness or alternation between the Hindu's worldly and otherworldly lives, "...in his spiritual activities the Hindu is like the dynamo, which generates electricity, and in his worldly life the motor, which expends it. Hindu spirituality and Hindu phenomenal existence are inseparable. They stand together" (315).

Chaudhuri remarks that the Way of Devotion (*Bhakti Marga*) was partly revived by the impact of Islam. He states further that the Hindu awareness of God was strengthened by the preaching of Christianity by the missionaries; and that the Hindus regarded their religious men as pious men, but never as holy men. He describes the Way of Knowledge (*Jnana Marga*) and the Way of Action (*Karma Marga*) as introvert expression and extrovert expression respectively of the Hindu spirituality.

An important observation made by Chaudhuri is that the Hindus did not attach great importance to intellectual understanding of life or empiric knowledge. True knowledge for them was a qualitative assessment. Most of the Hindu ideas were arrived at through intuition or super-animism. Their philosophical and ritualistic arguments contain the element of mystical exultation. Chaudhuri concludes his book by saying that the Hindu spiritual life has become pursuit of power through religion, and that the infatuation with power has nullified the greatest religious discovery of the Hindus i.e. passion.

Thus Chaudhuri's *Hinduism* offers a panoramic and objective historical survey of the bewildering and confusing religion that is Hinduism. Writing about the evolution of Hinduism or any religion is not a joke. It is as difficult to write about Hinduism as it is to catch a flying bird. Only an extraordinary scholar like Nirad Chaudhuri could dare to write such an authentic and research-oriented book on Hinduism, which is happily free from sentimentalism or glorification. Although the theme of the book is very wide, embracing the whole of India, he has written a little more about Bengal than about other parts of India, perhaps because of his being a native of Bengal, which is quite understandable. But one wishes he had written a little more about South India. One wonders why he does not refer to the protestant Lingayatism or Virasaivism popularized by Basaveswara, who rebelled against priest-craft and temple culture in south India, especially in Karnataka in the twelfth century. M.K. Naik complains that *Hinduism* is "a sketchy and one-sided presentation of a subject to which Chaudhuri returns again and again. The historical account is scrappy and the descriptive part makes too much of several taboos, which are only peripheral significance; while the analytical part makes no attempt to probe into the basic tenets of Hinduism and merely describes several cults."[2] When the book was published, the orthodox Hindu scholars like V.K. Gokak reacted strongly against Chaudhuri's views in the newspapers, but nobody showed the courage to disprove his views with sufficient documentary scholarship. It is true that Chaudhuri is an obstinate and provocative scholar known for his strong convictions and hard won insights. He easily disturbs and irritates the smug and pseudo patriotic. Although many scholars disagree with him, they are not able to disprove his views with their counter-scholarship. When the source materials about Hinduism are not properly organized by the earlier scholars, it is very difficult to reconstruct the history of the evolution of Hinduism. Hence it is not fair on the part of a literary critic like M.K. Naik to dub it as a sketchy and scrappy account of Hinduism. Besides, the intention of Chaudhuri is not to discuss the basic philosophical tenets of Hinduism (which is done by countless Indologists), but to show how Hinduism evolved over the centuries through the phases of transformation, nativization and localization. Again M.K. Naik has failed to notice the enormous importance of such solid writing. He further accuses Chaudhuri of making sweeping generalizations. But making such sweeping generalizations presupposes ability for deep thinking and perceptive observation based on abundant evidence. One may even venture to say that it is unfair to describe Chaudhuri's hard won insights as sweeping generalizations. One cannot but agree with *The Times*, which says that "Chaudhuri is a born writer. He makes delightful reading; imperative to anyone, who wants to understand India."[3] Similarly the publisher's words on the blurb describe the intention of the book correctly when he says that "General readers, who want to understand Hinduism, will appreciate Chaudhuri's new volume for the liveliness and clarity of its picture of Hindu life as it historically was and is. Scholars will welcome the book for the author's generally admired authority. The book rejects familiar assumptions about early Hinduism, makes dazzling reassessment of its formative influences, and examines the cult of the temple and image worship in general, as well as the three major cults of Siva, Krishna, and the Mother-Goddess."[4]

Notes

1. Nirad C. Chaudhuri, *Hinduism: A Religion to Live By*, New York: Oxford University Press, 1980. (All the page references are to this edition.)
2. M.K. Naik, *A History of Indian English Literature*, New Delhi: Sahitya Akademi, 1982. p. 269.
3. Chaudhuri, *Hinduism* Back Cover.
4. *Ibid.*

Chapter 11

Thy Hand, Great Anarch!: Autobiography as History

Whereas the *Autobiography of an Unknown Indian* depicts the first fifty years of his life, *Thy Hand, Great Anarch!* may be said to be an extension and a complementary sequence to it. There is no clear-cut division between the two autobiographical works as far as the time and theme are concerned. *Thy Hand, Great Anarch!*, which includes some facts of his early life, microscopically picturized in *Unknown Indian*, aims at giving a relatively vaster picture if his later life. If the *Unknown Indian* offers a close-up picture, *Thy Hand* offers a panoramic picture of Nirad Chaudhuri's life. In so far as it width and large rhythms of life are concerned; it assumes the dimension of an epic. It happens to be one the lengthiest autobiographies ever written in the world. The one autobiography that can easily be compared with *Thy Hand* is perhaps Bertrand Russell's. Normally autobiographies are likely to be arbitrary and slipshod, but writers like Nirad Chaudhuri have shown how even autobiographies could be written seriously, systematically and artistically. As Northrop Frye has pointed out, the writing of autobiographies involves artistic selection and concentration:

> Autobiography is another form, which merges with the novel by a series of insensible gradations. Most autobiographies are inspired by a creative and therefore fictional impulse to select only those events and experiences in the writer's life that go to build up an integrated pattern. This pattern may be something larger than himself with which he has come to identify himself, or simply the coherence of his character and attitudes.[1]

Although *Thy Hand* can be loosely called an autobiography, its detailed study shows that it is not a pure autobiography, yet it contains a heavy dose of memoir as well. An autobiographer records his own experiences as a participant in the events of life, whereas a memoir writer records his experiences as an observer of other people and events happening around him. Thus the heavy element of memoir, which is just a little less than half of the whole book may be said to be complementary to the autobiographical element in it. Thus Chaudhuri the participant supports Chaudhuri the spectator in giving a comprehensive picture of not only an extraordinarily sensitive Indian, but also of the large spans of historical events and movements.

As far as Chaudhuri's individual experiences are concerned, *Thy Hand* offers a greater number of details than the *Unknown Indian*. For example, he describes his intellectual growth by detailing the reading of important books. His reading of Falladon's *Recreation*, a collection of lectures delivered as Harvard University disturbed him deeply. But he immensely enjoyed reading Margot Asquith's *Autobiography* and was deeply influenced by Vallery-Radot's *Life of Louis Pasteur*, journals like *The Nation,* and *Times Literary Supplement* etc. These details are not mentioned in *Unknown Indian*. Chaudhuri describes the poverty, personal peculiarities, love affairs, outward callousness and inward tenderness of Bibhuti Babu very realistically and graphically. The reader is easily convinced about how and why Chaudhuri was deeply influenced and inspired by Bibhuti Babu. He acknowledges the help and encouragement he received from Bibhuti Babu to write and publish his articles in the British owned magazines like *The Statesman*.

Chaudhuri describes his mania for buying books even when he was unemployed and had his chronic poverty. His inability to pay the rent of his room (while trying to do his MA) and the dues to the booksellers and his humiliation by the landlord are narrated in a very touching manner. His poverty is closely associated with his unemployment. His temporary appointments with magazines like *Sanibarer Chitti* and *Prabhasi* did not solve his financial problems. But his appointment as a Secretary to Sarat Chandra Bose not only lessened his financial anxiety, but also enriched his experience of life in general and of political life of India in particular. Again he worked for *The Modern Review,* and *The Free Press Journal* (renamed as *Free India*) and many other journals including the Bengali ones. Because of his incurable poverty, he was compelled even to resort to ghostwriting, though it was not approved by his wife. Later he was appointed as a literary assistant to a very wealthy Bengali Ph.D. holder, namely Satya Churn Law for five years from 1939 to 1942. Since Dr. Law was an ornithologist and maintained many aviaries, Chaudhuri's close proximity with him helped him gain a scientific knowledge of Indian birds. But that did not solve his financial problem. A little later, Nalini Kanta Sarkar took pity on Chaudhuri and helped him to get a job in All India Radio of Delhi with a high salary, which was almost triple of what he used to get earlier. Thus Chaudhuri's long drawn poverty fortunately came to an end. His wife never complained or quarreled with him about his poverty—which is an evidence of greatness rarely found in modern Indian wives.

In the *Thy Hand,* Chaudhuri offers a detailed picture of his professional life, which is not given in the *Unknown Indian*. He mentions the details of his strenuous life. As he worked with two masters, i.e. Sarat Chandra Bose and Dr. Law, he had to shuttle between them almost all through the day. Consequently the strain of work told upon his health adversely. Though Chaudhuri was only forty years, he looked like a man of seventy years. But the great advantage of working with Sarat Chandra Bose was that it helped him enrich his experience of life and he could observe the Indian political life from very close quarters. He describes Sarat Chandra Bose's discipline, liberality, generosity, efficiency and anti-British views minutely. The diverse kinds of people including the young and the old, the normal and the peculiar, who used to visit Sarat Chandra Bose, extended Chaudhuri's knowledge of human nature.

Chaudhuri's appointment in the All India Radio at Delhi at the age of forty-five brought a remarkable change in his life as far as his financial security was concerned. He records his impressions about Delhi very honestly. He, for example, suffered a lot in the summer heat of Delhi and even had a heat stroke. But he was quite successful in his career as a military commentator and earned the admiration of British officers for his intelligence, good English (both spoken and written). Thus he had some temporary professional satisfaction in the All India Radio at Delhi. But this sense of satisfaction did not last long. At the time of retirement Chaudhuri's publication of his *Autobiography of an Unknown Indian* caused a great deal of jealousy among his colleagues, who tried to harm him materially. His service papers were not properly recommended or attended to, in spite of his serious attempts and appeals. Consequently he was retired on the due date, but his gratuity was not sanctioned to him on technical grounds. Thus his professional career ended on a note of disappointment. Finally after retirement he was offered a job of an editor of an English bulletin on a meager but fixed salary. *Thy Hand, Great Anarch!* thus, offers a panoramic picture of his professional life from his youth up to his old age with all the oscillation of his financial status. The reader cannot help pitying the financial insecurity of Chaudhuri in spite of the latter's being a brilliant scholar of international reputation. Chaudhuri has, obviously, shown how a sensitive soul is compelled to suffer in the callous bureaucratic set-up of India.

Chaudhuri's literary or scholarly growth is closely linked with his professional life. *Unknown Indian* has already described his scholarly quest microscopically, but *Thy Hand* offers some more details of his scholarly life, which are complementary to those of *Unknown Indian*. His scholarly attitude and obsession could be seen in his habit of voracious reading of encyclopedic range. Eager to find a direction for his life in the form of a vocation, he went on reading Margot Asquith's *Autobiography*, Vallery-Radot's *Life of Louis Pasteur* and journals like *The Nation* and *The Times Literary Supplement*. He mentions how his bibliomania in spite of his chronic poverty was disapproved by his relatives. One can easily perceive how in his life, reading, reflection and journalistic publication went almost hand in hand, thereby helping him consolidate his vision of life gradually and microscopically. Though he was initially interested in Bangla literature, he could not approve of the crude treatment of sexual life in it. He, therefore, grew disillusioned with it so much that he finally gave it up. But he kept his interest in journalistic writing in English alive and was appreciated by many intelligent British officers. Because of his scholarly pursuits, he was in epistolary contact with great scholars of the world. Being a student of history, he was in touch with the great historian Arnold Toynbee and used to get replies from him for his queries.

Thy Hand assumes the meta-autobiographical dimension in its description of the genesis, composition and publication of the earlier one, i.e. *Autobiography of an Unknown Indian*, which may be compared to a box within a box. *Thy Hand, Great Anarch!* thus achieves a sort of self-reflexivity and reveals several interesting details. Chaudhuri mentions how in 1947 he thought he might die within two or three years and how he decided to write his autobiography as he could not write a history of India for lack of facilities required for it. He is characteristically frank and honest in confessing that his insomnia and distress egged him on to write his autobiography. He mentions how he took nine months to write the first draft of it. He wanted to publish it abroad, but did not know any publisher. But luckily his colleague in the AIR, Melville de Mellow took the manuscript to England and arranged for its publication by the Macmillan publishers of London in 1951. Chaudhuri was naturally very grateful to Melville de Mellow. The book was reviewed favourably in the Western Press, especially in England and America, which gave him a sense of fulfillment. It also gave him some sort of material success. It widened the vista of his social life including the circle of friends. Consequently he was invited by the BBC to go to England for five weeks in 1955.

But there was a negative side to the publication of the autobiography. The Indian reviewer condemned the book totally. Krishna Menon, the Indian High Commissioner in London was said to be very angry about it. Chaudhuri's success created great jealousy among his close Bengali friends, who tried to harm him materially. A close friend of his wrote an anonymous letter to the Government of Department to proscribe the book. Though the green-eyed monster played havoc with Chaudhuri's life, he could not harm him totally. On the contrary, it inspired

Chaudhuri to write more and more so that he could scale greater heights of literary success.

The family life depicted by Chaudhuri in *Thy Hand, Great Anarch!* is more elaborate than the one briefly mentioned in his *Autobiography of an Unknown Indian*. The emotional ups and downs experienced by him are graphically described here and touch the chords of our heart. Like any autobiography written honestly and realistically, it offers a wealth of material for psychoanalytical critics. The first major event in his emotional life happens to be the death of his mother when he was only twenty-six. As he mentions, this event had a very deep influence upon his mind and made him very sad and pessimistic in life. Under the pessimistic influence of his mother's death, he wrote a short story about funeral ceremonies.

Although Chaudhuri had the juvenile habit of dreaming about a girl of seventeen years, he was not lucky enough to go in for a love marriage. Though he postponed his marriage about ten years, he was compelled by the contingencies of his life to get married finally to an educated girl in 1932. But after marriage, he never repented over it, as his wife happened to be not only educated but also very understanding and cooperative. Chaudhuri honestly confesses that marriage gave him an emotional stability and a direction to his life. That is the reason why he says, "Had I not married, my life would certainly have been lost like a river in a desert. Marriage made the river cut through rock and push through shoals to reach the sea."[2] He also mentions how he was lucky in the sense that although he was physically unimpressive, he was given the daughter by his parents-in-law considering his 'education'. Chaudhuri thus settled down to the regular matrimonial life. Later he narrates the expansion of his family gradually. He got a baby boy, who was pet-named as 'snubby' and christened as Kirti-Narayana. Again joy and sorrow went on alternating in his life. Chaudhuri, for example, lost his father when he was thirty-six-year-old. A little later he lost his mother-in-law also, who was about fifty-year-old and who was worried about his financial insecurity.

Chronic poverty seemed to be a very close companion of Nirad Chaudhuri. His life was not a bed of roses but one bestrewn with thorns all along. He was so impecunious that he could not pay the bill for the daily milk required for his children. Chaudhuri is very honest in acknowledging the humanitarian help of the milkman, who went on supplying milk to his family although he was not sure of the payment of his bill. Similarly, he records with gratitude a boy-servant's loyalty to him and his family. He acknowledges the greatness of his wife, who never complained about his poverty or quarreled with him. This is, indeed, a very rare quality in a normal Hindu wife.

Chaudhuri's honesty of expression and purity of character are at once revealed in his reference to an incident that happened in Delhi. When he was passing through a lane of Delhi, some pimp tried in vain to ask him if he wanted 'a pretty little wench from Bombay'. But the second pimp told the first that the gentleman, i.e. Chaudhuri never went to prostitutes. Chaudhuri rightly mentions that "that was the most resounding and prized certificate of character I ever got in my life" (713).

Chaudhuri's sense of humour may be seen in his description of himself as a 'Kuttawallah Bengali Babu,' a nickname given to him by the people of Delhi, who used to observe him going every evening with an Alsatian dog.

Chaudhuri happens to be a very keen observer of life around him and has a novelist's capacity to describe the scene in a very graphic manner. He, thus, brings the richness of fictive narration to the autobiography, which could have been a bald reportage in the hands of a lesser writer. His microscopic observation and almost photographic capture of the details of Nature and its beauty are remarkable. In *Thy Hand, Great Anarch!*, he has a few passages describing the beauty of Nature of different parts of India. For example, while he deplores the Bengali insensibility to Nature, he mentions his own sudden discovery of the beauty of Bengali Nature by saying that there is a close connection between water and Bengali life. Similarly, he refers to River Meghna and compares it with the other lakes and oceans of the world. He describes the autumn season in Bengal in 1935 including the dust in the street very minutely.

Likewise, Chaudhuri's description of the narrow lanes of Banaras and the serene sculpture of Sarnath is very graphic and almost photographic. It is because of his fascination for Nature that he studied the Himalayan hydrology and tried to learn some moral and political lessons from it. Similarly, his description of the Temple of Jagannath at Puri and the ocean is very elaborate and picturesque.

After getting a regular job at the AIR of Delhi, Chaudhuri migrated to Delhi, where the contrast between Calcutta and Delhi enabled him to observe the latter city very meticulously. He was really struck by the unimpressive look of the city of Delhi and suffered a heat stroke in summer. He honestly records the dust, dust storms and locusts of Delhi. His observations of Delhi and its life are very sharp. He refers to seven Delhis and calls New Delhi the eighth one. He observes the habit of the people of Delhi urinating at a wall or a post. He points out the dominance of commercial life in Delhi including wholesale business and import of foreign goods. He observes how the population of Delhi consists of Muslims and Hindus. He shows his scholarly admiration for the architectural beauty and grandeur of Red Fort and Qutub Minar, the melancholic grandeur of Tughlaqabad. He exhibits his perceptiveness of an art-critic and art-historian in his admiration for Islamic architecture, painting and civilization. He rightly opines that one can study the evolution of Muslim architecture from the 12th century to the 18th century of Delhi, although not all the greater monuments are there.

Chaudhuri's close association with Sarat Chandra Bose gave him a rich experience and knowledge of human nature in particular. This aspect of experience was not offered in *Unknown Indian* but it occupies a major portion in *Thy Hand*. Nirad Chaudhuri brings in the richness of fiction and its narration to his autobiography by offering a very graphic picture of his daily experience at Sarat Chandra Bose's house. His description of Bose's palatial house with all its paraphernalia like the furniture, garden, servants, maids, Eastern and Western type of cooking is very minute, elaborate and vivid. One easily gets the impression that Chaudhuri has written a chapter of a novel. Similarly, he captures the characteristic features of Sarat Chandra Bose's personality like his discipline, liberality, generosity, efficiency and anti-British views. Chaudhuri's close proximity to the great man taught him how to face the obstacles or crises of life immediately. He also came to know all the major cross sections of the Indian society—rich and poor; normal and abnormal; rational and irrational; educated and illiterate—which converted him from a taciturn into a relatively social man by rubbing off his rough edges.

Chaudhuri's autobiography *Thy Hand* has a big biographical chunk devoted to the life and career of Rabindranath Tagore. But he is very critical of both Tagore and Bengalis. The biographical-critical account of Tagore reveals as much about Tagore as about Chaudhuri's approach. Personally he had great respect for Tagore the poet, although he deplores the Bengalis' inability to understand or rate him in spite of their provincial vanity. He reveals some very interesting facts about Tagore's personal life and temperament. He mentions how Tagore was a product of interaction between European and Hindu life. He also points out Tagore's contempt for English novels (and even the Russian novel *Anna Karenina*) and even greater contempt for English criticism especially that of Dowden. He shows the paradox of Tagore's life by remarking how Tagore had to depend upon Europe for literary recognition and appreciation in spite of his dislike for British people. Similarly, he points out Tagore's alienation from the Bengali society and readership and contempt for their clichés borrowed from English literature. His mention of Tagore's further alienation from Bengali society after receiving the Nobel Prize for his *Gitanjali* in 1913 and his inability to get a D.Litt. degree from Oxford University and many other facts are very interesting revelations not easily available in Tagore criticism elsewhere.

One of the striking features of *Thy Hand, Great Anarch!* is that far from being a bald impersonal account, it projects a typically Chaudhurian point of view, which is critical and idiosyncratic at the same time. Being a highly original thinker and widely read scholar, Nirad Chaudhuri never accepts any fact or interpretation blindly. He analyses everything from his own rationalistic viewpoint and shocks the people including his readers by rejecting popular, fanatic and convenient views. It is not justifiable to brand his rationalistic views as only Anglo-maniac. He uses almost Bertrand Russellian type of chopping logic to deconstruct the meaning of people, things, events and movements. Among many things that Chaudhuri says about Gandhi, a few may be noted here. His opinion that Gandhi's upbringing in the Vaishnava atmosphere was responsible for his quietist views held later and that he did not have a higher Brahmanical Hinduism is sophisticated as well as acceptable. His attribution of the Western—especially Christian—admiration for Gandhi to the Christian pacifism is very insightful.

Chaudhuri offers a very subtle and contrastive picture of Nehru and Subhas Chandra Bose and admires their convictions and qualities. They were two towering personalities, who could never meet each other ideologically. Chaudhuri's interpretation of the collaboration between Nehru and Gandhi is interesting and realistic as he calls such collaboration opportunistic and calculated. In spite of his admiration for Nehru, Chaudhuri comments on his British leanings.

Similarly, Chaudhuri is very critical of the Hindu-Muslim as well as Indian-British relationship. He points out how the Hindus and Muslims distrusted and hated each other privately although they pretended to the contrary. Likewise he shows that the Indians and the British hated each other on political grounds, although they had cordial relationships in private emotional aspects. Chaudhuri does not spare the Indians either. He points out the paradoxical nature of Indians, who hated the British and yet tried to imitate them. He laughs at the Hindus' oscillation between xenolatry and xenophobia; between chauvinism and mindless imitation. Thus Nirad Chaudhuri's observation of the contradictions of people living in India is an evidence of his perceptiveness and clear-cut thinking backed up by his deep knowledge of Indian history.

That Chaudhuri is an extraordinary intellectual is evident in everything that he writes. That he is one of the great modern thinkers of India is incontrovertible. But his thinking is not an abstract one like that of philosophers, but a concrete one that is typical of historians, sociologists, ethnologists and political thinkers. Since Chaudhuri himself is a very perceptive student of history, his thinking is naturally backed up by a sharp historical sense and contemporary observation. From his childhood itself, he had a fascination for an intellectual life. He says, "I never lost my capacity to think even under the worst of conditions. In fact, it was during this period that I arrived at the ideas about our life, history and civilization, which have remained the basis of my interpretation of these things" (392). He had thus a great respect and capacity for 'mental creation,' but he did not like to be trapped in grooved thinking. He did not have any respect for a closed system of thought, which is normally enjoyed by a large number of traditional scholars of India. On the contrary, he has great love and respect for liberal thinking, which is based upon the past experience and revised by the fresh one. His intellectual sharpness, meticulousness, industry, precision and abundance of information are more than evident in *Thy Hand, Great Anarch!*. There is ample evidence in it to show how his intellectuality is supported by his bibliomania, journalistic career and intellectual interaction with great scholars of the world. The external evidence for his intellectuality may be seen in many of his brain-teasing books like *The Continent of Circe, To Live or Not to Live, Hinduism* and so on. His comments on the Indo-British relationship, the Indian National Congress and the International situation of the two world wars are pregnant with vast historical and contemporary knowledge.

It is but natural for an extraordinary intellectual like Nirad Chaudhuri to codify the philosophy of his life at least in the evening of his life. Whereas the *Autobiography of an Unknown Indian* was written during the meridian stage of his life, *Thy Hand, Great Anarch!* is written at the dusk of his life. There is, therefore, no attempt at the codification of his worldview in the *Unknown Indian*, but *Thy Hand* has a place for such codification as it helps him to look back at his past life—doubts, beliefs, dilemmas, frustrations and joys—and generalize the essence of his existence. Hence his generalization or codification tends to be philosophical and formulaic. The crystallization of his worldview is marked by his transparent honesty and scintillating ideation. He relegates the codification to the Epilogue of his epical autobiography and names it as *Credo ut Intelligam*, a typically pedantic label. The straightforward observations made in this section are very significant in that they help the reader unlock the mystery of Chaudhuri's life, worldview and interpretation.

Some of the remarks made by him are very interesting and comparable to those of many philosophical thinkers. His frankness as well as honesty could be seen in the confession of his loss of faith in Hinduism as well as other established religions at the early age of eighteen. Yet he developed some faith as a rational man though he did not care for intuition or supra-rational truths. He was more inclined towards the matter of fact or cautious interpretations than towards the imaginative ones of history. But the paradox of his life is that he prematurely realized that there is much sorrow in much knowledge. He honestly confesses that he suffered more from his rational outlook than from his crushing poverty.

Chaudhuri, in spite of being an agnostic, has developed a kind of philosophical faith. He says, "I have found peace in a new form of monism. I have been able to realize that the universe and I are one, and not at odds with each other. This is the very basis of my new faith" (945). He has achieved some kind of unity with the world. This union happens to be more an intellectual one than an emotional one. He also knows how he has to undergo the dark night of the soul before achieving the enlightenment of faith. "I would say that intellectual discipline is the purgatory through which a man must pass in order to reach the paradise of faith, and the passage can be, in fact, it often is, torture" (945). Chaudhuri has, obviously, passed through the purgatory to reach the final faith of his life, which, he says, is based upon his belief in biology and physics. One should specially note that his faith is not based upon religion and mythology. Thus he believes in a scientific or materialistic vision of life. He offers eight points of belief, which may be stated briefly: (1) The cosmos is not material in the ordinary sense; (2) phenomena or matter are subjective sensory perceptions; (3) the distinctions between matter and spirit are fictitious; (4) the universe is a flow or continuum; (5) there is no conflict in the cosmos as a process; (6) body and soul are not distinct;

(7) there is neither personal God nor are there many gods and (8) intellectual knowledge is partial knowledge and therefore it is only *credo ut intelligam*.

Many of Chaudhuri's philosophical observations are very deep and interesting and invite comparison with those of other serious thinkers of the world. According to him, man's body procreates, but his mind creates cosmos in a new dimension. Showing the difference between man and animal he says, "The animal is an automatic creator, but man, besides being that, is also a creator by volition" (952). He confesses, "I myself have arrived at a non-religious view of the universe as a creative process on the strength of the theory of evolution" (955). Though his faith is based on science, he knows that it is nearest to Hindu monism. He confesses that he believes in biological evil and not in theological or ethical evil.

Thus the philosophical strands of his worldview are made explicit at the end of his autobiography. The existential abundance of experience is followed by a process of essentialization. This kind of codification of his faith or vision of life naturally gives wholeness to the autobiography, which shows the transformation of the protagonist's experience into knowledge.

The most conspicuous aspect of *Thy Hand, Great Anarch!* is that only less than half of it may be called autobiography in the strict sense, whereas more than half of it has the quality of a memoir. In other words, Chaudhuri the spectator happens to be more dominant than Chaudhuri the participant. But what one appreciates in it is that the memoir element is organically linked to the autobiographical element. What disappoints the reader is that the memoir element grows far too unwieldy to balance the autobiographical one. In this respect *Thy Hand, Great Anarch!* invites comparison with Nehru's *Autobiography* in which Nehru the spectator appears stronger than Nehru the participant. A large part of the memoir element in *Thy Hand, Great Anarch!* is devoted to the depiction of the political pictures of India, especially the pre-Independence one. He offers an elaborate picture of the Hindu-Muslim hatred; the dynamic role played by Mahatma Gandhi, Jawaharlal Nehru and Subhas Chandra Bose; the Congress Party, governmental and civic politics in Bengal, India's struggle for freedom with exact dates, facts and documentary evidence. A large part of the book, which has the quality of a memoir about it, tries to relate Chaudhuri's individual life to the larger rhythm of national life. Yet one is compelled to say that this section is more enjoyable for political scientists and historians than for students of literature. The memoir element is so dominant that Chaudhuri's strictly autobiographical life appears to be rather insignificant comparatively. This is not to deny the evolutionary importance of the historico-political picture of India offered by Chaudhuri as a contemporary record of life. What is disconcerting to a literary critic is the disproportionate combination of the elements of autobiography and memoir.

Nirad Chaudhuri has given an artistic beauty to his autobiography by the use of his imagistic style. He exhibits his great scholarship in the employment of images borrowed from a wide range of fields of knowledge. The width of his field of references is almost Shakespearean. Geographical images are quite common not only in his autobiography, but also in his other works. For example, referring to his late marriage, Chaudhuri offers the metaphor of a river. He says, "Marriage made the river cut through rock and push through shoals to reach the sea" (343). Describing his experience of poverty and insecurity, he says, "It was like being on a raft after being picked up by a ship" (364). He describes the conquest of Bengal through a geographical simile, "The recovery and conquest of Bengal by Clive in 1757 was like the breaking out of a river through the highest section of a mountain range near its source, whereas in the period in which I am dealing in this book the river of the British Empire in India split itself into narrow and sluggish channels in a flat delta to be silted up wholly or to grope its way out in mangrove swamps" (394).

Being an ardent student of history, Nirad Chaudhuri is naturally inclined to use many historical images to highlight his point of view. Referring to the unromantic ugliness of New Delhi, he says that it could not be depicted in a very romantic style. He employs a historical image to convey his sense of irony, "Cleopatras did not lie on the beds of New Delhi bungalows and so there could be no question of raising the ghost of a rose in any of them" (730).

Chaudhuri employs many socio-political images to convey his ideas powerfully. He describes the shameless opportunism of Indian politicians, who showed their true colour after the transfer of power from the British to the Indians, through a very frank socio-political image, "All the nationalist beggars, who filed into the enormous buildings bequeathed to them by the fleeing British, realized what treasures were to be looted by them, and they must have thought their sacrifices were at last rewarded" (383). Chaudhuri's comparison and contrast between Mahatma Gandhi and Stalin is expressed through a political image, "In nothing else have Western writers gone more wrong about Gandhi than in overlooking his insatiable love of power and implacability in its pursuit. In this he was in no way different from Stalin. Only he did not have to kill because he could eliminate his opponents equally well by means of his non-violent Vaishnava method" (528).

Chaudhuri offers a very interesting animal image to describe Mahatma Gandhi, "On the animal plane Gandhi suggested the primitive terrier to me" (437). Such an image speaks of Nirad Chaudhuri's uninhibitedness and liberal imagination.

Likewise he is quite fond of using medical imagery whenever it is required. Pointing out the sympathetic relation between Bengalis and the Japanese, he says, "The truth was that the Bengalis, who had become nationalist drug addicts, were bringing down the Japanese to their level" (650). At some other place, Chaudhuri describes the Indian officers through a clinical image, "They were overwhelmed by the patriotism and self-sacrifice of Subhas Chandra Bose. He was the man, who wiped some of the filth from the body of these dirty military prostitutes" (787).

Many matrimonial images are employed by Nirad Chaudhuri at appropriate places. Describing the relationship between Subhas Chandra Bose and Mahatma Gandhi, Chaudhuri points out the period of waiting and anxiety for the two brothers through a matrimonial image, "For Subhas Bose and his brother

Sarat Bose these months were a period of fervid pre-marital honeymoon" (500). When in 1939 Paderewski sent a telegram to Gandhi for sympathy towards Poland longing for freedom, Gandhi sent a very sympathetic reply. But he also knew that "to ask the Indian people to have any sympathy for the Polish people at that time was like asking a wife to have sympathy for the cast-off mistress of her husband" (552). Nirad Chaudhuri's use of the matrimonial image to describe the political situation is an evidence of his liberal thinking and imagination.

Because of his wide range of scholarship and voracious reading, Nirad Chaudhuri employs a variety of literary images in *Thy Hand, Great Anarch!* as also in his other works. The international range of his literary scholarship could easily be sensed in his imagery. When Nalini Kanta Sarkar took pity on Chaudhuri and helped him to finally get a job in All India Radio in Delhi, Chaudhuri was very grateful to him. He describes his dire need through a literary image, "I accepted the offer at once. For me it turned out to be like the camel's thrusting of its nose into the Bedouin's tent" (405). Referring to the Bengali envy, Chaudhuri says that all that great Bengal produced in the 19th century was "a group of Dantean figures, in death sleeping far away from their ungrateful country" (665). Chaudhuri describes his own rational growth in a literary-cum-eschatological image, "I would say that intellectual discipline is the purgatory through which a man must pass in order to reach the paradise of faith" (945).

Nirad Chaudhuri is very fond of using Biblical imagery (which is part of literary imagery) to describe various situations of life. It shows his subtle understanding of the Biblical lore and his imaginative capacity to use it appropriately. He employs a Biblical image to describe Mahatma Gandhi's relationship with the Working Committee to the Congress, "Mahatma Gandhi was never a member of the Working Committee. But he hovered above it like the Holy Spirit, and sometimes even descended in the form of the dove of peace" (444). Referring to the corruption of the Congress members, he says, "It was as if the Congress organization as Adam had been coaxed by the practical leaders as a Congress Eve formed out of the ribs of

Gandhi, to eat the forbidden fruit" (445). Chaudhuri opines that Indian politicians like Subhas Chandra Bose would be happier in prison than being pestered by visitors. He, therefore, says, "Forced imprisonment was for them what self-imposed retreats were for devout Christians" (478). Chaudhuri makes very harsh comments on Nehru's pro-British policies, "Joan of Arc was inspired in her patriotism by the vision of the Virgin, but Nehru was both inspired and sustained in his by the apparition of Britain as the Evil One" (543). All these Biblical metaphors testify to Nirad Chaudhuri's sound knowledge of Christian theology as well as very perceptive observation of Indian things, beings and situations.

Since Chaudhuri knew the private as well as the public face of the Gandhian Congress, he describes it through a theatre image, "or varying the metaphor, I would say that I saw something of the greenroom behind the lighted stage and the actors without the make-up as well as with its application" (434). One may easily understand how the metaphor is resonant of many things connected with drama acting.

Sometimes Nirad Chaudhuri uses architectural imagery to drive home his point. That is ascribable to his sound knowledge of art-history and theory. He describes the ICS officers and clerks through an architectural image, "When Llyod George described the Indian Civil Service as the steel frame of the Government of India he forgot to mention that the Bengali clerk was its concrete foundation" (729). Referring to Gandhi's encouragement of bogus membership of the Congress by rich people, Chaudhuri says, "While this was happening on the ground floor of political life, on the upper floors there was vicious competition for office and other profits" (456).

Thy Hand, Great Anarch! is thus an important autobiography, which gives a very honest picture of Nirad Chaudhuri's life of continuous struggle and of the major historical events of Indian life in general. Although one may not like the disproportionate elements of autobiography and memoir in it, one feels that both the student of literature and the student of modern history may benefit from it by turns. It is easily one of the great cultural records of India with epic proportions.

Notes

1. Northrop Frye, *Anatomy of Criticism*. New York: Athenium Press, 1970, p. 307.
2. Nirad C. Chaudhuri, *Thy Hand, Great Anarch!* London: Chatto & Windus, 1987, p. 343. (All the subsequent page references are to this edition.)

Chapter 12

Chaudhuri's Prophetic Vision in *Three Horsemen of the New Apocalypse*[1]

A writer who can produce an important book even at the age of ninety-nine is someone very rare and remarkable in the literary world. Nirad Chaudhuri's *Three Horsemen of the New Apocalypse* (1997) happens to be a semi-philosophical treatise on the life of the twentieth century man. It contains the quintessence of his life-long thinking on human life expressed in a crystal clear style without getting himself lost in the labyrinth of details. Being an extraordinarily serious scholar of interdisciplinary kind, he has followed similar gigantic scholars of the world for a model of his own writing. As he has put it clearly in his Preface, "But I shall at least lay my cards on the table. In choosing the form of the book I have taken Machiavelli, Thomas Hobbes and Alex de Tocqueville as my models. These great thinkers and writers were not given to looseness of thinking or imprecision in writing. Of these qualities I shall try to give an imitative display. But that is also likely to create mental resistance to what I shall say..." (Preface). He forestalls the critical opinion about his so-called prejudices by saying that "I have never allowed my likes and dislikes, my predilections and prepossessions to influence my presentation of my subjects. I have so to speak, tried to keep the lens of my mind free from chromatic aberrations" (Preface). He goes further to confess that it is the expression of his vision of life. "It consists in thinking that I am not the real creator of my books but only the medium or amanuensis for the self-revelation of the subjects I deal with" (Preface). Chaudhuri quotes from the 27th Canto of Dante's *Purgatorio* to illustrate the relation between reason and faith. Virgil, who conducts Dante through the first two post-mortem regions, tells him that, being a pagan, he cannot take Dante further. Dante, therefore, takes the guidance of Beatrice. Whereas Virgil represents reason, Beatrice represents faith.

Chaudhuri believes in the close connection between the earthly or human life and the larger cosmos. He clearly states that he accepts the theories of contemporary scientists about the nature of the universe and rejects their views about its duration. He believes in the cosmological view that the universe is not a material body or has a material structure and that it is a process and a flow of energy in different directions. But nobody can define the cosmic energy, which may be comparable to a TV. He describes the spiritual/dynamic power or energy through a scientific, especially a technological metaphor of television, "...the universe is really cosmic TV show run by some power who designed it for some purpose known only to itself" (12). Chaudhuri's belief in the cosmos as a process is easily comparable to Whitehead's philosophy of process and becoming. He explains the human happiness in terms of illusions or of Vedantic concept of *maya*: "Man's happiness lies in living on the strength of his illusions. It is the *maya* of the Hindu philosophy of Vedanta" (12).

Chaudhuri rejects the modern scientists' postulate about the end of the universe according to Thermodynamics, as he considers it as an expression of scientific nihilism. Chaudhuri rejects the futility, meaninglessness and purposelessness of human life propounded by these theories. These theories imply that "Everything that man does becomes a tale told by an idiot signifying nothing" (13). He, therefore, emphasizes the importance and necessity of faith in human effort. Faith need not be connected with religion. "Faith in human endeavour is enough" (13).

Although Chaudhuri is dismissed in India as a controversial writer, he does not accept this view, as he has never indulged in any controversy with any scholar. Any indulgence in such a controversy is deleterious to his writing career. As every writer follows his own method to arrive at his conclusions about life, Chaudhuri makes it clear that he has followed his own method and expatiates on it in the first chapter entitled "The Reason for this Methodological Prologomena". If there is no meeting between two methodologies, there cannot be any alignment in the views expressed by two scholars. Hence Chaudhuri warns the reader to note the particular methodology followed by him. He further clarifies in his second chapter, "On the Method," that he does not believe in the statistical method of understanding truth, but prefers to dwell on the essential aspects of truth. "I reject the statistical method of finding the truth and refuse to accept the average as any kind of truth. I follow Sherlock Holmes in this. He said the first step in deletion is to find the essential fact among a whole number of them, which might all be connected with the crime. But this calls for an extremely perceptive and keen nose" (9).

Chaudhuri makes it very clear that his views on the 'Decline and Fall of Western Civilization' are not a mere extension of Spengler's views, but are the products of his life-long observation of the world. He makes a very insightful observation when he says that "Western civilization today is no longer exclusively Western" (10), and that it can be divided into two divisions: "There is an inner circle, which is fully lighted and is occupied by peoples of European origins; around it is a very much larger circle, which is the penumbra of the central sun and is occupied by diverse non-European peoples" (10). It is in this faith in the continuity of the world that has given him the will and energy to pursue his vocation of a writer till his centenarian year.

Although Chaudhuri disbelieved in the purposefulness of the world or its evolution in his childhood, in his later years, he accepted the purposefulness of evolution: one restricted to better adaptation to the circumstances of existence of all species; and the other extended to the creation of new forms of animal existence. He firmly believes that the purposelessness of evolution is absurd. He believes that the purposefulness is not complete, but is in the process and therefore incomplete.

He believes that man is united zoologically and in the next stage, he has to be united socially and culturally also. But how is that possible? For this question, Chaudhuri has his own answer. According to him, the zoological evolution has almost been complete as there has not been any emergence of new species. But the zoological evolution is replaced by psychological evolution. This idea of Chaudhuri may not be easily accepted by people as any new view is not accepted immediately by some people.

He firmly believes that the individual's life cycle is more or less clearly repeated in the lifespan of nations. Birth, growth, static stability, deterioration and death—are common to individuals and nations. A distinct genetic group or an ethnic group of different genetic origins united by a common culture, with a common language; development of political power and cultural achievement; acquisition of group consciousness with self-assertiveness; political and cultural expansion, stable staticity, loss of vitality and decline or metaphorical death—happen to be a common pattern of human life according to Chaudhuri. Nations in their old age can have either a golden augustianism or an ignoble existence in a figurative brothel.

Chaudhuri makes it very clear that all opinions are made to obey the historical trends and change the society in turn. For example, he illustrates this formula by citing the example of how a portion of India was effected by the British Government in spite of the opposition to it by the Indian leaders and how the opinion changed suddenly within a short span of seven days. Thus opinions are determined by historical trends and not vice versa. Chaudhuri does not deny free will by preaching mere determinism. He calls it 'a very special and restricted kind of determinism,'—a determinism operating in a part of the process of evolution, not in the whole. He further clarifies that the end or goal of man is determined, but the course of his action or growth is irregular. He explains it through a geographical simile; "This process is very much like a river flowing down to the sea with many windings, never in a straight course" (20). He supports his argument with the examples of the Ganga and Thames Rivers.

Chaudhuri offers the example of costumes. Although costumes are broadly determined by climate, they have a sexual motivation behind them and cannot be explained very rationally as fashion is always sub-rational. Even the evocation of sexual desire is determined by historical trends. "An age of elegance creates elegant clothing. But vulgar age will not only create vulgarity, but even persecutes everything that is not vulgar" (21). Fashions, motivated by sexual desire, can be sophisticated (a rapier of sensuality) or shabby (a bludgeon) and are next only to the greed for money. Chaudhuri makes a bold statement that there is no 'taste' in the contemporary world.

Chaudhuri brings in a personal note by saying that he had not seen the death of his parents or in-laws and prepared himself to see the inevitable death of his wife in 1994 at the age of eighty-five. He accepts the inevitability of death or 'The Night of Time' (in Thomas Browne's words) and says how the death of his wife made him lose all his interest in life.

Chaudhuri has selected the three horsemen to represent three ideals of the modern world. The first one is a white horse symbolizing individualism; the second one is a red horse symbolizing nationalism and known for murderous ness. The third one is a black horse symbolizing democracy and known for its balancing capacity.

He begins to discuss the subject by giving a history of the word 'individualism'. He opines that the concept of individualism (symbolized by the white horse) was given currency in the nineteenth century and pleads for the beliefs in the individual's supreme worth and importance as well as in his right to act as he pleases. Chaudhuri points out the mistakes made by the American professor in the *Encyclopaedia Britannica* by saying that Tocqueville is not the man who used the word 'individualism' for the first time (28). He succinctly summarizes Tocqueville's idea of individualism in the United States as "the right to pursue self-interest in the form of acquisition of money and fulfillment of all desires, good or bad, also amenities of life, without external constraints" (28). He further points out how in America this is slightly modified in the sense that while the individual's self-interest is pursued liberally, it should also recognize the right of other individuals to pursue their self-interest. The American Declaration of Independence recognizes the inalienable rights of man like "Life, Liberty and the pursuit of Happiness" (29).

Then Chaudhuri quotes five meanings of individualism from two famous dictionaries: (1) The *Oxford English*

Dictionary differs from Tocqueville in so far as it makes a distinction between individualism and egoism (30). (2) The second meaning of individualism, according to *OED* is 'the social theory advocating the free and independent action of the individual as opposed to communistic method of organic action and State interference (30). The third meaning, according to *OED* is 'metaphysical' in nature recognizing the individual as 'a self-determined whole'. Likewise Chaudhuri examines the other meanings of individualism offered by the two dictionaries (*OED* and *Webster International*) and opines that none of these meanings is adequate to throw light upon the individual's own life and activities (31). Herzon also does not clarify as to why an individual wants liberty. Chaudhuri attributes Herzon's apparently irresponsible assertion of liberty to the background of authoritarianism in Europe from 1815 to 1870 (32). Individual freedom was not encouraged in Russia. Chaudhuri opines that the doctrine of liberation was challenged in France also. For him, individualism is closely connected not with equality but with liberty (34).

Chaudhuri points out the ubiquity of authoritarianism in the world. According to him, authoritarianism, especially papal infallibility was practiced in the Second Empire in France. The Catholics had no right to private opinion on Christian beliefs. The Anglican Church in England also practiced the same kind of religious authoritarianism. Chaudhuri comments that all religions remain intolerant and heresy hunting is natural to them. Even Protestantism was limited in its liberation. Islam remains more intolerant of other religions. Every Muslim is a Fundamentalist or no Muslim at all. Hinduism is also intolerant in its own way. It has no creed and hence no doctrinal heresy in it.

Then Chaudhuri examines authoritarianism in Europe. He points out how political authoritarianism was practiced in France. The French were anti-democratic as late as 1910. Writers like Charles Maurras and Maurice Barres preached royalism and Nationalism. Maurras shows that the French Government in India is authoritarian. Chaudhuri applies this principle to the British Government in India who succeeded in controlling the country through their authoritarianism. Even the French writers supported the French authoritarianism as against the Paris Commune. In the First World War, the Soviet Regime in Russia, the Fascists in Italy and the Nazi in Germany were all authoritarian. In the Second World War, there was a fight between freedom and authority. Chaudhuri makes an insightful observation when he says that "The degradation of the individual was an extreme reaction to the evil authoritarianism that brought about the War" (43). He deplored the degeneration of individualism into unrestrained self-indulgence especially in regard to money and sex. He calls it primarily an American product spreading over to other countries relentlessly. He believes that he is only a particle of the universe—intellectually, morally, spiritually and physically. The Ambassador of Switzerland in India, a theologist said that Nirad cannot be a Christian.

The basic assumptions of Chaudhuri's individualism are as follows: Man is part of the universe. "In short, man is a microcosm in a macrocosm, comparable to an electrical battery" (44). Man is only limited in quality and duration of his existence. But the relationship between man and the universe is not direct, but indirect i.e. through the earth. The relation is qualitative. Smaller the quality, greater the power. Man is an agent of the universe for a cosmic purpose. Man's primary functioning is zoological, like any other animal's. Sex is the means of procreation cosmically. Sexual intercourse as an end in itself is a modern perversion and irrationality. The use of contraception is a revolt against biology and a repudiation of ethics. The religious view is totally opposed to biological view of individualism.

Then Chaudhuri examines the religious views about life and death. Religion views death as unimportant and that man is only a sojourner in life. Religion, especially Christianity considers the world as full of evils in which man can be protected only by the grace of God. The world is a wicked one in religion. Man is supposed to renounce the wicked world. Chaudhuri's question is: If the world is wicked, why did God send man into it? If death is certain, what about life? Isn't life uncertain according to religion? Chaudhuri concludes by saying that the religious view of life is anti-biological. He further examines the difference between the biological view and the religious view of life. The individual's life cycle is biologically determined and the observable life cycle of human life has an obverse and a reverse. But the biological life cycle of human life is dismissed by all religions. But although death puts an end to all the human vanity, man emerges as a victor finally. He is not rendered a superfluity on account of his mortality. "He is a necessity like the leaves in a tree which maintain photosynthesis. The Cosmos is the everlasting deciduous tree which is kept alive by its leaves, growing anew and falling seasonally in turns" (50).

After commenting upon the various aspects of individualism, he goes on to discuss nationalism (symbolized by the red horse). He quotes six meanings of 'nation' from three famous dictionaries and points out how the earliest use of 'nation' was in 1300 A.D. and how its derived abstract word appeared only in 1836. 'Nation' is primarily a political term, which is different from 'state'. Whereas nation is real, state is accidental. 'People' is preferred to 'nation' in historical and sociological terminology.

Chaudhuri points out how earlier wars were monarchical and dynastic or state-conducted. According to him, national wars began only in the 18th century like the American War of Independence (1775-83), the Second War of American Independence and the French Revolution from 1792 onwards. He points out how Nationalism and Militarism were combined in the Russian War of Liberation. Similarly, he shows how there took place three wars of national liberation in the 19th century (1) in Germany, (2) Peninsula War in Spain and (3) Liberation of northern Italy from Austria in 1859.

Chaudhuri shows that the general American notion is that nationalism is opposed to imperialism. But he clarifies that "In reality, nationalism and imperialism are of the same political urge, the first being its defensive aspect and the second it's assertive. Nationalism becomes imperialism when a nation becomes so powerful that it seeks to bring other nations under its domination" (56). He further defines an empire as a conglomeration of different nationalities—with the hegemony of one of them over the rest—with a hierarchical order within it.

Chaudhuri warns that imperialism and colonialism should not be confused with each other. There is no 'decolonization'. All colonialism has become permanent. He offers the examples of America and India as instances of permanent colonization. He offers the historical examples to show how the Europeans were colonists in North America and South America, East Africa, South Africa, Australia and New Zealand, but they were imperialistic in West Africa, India, Burma, Malaya, Indonesia and Indo-China.

Chaudhuri points out that imperialism and nationalism have disappeared from the world, but a new 'Nationalism' has emerged. He highlights the characteristic features of the new 'Nationalism' as follows: (1) It is a self-sufficient and disinterested passion. (2) It is a strong sense of identity or we-ness and is accompanied by xenophobia (which is quite aggressive). (3) It is the political passion of the 'freed-nations' from European imperialism. A national pride and nationalistic inferiority complex are associated with it. (4) A sense of grievance leading to impotent hatred. Then Chaudhuri points out the four ethnic conflicts: (1) Hindus and Muslims in India, (2) Arabs and Jews in the Middle East, (3) Roman Catholics of Ireland and Protestants in the British Isles and (4) Whites and Blacks in South Africa. He generalizes in his typical way, "...friendship between nations is fragile, while hatred is ineradicable. In respect of strength, love can never be equal to hatred" (61). He further shows how this hatred has increased the military preparation and expenditure and terrorism in Asia and Africa.

Then Chaudhuri discusses democracy symbolized by the black horse. He defines democracy as the domination of the Demos or majority. Talking about the history of democracy over 2500 years, he says that democracy is a form of government taught by the Athenian philosophers like Plato and Aristotle and that Greek democracy was formed by the citizens belonging to old families. He rightly points out that modern democracy is really American democracy and cites Lincoln's definition of democracy as a government of the people, by the people and for the people. Once Lincoln said, "You can fool all the people some of the time and some people all the time, but you cannot fool all the people all the time" (63). But Chaudhuri adds satirically, "Lincoln could not foresee the power of television to fool all the people all the time" (64). Then he shows that Britain and America accepted political democracy after World War I. He opines that total democracy has become assertive and aggressive today and that it is elitist and a champion among the English people.

Modern governments want to adopt the policy of egalitarianism and create a classless society. Chaudhuri points out how the French egalitarianism is different from the American one, and how the real egalitarianism is accepted in respect of mental powers and not in physical powers. He also points out rightly that the creative function of man is exercised by the mind and that all creation is creation of inequality. According to him, there is inequality in modern egalitarianism.

Chaudhuri opines that there has been a decline and fall of not only Western civilization but also of eastern civilization in general. "I shall only assert that the decline and fall of civilizations is real historical phenomenon, which has again and again been seen in history" (71). He shows how the great civilizations of ancient Egypt, Mesopotamia, Iran, Greece, Rome and China fell. Likewise Chaudhuri believes that the ancient Indian civilization also declines and disappeared although it is not accepted by the present Hindus.

The most accurate definition of 'decadence' is that it presupposes a previous maturity and a high degree of excellence reaching the high peak of its development and then declining gradually by losing its political and economic as well as cultural creativeness. Then Chaudhuri rightly points out that there can be a national or collective decadence as in the late Hellenistic stage of Greek civilization and the last stage of the Roman Empire. "I might add flippantly that I consider Mrs. Thatcher (defined post-premierly as the Baroness Thatcher) as the British Diocletian in a female incarnation" (73). He further points out how decadence after the peak of achievement or golden age is a natural order of evolution of human life in recorded history. 'Golden age' always belongs to the past. Even our epics show (according to Chaudhuri) the story of a great victory followed by a disconcerting defeat.

Chaudhuri noticed in his first visit to England in 1955 that the English people were so thoughtless about their future. His later visits to England in 1967-68 and his permanent domicile in England in 1970 confirmed his view about the onset decadence in England. He opines that the decadence has spread to all aspects of English life—like national personality, politics, social, economic, academic and cultural aspects. He sees the English decadence in the Englishman's attitude to expenditure of money. Although this is a trivial matter in the national life, it provides an important clue to the English character and personality. Chaudhuri comments on the English people's preference for cheap items. Likewise, he sees 'decadence' in the English attitude to beauty. According to him, Princess Diana is not as beautiful as she is said to be the English people. His reading of English history has made him disappointed with 'the decline in the character of the Spencer family of Althorp. "Certainly, Princess Diana has neither the looks nor the air of Georgiana, Countess of Spencer, nor of her young daughter, as represented in the painting by Reynolds, which is at Althorp" (77).

Chaudhuri gives a detailed picture of the decadence of the Spencer family at Althorp from the past grandeur to the present economic compromise. His reading about the past glory of the family and his observation of the present situation creates a blatant contrast between the past and the present. Earl Spencer, the Princess of Wales' brother, hiring the palace to hoteliers to meet the expenditure of 400,000 pounds a year for its upkeep shows the economic decadence of the royal family.

According to Chaudhuri, the English decadence is of two kinds: one, general; two, malignant. The general decadence is like a chronic disease, not frightening on the surface or in symptoms, but very fatal in effect. The malignant decadence is alarming like the sudden outbreak of a plague, smallpox or cholera.

Chaudhuri is very critical of British life. According to him, the English people do not live naturally, sincerely and unself-consciously. On the contrary, they believe in false behaviour and become poseurs. "It has become posing, men and women appearing as actors and actresses" (79). Posturing and advertising has become the order of the day. Names, labels and titles are more important than substances. Among women, becoming a model has become the supreme ambition of their life. Chaudhuri is stunned and irritated by the artificiality of this posturing in England. The examples of posturing can be seen in 'stills' in statues in shops and 'movies' through TV and video. The "transformation of experience of life into vicarious experience is one of the most noticeable features of contemporary decadence" (80).

Chaudhuri points out further how the English women, especially the young, have fallen for the Oriental habit of overloading themselves with jewellery even in their daily life—like synthetic pearls and fake gold—absurdly with jeans pants. Likewise, decadence may be seen in the English women's (especially young ones') treatment of hair. Use of a variety of wigs and colouring the hair differently on different days according to their whims—is also part of decadence.

According to Chaudhuri, the government has also grown decadent in three aspects: (1) bureaucracy, (2) high taxation and (3) debasement of money. Such decadence may be seen in the Roman Empire, Czarist Russia and England. The behaviour of bureaucrats in England was not dignified. Chaudhuri, therefore, was depressed by the sight of it, "...to all politically minded Indians the House of Commons was like the political Mecca with its stone of Kaaba" (85). Chaudhuri comments that the English people have lost not only their political ambition, but their zest also in politics. The catchwords were used in inverse proportion to their truth. The British parliamentarians' behaving in a false manner—actors and poseurs—shows the decadence of the government. Chaudhuri's honesty and courage may be seen in his remark that the British Prime Minister Mrs. Thatcher or Mr. Major behave like a dictator.

Chaudhuri remarks that in modern England, people practice their religion according to their whims and fancies instead of conforming to the strict injunctions of religion. This is religious decadence according to him. He further remarks that those of the Anglican Church have started obeying the voice of the people instead of the voice of God. In England people have lost their faith in Christianity but have become more superstitious. With the loss of faith in Christianity, the English people have liberated themselves from morality also—from moral inhibitions—in respect of sexual life, stealing and homicide. Chaudhuri describes the English decadence in Biblical style, "Decadence crieth without; she uttereth her voice in the streets; she crieth in the chief places of concourse" (88). Chaudhuri offers further details of decadence in England. Decadence may be seen in the increase of adultery and homosexuality, which are considered to be natural. Abortion, which is a revolt against biology and morality, has become very common. The English people reject morality under the pretext of rejecting Victorian morality. Chaudhuri's anger may be seen in his metaphorical attack: "This is like giving a dog a bad name in order to hang it" (88). Then Chaudhuri summarizes it epigrammatically, "Corruption of the best is the worst corruption" (88).

Chaudhuri proceeds to comment on the decadence of the English social life. The social life of the English people has been brought under the power of the State. People have been made helpless against the power of the State. The absolutism of the English State is equal to monarchical absolutism. Instead of people taking care of the government, it is the government, which has to take care of the people. Chaudhuri is really puzzled by this reverse phenomenon.

Family is consubstantial with society, but such family is threatened in England. Hindu society has survived today though political regimes have disappeared. In England, family is in shambles today. Marriage has lost its sanctity and status. Illegal living together of a man and a woman or divorce has replaced the marriage. He points out how men and women live together outside the religious and legal tie in England and how 'partner' has replaced 'wife'. A new type of family—'one parent family' i.e. a young woman, especially unmarried mothers, have become common in England and are given special privileges by the government. These women cannot assert who the real father of their child is. Words like 'lover' and 'mistress' have been replaced by 'boy friend' and 'girl friend'. Chaudhuri is really amused by the elderly people's reference to their 'girl friends'. He, therefore, remarks rightly "Decadence, however, degrades words and phrases as well as living" (91).

Chaudhuri has noticed decadence in family and education also. According to him, in the past, home was a seat of education and school was an adjunct or extension of home. But now the happy relationship between home and school has been destroyed. The school can give only technical skills and never bothers about the cultivation of character of the student.

Chaudhuri has noticed decadence in the modern language also. It has shrunk from the widest to its narrowest compass. In the past, aristocratic ladies appointed lectrices to read aloud literature to them thereby improving their literary taste and influencing the writers. But nowadays these ladies have themselves become writers without influencing the taste of others. The *salon* has disappeared now. This is linguistic decadence according to Chaudhuri.

In Chaudhuri's view, decadence may be seen in the disappearance of parental authority over children. The misadventure of children is due to the lack of parental authority and responsibility. Chaudhuri offers an example of a child who admitted robbers into the house and helped them carry the money. This is an example of too much of freedom given to children. Sometimes this freedom of children has led to juvenile mafias, which murder and rob in a professional manner. Sometimes the exercise of freedom approaches criminality. For example, sometimes young boys murder children out of curiosity. The least harmful exercise of freedom by young people results in vandalism i.e. in breaking glass or damaging seats in buses and trains.

Chaudhuri then goes on to comment on cultural decadence in England. Nowadays 'culture' has been replaced by 'civilization'. The decadence of the British Government may be seen in Thatcher's conversion of the Socialist Welfare State into a Capitalist Welfare State. Chaudhuri considers the Welfare State as a decadent state. Mere economic prosperity of a nation cannot enrich their culture. According to Chaudhuri, culture has to be animated by a great passion.

Chaudhuri deplores the decadence of British literary culture. The decadence of the English mind is expressed in the careless and penurious use of language—without precision, adequacy and elegance. Decadence may be seen in the shrinkage of vocabulary, absence of colour in diction, monotony of rhythm and ungrammaticality. Chaudhuri is sorry to notice that "the English mind, too, is losing its depth, its intensity and its capacity for making distinctions" (95).

Chaudhuri sees decadence in the changes in the religious diction by the American church. He believes in the view that the "popularization of diction will not save English Christianity" (95) and that all religions have remained staunch, conservative in regard to language. If a man is religious, he will understand the conservative language of religion. "No one understands religious diction unless he is religious" (96). Chaudhuri, therefore, concludes, "Popularization of religious diction then indicates the religious decadence" (96).

According to Chaudhuri even the 'secular' employment of English language has become decadent these days. The new English has been vulgar English, which has not developed a homogeneous style. "There have appeared styles as varied as are the fashions in women's dresses" (96). Politicians, preachers, and teachers especially journalists have vulgarized the English. Today's journalese is an extraordinary mixture of colloquialism, slang, figurative diction, recondite allusions, figures of speech and bad puns and of the use of French and Spanish in wrong places or contexts. Chaudhuri offers examples of degradation of words like 'sex' and 'gay' and employment of sensational titles in newspapers to redeem the dullness that follows. Chaudhuri comments on this phenomenon in his typical manner, "But I say wickedly that those who need such headlines to be induced to read the news are exactly like those who need aphrodisiacs to perform the sexual act naturally" (97).

Then Chaudhuri shows the impact of decadence on the English personality also. It is seen in the following habits and practices: race and colour consciousness. The Englishmen were and are notorious for their contempt for the Indian 'niggers' and black men. They called even a fair man, an M.P. Dadabhai Naoroji a 'black'.

But nowadays, the British do not mind the black people in their country, as they want to make it multi-cultural and multi-cultural and enrich their life. Chaudhuri, therefore, quips, "Today, apparently, the distinction between words adulteration and enrichment has ceased to be recognized" (98). He comments on the special prize of 3000 pounds instituted to be given to any black writer born in Britain or Ireland. Chaudhuri refuses to be considered as an Indian writer and holds the view that "Writers should be classified only by the language they write in and not by country, race or complexion" (98).

Chaudhuri points out how decadence expresses itself in the hard core of racial and colour prejudice in England. "Both remain in the marrow of their bones" (98). All the Indian administrators, individuals and especially university teachers in England feel this. "I can say in a general way that an Indian has to possess at least twice the competence of an Englishman in order to have equality of recognition with his or her English colleagues" (98). Then he generalizes, "Our general rule about the effect of decadence on any people is that it always weakens their good qualities, but leaves the bad ones as they were" (98).

In Chaudhuri's view, modern decadence may be seen in not praising of our great men. In other words, scandal mongering has become a common habit, especially in writing biographies and exposing the private (or public) weaknesses of great men. He shows how Empress Theodora was exposed as the "most shameless harlot in her young days as a dancer" by the historian Procopius. The modern English biographers are interested in finding out if a great man is a 'bastard' or a 'bugger' forgetting the fact that the most illustrious William the Conqueror and founder of the English State was a 'bastard'. This is the decadent habit of writers, their views being coloured by rancour and malice.

Erosion of delicate sensibility is the last kind of expression of decadence brought about by audio-visual providers of entertainment like TV and electronic devices. Chaudhuri opines that audio-visual exploitation of literature has destroyed the literary culture. BBC is the worst villain guilty of this. TVs distort and misinterpret literature. Chaudhuri offers an example of Jane Austen's *Pride and Prejudice* to illustrate this kind of distortion. In it, Darcy kissing Elizabeth on the mouth in the TV film is not warranted by the novel. Chaudhuri, therefore, says that in "an age of decadence even respect for delicacy disappears" (102).

Then Chaudhuri expatiates on the malignant features of English decadence. Large majorities of any nation are passive and thoughtless and submit to the active minority in power. He deplores the criminality of the English masses. There is a good deal of sympathy for criminals in the modern society. The masses have a criminal 'libido' in them which makes them sympathetic to criminals. They, therefore, become vicarious criminals. The sympathy for criminals shows the loss of vitality of a nation. Criminality becomes a norm and acquires the cancerous malignity.

Drug addiction is another form of decadence according to Chaudhuri. The crimes of the English people are (1) armed robbery on banks and post offices; (2) robberies on private homes accompanied by murder, especially of lone elder women; (3) murders of wives by husbands or vice versa, caused by extra-marital affairs or ill treatment etc.; (4) murders committed from homicidal mania; (5) rape on very young girls below sixteen or on old women followed by murder; (6) juvenile crimes committed out of curiosity; (7) stealing babies or murdering babies by unmarried mothers and massacre of young children. Such crimes are irrational and cannot be explained satisfactorily. The Christian Church parading the murderers of children (Mr. Hamilton), i.e. Christian charity puzzles Chaudhuri who feels like running away from England.

Chaudhuri has been aware of decadence in India from his childhood itself. He states that there have been two decadences in Indian history. The first decadence for two hundred years before the Muslim conquest at the end of the 12th century brought about the extinction of the ancient Hindu civilization. The second decadence in the 16th century, after the death of the last Mughal emperor Aurangzeb brought about the extinction of the Indo-Islamic civilization. Again Chaudhuri noticed decadence in India in 1947 when the national life was 'devoid of colour and changed with tedium'. It had become stagnant and died like a lagoon. Chaudhuri noticed 'unadulterated decadence' in the spiritual, moral and material life of India in 1947. His view of Indian decadence culminates in the recognition of *Thy Hand, Great Anarch!*. The descent of India is endless. The Indian decadence does not exhibit the British kind of 'malignity' but seems to be in a 'comatose senility' (111). Chaudhuri sees aspects of decadence in India in (1) the complete ineffectiveness of the State in preventing the foreign invasion in spite of its suppression of Hindu-Muslim riots; (2) expediency and opportunism and dishonesty in giving concession to people; (3) exhaustion of Muslim political power and the process of Indianization in giving power to Hindus (especially Baniyas) and Indianized Muslims; (4) promotion of private interests under the garb of political life and service'; (5) the Marathas and the Congress having similar characteristics like (Marathas') negative xenophobia (especially Muslimophobia) of the Hindus and the mercenary motive of plunder and exaction; (6) the effect of the decline of the State on the masses resulting in the mass's loot, murder, robbing and Pindari and (7) tolerance of anarchy and corruption or resignation to them.

Commenting on the aspects and stages of political decadence in India, Chaudhuri says categorically that "The most striking aspect of the Government of India after the gift of independence by the British people was its total falsity. Nothing was authentic, nothing sincere, nothing disinterested in it" (113). Chaudhuri opines that Nehru was not a scoundrel or a counterfeit but that he was a dictator without dictatorial will and that he was imprisoned in the bureaucracy. "He was wholly genuine, as an Englishman of radical views. But he was not endowed with practical political capacity. As soon as with independence he abandoned his former role of demagogue, he became an ineffable ideologue, flapping his wings against the bars of the cage in which he was put by the bureaucracy" (113). Chaudhuri makes a very hard comment on Nehru when he says that Nehru was neither a dictator nor a practical democratic statesman, but took refuge in escapism. The large dams and buildings got constructed by Nehru are described by Chaudhuri as "the pyramids alas! Not as lasting as those of Gizah" (114). He further comments that Nehru passed on the task of governing and legislating to the officials and the Congress politicians notorious for their opportunism and adventurism.

Chaudhuri comments that Nehru encouraged only the foreign (especially Cambridge) educated people around him and that they were great opportunists. "Thus India under Nehru Government was like castles in Spain resting on kitchens if not sewers" (114). Nehru was an Anglicized Indian. Chaudhuri offers a musical metaphor for the dictatorship of Nehru family. "The dictatorship of the Nehru family continued with short interruptions, which were like the 'accidentals' in a musical composition. The normal key was quickly restored" (115). He comments on Indira Gandhi's power mongering and unscrupulous behaviour. "The position brought about a transformation in Mrs. Gandhi's character paralleled only by the promising Ivan Romonov's becoming Ivan the Terrible" (115). She was, therefore, murdered by the agents of the fanatical Akali Sikhs.

Then Chaudhuri comments upon the present regime of the Indian Government. According to him, personal rule has been replaced in India by rule by a fraction or an opportunistic combination of many factions. Further he points out how the present Indian Government remains British in spirit, though the British personnel had left India in 1947. He rightly shows that the Indian Government is in the hands of bureaucrats—from highest officials like IAS to the lowest clerks and that India is caught in the 'net of Babuism'. Babu means a Bengali clerk. Government by such bureaucracy is a decisive sign of decadence. The 'dealing clerk' is the motive force of all action by the government. The dealing clerk can stop the governmental action by playing truant or going on leave.

Commenting on the social and cultural decadence in India Chaudhuri says that there has been a decadence of mental life also in India. The Hindus did not have a picture of ancient India until the European Orientalists presented it to them. He points out that the British rule in India established a close relationship between the political regime and the Indian people (social order) by creating a Hindu official class and a Hindu professional class.

According to Chaudhuri, the American influence on Indian decadence has been greater than the English. In India there is a popular and lowest expression of Americanism. Many Indians want to migrate to America and settle there which is their cultural home composed of its 'sansculottes'. He offers details of social and cultural decadence in India. Single-minded pursuit of money by Indians is a mark of their decadence. There is a rise of the upstart class of new rich. Licentiousness is practiced openly in India and not secretly as in the past. Yet it is less than seen in England. Chaudhuri discerns two reasons for such an open practice of licentiousness: one, disappearance of *purdah*-system and unrestrained meeting of men and women and two, the Hindu law of divorce, especially the husband's friend being the cause of it. Chaudhuri sees a change in the mores of India. According to him, decadence in India may be seen in the absence of strictness in speech, dressing habit and eating habits. Indians reject their regional dress and accept the Western ones. Abandonment of conservatism in respect of eating is a mark of decadence.

Then Chaudhuri highlights a special Bengali feature of decadence. Being himself a Bengali, Chaudhuri has observed the decadence in Bengali life also. According to him, the disintegration of 'bhadralok' (equivalent of English 'gentlefolk') is a feature of decadence. The Bengali bhadralok believed in blue blood and not in money and therefore a rich man married a poor girl. But now this habit has disappeared. They had massive solidarity of the class, which ignored money. But this process of disintegration began in 1920s and expedited by three events like the provincial self-government, the World War and the Indian Independence in 1947, which gave an opportunity to people to become rich through political power. This division has created class hatred between the rich and the poor especially in Bengal.

Turning his attention to America, Chaudhuri confesses that he does not have as close knowledge of America as of England, but sees decadence in America also. Rape and murder are not very common in U.S. as the bond of marriage is very loose there. General permissiveness does not necessitate rape and murder. Young people in U.S. hire jewelry for their engagement rather than invest huge amount of money. Divorce has been very common. After divorce, the couple lives as mere 'friends'. This is a mark of decadence in America according to Chaudhuri. Until the third quarter of the nineteenth century, marriage was indissoluble in America, but now many marriages and divorces are common there.

According to Chaudhuri, Henry James's *Portrait of a Lady* (1881) provides a true picture of traditional American marriage. Even an intelligent woman like Isabel Archer is deceived by an expatriate with self-interest. *The Europeans* is also a great novel. Americans have abandoned old values especially about man-woman relationship. Chaudhuri believes that the progress of American technology has added up to their decadence. He points out how the word 'techne' is a Greek one meaning craft and how 'technology' is a neologism and a discourse or treatise on the practical or industrial arts and on the handling of matter. He further points out how in America there a greater importance is given to practical application of science than to theory. There is no divine love of truth as in an aristocratic society. Americans care a lot for material welfare. The American obsession with the 'material enjoyments' and comforts may be seen in their use of electric lighting and incandescent bulb especially in the kitchen, vacuum cleaner, sewing machine, refrigerator, telephone, gramophone, typewriter in the office and air-travel.

According to Chaudhuri, technological achievements coexist with decadence. The U.S. has become the center of diffusion of decadence all over the world. He then offers a historical picture of decadence in the world. Till the 18th century, the economic basis of all civilization in the world was agriculture accompanied by handicraft. Decadence happened within that economic world.

But the present decadence happens in the machine age. The Hindu and Islamic fundamentalism is the resistance of the old Hindu and Islamic cultures both to modernization of human life and to Western decadence. "So decadence may now be said to be triumphant, no longer militant" (135). Chaudhuri further points out how the application of nuclear power in America is very great and how it is used for military power i.e. war and how even space-research is used as a means of competition of power. But Chaudhuri is also aware of the fact that space research has given unprecedented knowledge of the cosmos. Nuclear weapons are used as deterrents rather than for positive employment. Nuclear power belongs to the latest industrial basis of human existence, whereas civilization belongs to the old agricultural basis. Finally, Chaudhuri points out how nowadays decadence is regarded as the normal condition of human life, though not as the most desirable one. There is a fanaticism behind decadence, a form of hubris never seen before. The world has become a continent of Circe and there has been a note of despair in the world. Chaudhuri has thus discussed at length how decadence has grown all-pervasive in the modern world. Although his views seem to be pessimistic and nihilistic, they express the harsh realities of modern civilization. His apocalyptic vision, which is negative and satirical, happens to be an extension of his earlier vision articulated in all his works.

Note

1. Nirad C. Chaudhuri, *Three Horsemen of the New Apocalypse*. Delhi: Oxford University Press, 1997. (All the page references are to this edition.)

Chapter 13

From the Archives of a Centenarian[1]

1. NATIONALISM IN INDIA

In "Nationalism in India" (originally published in *Survey*, April, London, 1968), Chaudhuri makes it clear that there is not one but are many nationalisms in India. In its external aspect nationalism determines the Indians' attitude towards all foreign countries. But in its internal aspect it is an assemblage of separate and different nationalisms, depending on the internal evolution of the Indian peoples. The external nationalism of India is "virtually pure xenophobia" (1). It recognizes the fellow (the other) and not the self, whereas, the internal nationalism is a collection of nationalisms based on linguistic unity. It is really the provincial nationalism dubbed as regionalism. Chaudhuri's political insight may be seen in his subtle observation that the internal and the external nationalism of India really co-exist and run parallel to each other and that this duality is found nowhere in the world.

The external nationalism with which Nirad Chaudhuri wants to deal is anti-British nationalism. Its aim was negative. He points out that the Indians became monomaniac about political independence and that the politics of nationalism was itself wholly negative—like agitations, boycott of British goods, etc.—which bred hatred for the British Rule in India.

The external nationalism, according to Chaudhuri, identified itself with the other nations who were anti-British and so it became pro-French and Bonapartist, pro-German and pro-Soviet from 1917 to 1941. The Indians, because of their concern for political freedom, began to read the accounts of American War of Independence so eagerly. Similarly Indians took to foreign political doctrines because of their anti-British stand:

> ...the anti-British feeling made Indians take to foreign political doctrines and systems without any regard for logic or coherence. They felt attracted equally to communism, fascism and Nazism because all of them had explicit or implicit anti-British implications. Indians saw no inconsistency between admiring Lenin, Mussolini, and Hitler equally, nor did they find it difficult to reconcile their sympathy for Ethiopia and the Spanish Republicans with their admiration of Hitler's seizure of Czechoslovakia. A number of Indian leaders had even liaisons with the official Fascist Party. (7)

Chaudhuri rightly points out that the Indians neglected the extensive power of Pan-Islamism, which heightened the Muslim self-consciousness and led to the final partition of the nation. He remarks how the Hindu exclusiveness (based on birth and genetic tie among its members) and prevention of conversion was further strengthened by the Muslim invasions from eighth to twelfth centuries. He points out further that the Hindu xenophobia was accompanied by a hyper-trophied megalomania.

Chaudhuri shows the dual approach of Indians to the British presence in India. When the British Rule replaced the Muslim Rule, the Indians hated the British people, but welcomed their government for bringing some order in Indian life. He points out how the Indians' aping of the West in external habits has sterilized their own solid and native culture brought about by this superficial imitation.

Since Indian poverty and backwardness is attributed to British exploitation, the Indians accept gifts from the West (Britain) without any obligation and by thinking it to be a privilege:

> They have been taught to attribute their poverty and economic backwardness to British exploitation, which was a part of Western imperialism. So the whole of the West is expected to pay reparations without any claim to gratitude.

> Over and above this, the claim to western money is strengthened by two attitudes which Hindu traditions have made both widespread and normal in India. Among the Hindus holy and learned men have always been supported by the wealthy, and the acceptance of gifts without any obligation has come to be regarded as a privilege almost the prerogative of the morally and spiritually great. Their nationalism with its self-conceit makes all Indians feel that they stand in the same relationship with the wealthy nations of the West as their holy men stand to themselves. (15)

Chaudhuri points out the ambivalent attitude of Indians towards the English language. Whereas the aristocratic people might like the English language as a means of power and privilege, the lower middle class people are violently prejudiced against the English language.

2. INDEPENDENCE AND THE INDIAN MIND

In his essay, "Independence and the Indian Mind" (published in *The Statesman, Independence Day Supplement*, August 14, 1955), Chaudhuri thinks loudly about whether the political freedom has brought about any physical or mental change in India. He wrote this essay only after six years of independence. He wanted to highlight the psychological consequences of political independence. He has noticed two groups of people holding contradictory views about this aspect. One group thinks that there has been a remarkable change in India, whereas the other group thinks that there has been no change at all. But the truth lies somewhere between the two.

After commenting briefly on the climate of public opinion, Chaudhuri offers his own insightful views about the psychological consequences of political independence. For example, his remark that the Indians have overcome the social barriers between Europeans and themselves is true. But the radical Indians were frustrated to know that no fundamental economic and social revolution took place in India and that national sovereignty has come to India rather too late.

Chaudhuri makes an insightful observation that there has been a psychological revolution in India as part of its profound cosmological outlook (as pointed by Whitehead). For example, he rightly opines that Indians have gained in dignity to a great extent by overcoming their inferiority complex. Another aspect of political freedom is her awakening of awareness about spirituality. Chaudhuri identifies two groups here, one, specifically Hindu and conservative (represented by Bankim Chandra Chatterji and Swami Vivekananda) and the other, liberal and cosmopolitan, which pleaded for a synthesis of cultures. But Chaudhuri is alert to notice that the contemporary India has grown up her old concepts and embarked on a thorough going material revolution and been passing on to a new concept of national regeneration and greatness. Because of these new concepts India has become a heaven for economists and a dark room for philosophers. He expresses his view through a double metaphor of Greek and Christian mythology and religion as follows: "Under its impact the country of Vedanta has become an El Dorado for economists and a place bleaker even than the proverbial church for the mice of philosophy" (25).

Commenting upon the importance of technology and the relative subordination of economists in India, Chaudhuri expresses his satirical view through a royal/court metaphor: "In actual fact, she is run by a technology, and the young Indian technicians trained in the West who constitute this technocracy, are the most powerful human motive power in the country. The economists are, so to say, their court pundits" (25).

3. THE ART OF POLITICAL ANTICIPATION

In his essay, "The Art of Political Anticipation" (originally published in *The Statesman*, December 5, 1964), Chaudhuri attacks the behavior of Indian politicians, who are generally ignorant about what happens in future in their country because of their ignorance and short-sightedness. Chaudhuri is bold enough to comment upon their behavior in a very analytical fashion. "If I say that the political leaders of a country, who hold the fate of millions of human beings in their hands, should be able to foresee the consequences of their policies, decisions, and actions for at least ten years to follow, I think there would be agreement with me. Perhaps there will not be much dissent either if I add that this is precisely the faculty in which those who are ruling us today are most lacking. Almost every effect of every obvious cause takes them by surprise. They began with a ghastly failure by being incapable of foreseeing the catastrophic consequences of the partition of India, and have kept up their record ever since" (26). In support of his argument Chaudhuri offers the examples of the partition of India, the Hindu-Muslim separatism and the failure of unity conferences. That is because the Indians' (Hindus') behaviour is characterized by self-interest and inefficiency in the political office that they hold rather accidentally rather than in a deserved manner.

4. THE HINDU-MUSLIM PROBLEM IN INDIA

In his essay, "The Hindu-Muslim Problem in India" (originally published in *The Times of India*, December 12, 1982), Chaudhuri takes up the burning problem of India and shows how the Indian politicians including Mahatma Gandhi failed to solve it. He shows how there was an unholy alliance between the nationalists and the Muslims brought about by a very short-sighted opportunism on the part of Mahatma Gandhi and the Congress. Chaudhuri's political insight could be seen in his observation of a change of attitude in Muslims after the failure of Khilafat movement and Kemal's abolition of the Califate. "But instead of any kind of resentment against Kemal for that, they redirected their thinking on their position in India, to which they saw a threat in the nationalist movement. They came more and more strongly to feel that they stood nowhere as Muslims unless they had a territorial base in India. There was a complete turnabout from extraterritoriality to territoriality in their political thinking, and the conception of Pakistan was a natural consequence of that revolution in ideas" (35).

The group-identity of Muslims prevented them from being assimilated into Indian culture and finally it resulted in a separate territorial base of Pakistan. Chaudhuri points out how the Hindu-Muslim divide could not be solved by any politician of India. One has got to accept this harsh reality of the Indian political life.

5. THE PROBLEM OF BENGAL

In his essay, "The Problem of Bengal" (originally published in *The Times of India*, Delhi, December 14, 1967), Chaudhuri comments upon the Centre-State relation, with particular reference to Bengal. He says that the Congress Party in India enjoyed a lot of power for several years simply because there was no powerful opposition to it by any single, major party. Then he shows how the United Front was a popular and powerful party in Bengal. Then he comments upon the Bengali provincialism and separatism and superiority complex. "During British rule the Bengalis acquired a sense of superiority over the people of the rest of India. Taking to English education first, they took the lead in creating the modern Indian culture—they created a fine literature of their own, initiated religious and social reform and were the first to launch a national movement. There was even a sort of Bengali imperialism in northern India" (42). They could neither separate from India nor live within India by losing its importance.

In a way Bengal was historically lucky because of their earliest contact with the British rule and English culture. They entered the government offices in large number, got themselves educated in English, produced good literature under its influence and paved the way for nationalist movement. Thus, they enjoyed a superior position and responsibility. But Chaudhuri shows how this was changed suddenly by a historic event, i.e. the transfer of Indian capital from Calcutta to New Delhi. When the political centre moved from Calcutta to New Delhi, all the Bengalis seemed to have lost their central position and being pushed to the margin as it were. For example, in literature the non-Bengalis began to vie with them. In politics, leaders like Mahatma Gandhi took the lead and the Bengali leaders had to fade into insignificance. Finally the Bengalis have started suffering from a sense of alienation from the rest of India and are in a pathological state.

6. CHASM BETWEEN INDIAN OPINIONS AND ACTIONS

In his essay, "Chasm between Indian Opinions and Actions" (originally published in *The Statesman*, April 29, 1970),

Chaudhuri points out the conspicuous gap between Indians' opinion and action and remarks how their opinions are never translated into action and comments upon how the foreigners are misled by the Indians' expression of their opinions in the press. He says, "In discussing public and private life in India I have adopted for my methodology the basic principle that the ills from which we are suffering today arise out of certain deep seated inadequacies in our psychological constitution, and not from mistakes in immediate diagnosis and prescription. One of these is the dichotomy which exists between our opinions and our actions. No Indian follows up any drastic or revolutionary opinion of his own with any kind of action to put it into effect. It is not a question of dying in the last ditch for one's convictions. He does not even raise his little finger (so far as that is a symbol of action) in support of his opinions if that would harm his self-interest according to his invariably timid calculations. In simple words, his opinions and his actions exist in separate worlds: the first in a world of vicarious enjoyment and the other in a world of cowardly conformity. This incapacity to combine the two in a coherent pattern of behavior is really a moral, and not an intellectual failure" (44). Chaudhuri offers three to four examples to support his argument. He remarks that Indians are not able or willing to achieve anything great in public life. He sees self-deception and hypocrisy ingrained in the Indian's (the Hindu's) behavior. For example, he highlights the Hindu hatred of Muslims for vicarious purposes but cultivating the same Muslims for their promotion, especially during the Mughal Rule. For a Hindu or (an Indian) the first interest is home, private life and self and next comes the nation or public life. And that he suffers from some kind of moral dementia.

7. DISLIKE OF WORK: ECONOMIC PROGRESS

In his essay, "Dislike of Work: Economic Progress" (originally published in *The Statesman*, February 7, 1966), Chaudhuri repeats his observation about the Indians' aversion to work or hard labour or consistent work, due to a variety of reasons. They lack the will to work. He comments on their abstract planning which is not followed up by any productive labour. He points out how it is difficult to get the services of a craftsman, a carpenter, mason or plumber, even if you are willing to pay him extra. In addition to the subjective lethargy of Indians, Chaudhuri reminds us repeatedly that the horrid climate of India is also partially responsible for Indians' laziness and shirking of work. He has expatiated on this topic in his *Continent of Circe* also. He says, "It must not be forgotten that in a cold country physical activity is a physiological necessity and a requirement of health and bodily comfort. In the tropics, on the contrary, it is the abstention from work which is an element of well-being" (51). He shows this principle operative in the academic field also. "In every walk of life there is a tendency to rest on the oars, and to live on the little capital of position and reputation once acquired. Thus the first book of an Indian writer is as a rule his best book, and the university teacher is most knowledgeable in his first year of employment" (52-53). But Chaudhuri does not know the present situation in Indian Universities where many professors retire without having produced a single worthwhile book in their entire career.

Chaudhuri points out the widespread dishonesty and corruption in Indian public life and relates them to their general lethargy. They are very enthusiastic in buying great furniture or building big houses or starting a big project, but are never bothered about maintaining them properly and regularly. "So, in India, the greatest obstacle to a high standard of living is maintenance. People might buy furniture, cars, or houses, but they will not take care of them. They seem to think that material things especially machines and appliances, can recoup themselves like living organisms. As a result, these never yield even half the return in use and enjoyment which can be expected from the capital outlay and a high standard of living is exhibited by us only in periodic saturnalia of garish ostentation, as in weddings" (52).

On the whole Chaudhuri shows how the Indians hate and shirk hard work of any kind and try to make a religion of their lethargy and quietism.

8. ENVY AS PART OF OUR NATIONAL CHARACTER

In his essay, "Envy as Part of Our National Character" (published in *The Illustrated Weekly of India* in June 1973), Chaudhuri takes up the psychological evil or disease called envy or jealousy and defines its nature. The Hindu philosophy refers to the six enemies of man and envy or jealousy happens to be one among them. Quoting from the *Mahabharata*, he differentiates between envy and jealousy by saying that it is gratuitous, furtive, cowardly and more irreconcilable than hatred and transforms the good of others into one's own sorrow.

After making a general observation on envy, Chaudhuri offers an example of literary envy. For example, when his friend, Bibhuti Bhushan Bannerji (author of *Pather Panchali*) told him about an appreciative review of one of his stories (in a magazine) an established writer enviously remarked, "Yes, yes, these do appear if you have cousins."

Then Chaudhuri offers his example of being the target of envy by his friends. For example, when his belated book, *Autobiography of an Unknown Indian* was accepted by Macmillan Publishers of London, the publishers paid great tribute to Chaudhuri's scholarship and insightful analysis and description of his society and its relation to him as a sensitive observer, Chaudhuri was quite elated by it and showed it to a family friend of his, who read it and felt so envious that he dropped the blurb to the floor, instead of showing it to his wife. Chaudhuri confesses that he wanted to take revenge upon the envious ones by growing more and more successful in his writing career. But others do not know how to fight the envy by friends and people.

From these examples, Chaudhuri goes on to generalize, "...in India the suppression of talent and enterprise through envy has become a national evil. Of course, envy is a universal human phenomenon, but the degree to which it exists and can do harm matters and I think in regard to both, Indian society is exceptionally malignant" (58).

After generalizing about the Indian national character, Chaudhuri comments upon the Bengali envy, "From my experience of Bengali life, I would, however, say that it seems to me, a Bengali, that my fellow Bengalis have the feeling in its lowest form, besides having it in the largest measure. This is not my opinion alone but that of many great and famous Bengalis" (58).

Chaudhuri offers some concrete examples of Bengali writers and thinkers being the targets of envy by the fellow Bengalis. For example, Bankim Chandra Chatterjee was transferred to an out-of-the-way station in Orissa as a Deputy Magistrate, by the machinations of many fellow Bengalis, because he wrote *Anand Math*. Similarly, Rabindranath Tagore and Swami Vivekananda suffered due to the envy by the fellow Bengalis (59).

Chaudhuri mentions how envy is felt by the members (especially daughters-in-law) of the family or between relatives. Then he mentions how the Kashmiri, the Tamilian and the Punjabi complain about the Kashmiri, the Tamilian and the Punjabi respectively. Chaudhuri in his typical fashion attributes this envy to one effect of Circe's spells, traceable to disinclination to hard and honest work due to the horrid climate of India.

Chaudhuri points out the inability of Indians to do sustained work and to recognize talent or any exceptional gift in others. Though he was an object of envy by others, he succeeded in getting due recognition for his work (61).

9. PERVASIVE PARASITISM

Chaudhuri comments on the Indian intelligentsia's obsession with isms—like nationalism, socialism, capitalism, communalism, asceticism—and points out how these isms are only verbal euphemisms to camouflage the bitter truths (63).

He shows how there is a hierarchy of parasites in India—higher and lower—like bureaucrats, politicians, managerial class and their nepotism, bribery and ingratiation. He points out how there the lower parasites depend upon the higher parasites. He points out how the Indians have a tendency to avoid work and labour and consequently their laziness leads to corruption and dishonesty and that work is a great evil in India.

Chaudhuri in his typical satirical manner says that parasitism is the most popular ism rigorously practiced in India. Similarly, he comments on the socialism and socialists. A socialist state, according to him, has to be a bureaucratic state. A bureaucrat has to be offered chairs, desks and salaries. "There is hardly any Indian socialist for whom the chairs, the desk and the salary are not the major attractions of socialism" (64).

Chaudhuri comments on the most shameless class of India, i.e. of politicians as follows, "The newest and the most upstart parasitical class in India is the politician class. Politics among us is the possession of living on the public revenues. If the politician is also a holder of office he is given the right of making unlimited drafts on these revenues" (64).

He points out further that there is a second phenomenon of parasitism to be seen in the new influential managerial class in the commercial and industrial concerns of the country. In the industrial and commercial concerns, it is profitable to employ sons and relatives of the politicians and bureaucrats and use them as contact men. Chaudhuri codifies it as follows, "To have a father, a son, or a brother in the higher ranks of politics, administration and even civic affairs, this is a form of super-tax, and at the worst a form of bribery, which they do not mind" (64).

Nowadays the young men from the middle class have been moving into the professional sphere, because his earning is four times or even twenty times bigger than that of an ICS official. Chaudhuri expresses his opinion through an entomological image, "It is also interesting to find how readily the Indian technician transfers himself to the desk from the workshop. In the factory he has to be a working bee, however well paid, in the office he can be a drone, and his wife a queen bee" (65).

Chaudhuri points out that the labour class in India has been growing more and more parasitical by depending more on the employer and producing less and less.

The Indian student has become another parasite, who wants to depend upon his father or growing brother, who should help him to get a scrap of paper called diploma or degree. He serpents the English language as he does not want the labour involved in learning that language.

Chaudhuri makes an interesting observation, "Work is the great evil in India, and no other evil half as bad" (66).

10. I HAVE SEEN CHANDIGARH

In his essay, "I have seen Chandigarh" (originally published in *The Hindustan Times Weekly,* New Delhi, 1969), Chaudhuri records his experiences and impressions of Chandigarh, which is the stronghold of the Sikh people. He offers a comparative picture of two big cities of India like Chandigarh and New Delhi and shows his preference for Chandigarh as it is superior to New Delhi in its architectural planning and beauty. Chaudhuri exhibits his fine aesthetic taste and hence appreciation of Chandigarh as if he is an excellent art-critic. But he criticizes the Indian, especially Hindu behavior of acquiring something great not caring sufficiently for its preservation or maintenance. First he mentions the reasons for his liking for Chandigarh. "What struck me most at first sight in Chandigarh was the symmetry, breadth and mass of its layout. In respect of these I considered the city to be superior to the two examples of town-planning in India which come to my mind when I saw it, namely, Jaipur of Sawai Jai Singh II and the old New Delhi of Lutyens. British New Delhi was spacious without possessing mass, it was without a sky line. Jaipur, on the other hand, had mass without the counterbalancing space. In Chandigarh the empty spaces and the mass of the buildings were perfectly matched. So were the colours, or rather the intended colour scheme, which may have been intuitively felt rather than deliberately thought out, and this was made up of the blue of the sky, the red of the buildings relieved by the studded decorations in glass or tiles and the green of the grass and the shrubs" (68).

As a contrast to the beauty of Chandigarh, Chaudhuri points out the ugliness of New Delhi in its various details. "I wondered why the new New Delhi which has grown up since independence could not rival Chandigarh in the architectonic quality of its layout, because both were created by the partition of the Punjab. The common cause withal, there is a vast difference between Chandigarh and even the most pretentious part of new New Delhi, namely Chanakyapuri. I attribute the difference, in the first instance, to the presence of a single directing mind at one place and a jumble of disparate individual minds in the other. Over and above, the foreign legations have made the quarter of New Delhi a museum of architecture. Secondly, the difference was bound to appear because it was inherent in the architectural concepts behind the two cities. In Chandigarh one sees a new example of the original and genuine modernistic architecture of Europe, whereas in New Delhi one sees only its mechanical imitation by Indians. There is no integrity in Delhi, and the name of Chanakyapuri by itself is illustrative of this" (68).

Chaudhuri has special admiration for the artificial lake of Chandigarh. "What I admired next was the placing of the city. The idea of creating an artificial lake was an inspired one, for without that stretch of water Chandigarh would never have been what it is. I have walked along the Embankment of the Thames, the Quays of the Seine, the Lungos of the Tiber, by the side of the Jumna in Delhi, and by the Hooghly in Calcutta. Never have I felt greater peace and internal renovation than what I did, walking along the embankment at Chandigarh. The lake gave to Chandigarh a background, and to my thinking it is rivaled by only one other city—city I have seen—that of Cuttack in Orissa" (68-69).

By contrast, Chaudhuri finds the buildings of Delhi rather ugly, especially the buildings of Delhi University look like magnified hovels. Whereas the buildings of Chandigarh are authentic, those of Delhi are pastiche and even spurious. "But I must state honestly that I have no admiration for the three individual buildings by Le Corbusier that is, the Secretariat, the Assembly, and the High Court. If the first were not by him nobody would have had any hesitation in ranking it with the Ashoka Hotel in New Delhi: the symbolism on the roof of the Assembly is extremely unconvincing and ugly to look at; and the High Court as seen from the river front, is like a grandstand of racecourse" (69). Similarly Chaudhuri finds the historical Delhi also grand and ugly at the same time. "The European travelers saw Shah Jahan's Delhi as a paradoxical combination of magnificence and squalor in which palaces in stone stood cheek by jowl with *jhuggis* of mud and grass" (70).

Then Chaudhuri comments on the Indians' habit of drying their clothing in the front balconies of their houses and lodges without bothering about disfiguring the beauty. "As regards drying clothing, it is considered to be one of the birthrights of freedom in India, and thereof I am surprised that it was not incorporated in the chapter of Fundamental Rights in our Constitution. Last year, happening to be staying in the fine railway hotel at Puri, which looks out on the beaches and the sea, I read notices on both floors: 'Residents are requested not to dry clothes in front of the hotel, upstairs or downstairs.' When I asked the reason for the notice the staff only shrugged their shoulders, but I understood that the worst offenders were the privileged order of the political leaders or rather their wives" (71).

Similarly, Chaudhuri comments on the Indians, especially the officers not watering the grass or lawn in public places or in front of government buildings properly or regularly as they are not bothered about the beauty of their campuses or regions. Sometimes, they go on burning the grass regularly in the summer season without caring for the ugliness that will result from that burning. Chaudhuri, therefore, concludes rather sadly, "I am taking only these three aspects of the neglect in Chandigarh to drive home the point that it is a deeper affair than casual inattention. To counteract the neglect will not be easy, because it is in the bone. We create and build on a sudden impulse of megalomania, and the creation and the building crumble away in obedience to the natural inertia of our life. So, taking a philosophical view of the matter, I am not surprised by the early decadence of Chandigarh. But it is difficult to be philosophical when a man loves something and, above all, beauty in human life, and finds it perishing before his eyes" (72).

Thus, Nirad Chaudhuri admires the beauty of the city of Chandigarh as contradistinguished from the ugliness of New Delhi, he also deplores the Indian habit of neglecting the upkeep of that beauty due to their lethargy and lack of aesthetic sensibility.

11. TAGORE AND THE NOBEL PRIZE

In his lengthy essay, "Tagore and the Nobel Prize" (originally published in *The Illustrated Weekly of India*, March 11, 1973), Chaudhuri offers a general picture of the effect of the award of the Nobel Prize on Rabindranath Tagore and the Bengali writers. This award created quite contradictory feelings in the minds of Tagore's admirers and detractors. The local, national and international awards are known for their unpredictability but are certain to boost the sale of books by the award winner. The Nobel Prize is not an exception to this rule. Chaudhuri comments upon this phenomenon in his typical manner, "The ways of the Swedish Academy, like those of Providence, are inscrutable—which is the best view to take of them. The winners of this prize are like those who neither sow nor reap, yet whose Swedish Father feeds them" (73).

Chaudhuri attacks Tagore for cold-shouldering the Bengali fans who went to Bolpur to honour him. Tagore did not like their behavior of showing their respect to him after he had earned recognition from the West. "Tagore likened their conduct to that of village boys who tie a tin to the tail of a dog and chase it through the streets with shouts. He also said that, as they were walking back to the station on foot, Tagore drove past them in a trap, with Jagadish Bose by his side, scattering dust on his admirers. He even added that no refreshments were given to them at Santiniketan, but some *bundia* was distributed at the station" (74).

Tagore's earning the Nobel Prize created a lot of jealousy in the hearts of Bengalis. Tagore himself was aware of the unexpectedness of the honour, but did not want to be intoxicated by it.

Chaudhuri states quite impartially that Tagore was free from charlatanism and that his literary status was higher than that of the other thirteen winners. "I would loudly proclaim that the status of Rabindranath as a literary man was higher than that of all the thirteen Western writers who had received the Nobel Prize from 1901 to 1912" (76).

Chaudhuri points out the irony of literary response by the reading public in India when he says that Tagore was underrated by his detractors until he earned the Nobel Prize. For example, D.L. Roy did not like Tagore's poem, *Sonar Tari* (Boat with Gold). But he was admired only by a small group of *bhaktas*.

Tagore's supersensitivity turned out to be his hypersensitivity. The Bengalis' malicious underrating and insulting remarks hurt him deeply. He did not have the practical sense of Bankim Chandra Chatterjee to ignore them. He was hurt so much by the remarks of his detractors that he expressed his feelings his four letters. In one letter, he wrote that he wanted to die at the earliest. In his second letter he wrote how he was hurt by somebody's remark that he had got the Nobel Prize by a subtle trick and that his poetry was written by a certain Englishman. In his third letter, he pointed out how slandering him profitable to some Bengalis. In his fourth letter he articulated his strong desire not to be reborn in Bengal. Chaudhuri states that Tagore died without being reconciled to fellow Bengalis.

Chaudhuri finds the reason for this alienation between Tagore and his people on both sides. First he examines the people (i.e. readers). He classifies the Bengali readers into three categories: one, passive large group; two, small group of *bhaktas* and three, the active group crazy with envy by his fame, success and achievement. Chaudhuri points out that this was the general pattern of behavior among the Bengali *bhadralok*. The envious people would go to any extent in maligning the poet. A nationalist daily of Calcutta reproduced the story from some foreign magazine that he was not even a pure Bengali but had Portuguese blood. It was quite common among the Bengalis to make indecent comments on one another, sometimes transgressing the limits of decency by casting aspersion on the character of their wives also.

Chaudhuri attributes the jealousy of Bengalis towards Tagore to their lack of knowledge of English language and Tagore's antipathy to Hindu obscurantism and chauvinism. "Over and above, the creative writers in Bengali never knew English well and in any case could not write it well. So, when Tagore got the Nobel Prize on the strength of a book in English, they treated him as the jackdaws treated one of their fellows in the borrowed plumes of the peacock. A conviction which they could not resist, that the English of the *Gitanjali* might really be Tagore's own, made them even wild. In addition, he gave a handle to his critics and created a prejudice against himself by unsparing criticism of Hindu obscurantism and chauvinism. By and large, the great majority of Bengalis were unsympathetic to him. What must have irritated Tagore more was the worthlessness of the criticism. The animus against him was never redeemed by intellectual competence, and what was worse, he admirers did not also reach a higher level. So he felt abandoned intellectually, and could not ignore his critics, which Bankim Chatterjee was quite able to do. Chatterjee has left a very amusing skit on the average run of Bengali critics, representing them as monkeys pronouncing their judgment on the discourse of a tiger, of course, only when that dangerous animal was out of hearing" (80-81). Unlike Tagore, who was highly sensitive, Chatterjee could do so because of his strong practical approach to life.

Chaudhuri points out the triviality of Bengali critics who enjoyed accusing a writer of being guilty of grammatical mistakes in some piece of writing that they could not understand. Tagore suffered because of his hyper-sensitivity to his critics. Chaudhuri shows how other sensitive writers like Dinabandhu Mitra also suffered on account of bilious critics. Chaudhuri remarks how people relish scandals because of their deep-seated envy and points out how even great men like Rammohun Roy, Keshub Chunder Sen, Bankim Chandra Chatterjee, Ishwar Chandra Vidyasagar suffered at the hands of enemies, i.e. the so-called intelligentsia of Bengal.

Commenting on Tagore's hyper-sensitivity, Chaudhuri makes a beautiful observation. "He did not possess the aristocratic worldliness of his grandfather which could place Brahmanic and English arrogance in their place, nor the aristocratic self-sufficiency and dignity of his father. He lacked the robustness of both in dealing with the world. It should not be forgotten that he lost his mother in childhood, and never felt that he was fully protected. His formidable father was more or less unapproachable, though affectionate and very scrupulous about his duty as a father" (83). One may easily see how Chaudhuri has played the role of an excellent psychological critic of Tagore as a writer here.

Chaudhuri points out how Tagore's sensitiveness made him intolerant of external discipline, especially the institutional one. That is why he could never endure schools or universities. Chaudhuri points out further how basically Tagore was unsocial and a practical anarchist in his individualism and that he was not made to face the rough and tumble of life. Chaudhuri shows that Tagore had a special love for rural Bengal and felt inspired by it; that he lived in a house-boat on River Padma, where he wrote his greatest work and realized his essential nature.

Chaudhuri points out Tagore's aversion to European literature, especially the realistic one for its drabness and ugliness; and that he disliked Tolstoy's *Anna Karenina*. He quotes from Tagore, "Tried to read *Anna Karenina*, but found it so unpleasant that I could not go on. I do not understand what pleasure can be got from reading such sickly books. I want the kind of writing which is simple, beautiful, sweet and generous and cannot stand for any length of time these complicated, bizarre, and tumultuous goings-on" (85). But Tagore loved some Vaishnava poets.

Another insightful observation of Chaudhuri about Tagore was that his Bengali nature also remained dead to the glory of the English landscape. He shows the contrast between Rabindranath and his elder brother, Satyendranath: whereas the latter liked England, the former called it 'the wretched land'. The same Bengali nature of Tagore recoiled from English social life.

The Western recognition of Tagore in the form of the Nobel Prize acted as a sort of compensation for his sense of humiliation at the hands of bilious Bengali critics. Consequently he grew to regard the Western world as his sphere of action and became an international moral influence. But this recognition offered him a stage and he became an actor. The recluse by nature began to give public performances. Chaudhuri is bold enough to remark that Tagore's literary influence on the Western world was also unfortunately not very substantial. "But the mistake it led to was even more disastrous. His resentment against his people made him think that the Western recognition was going to be a compensation for him, that henceforth he could regard the Western world as his sphere of action and become an international moral influence. He could never become that, for what the West found in his writings was, in a manner of speaking, a sweetly scented room-freshener, for the stuffy atmosphere of its mental life before the First World War" (87).

Chaudhuri's perceptive observation about Tagore is noteworthy, "Of course even in the West he remained partly a writer. But that writer was not the Tagore of Bengali literature. In his English writings he is not the Bengali poet in flesh and blood, but another personality in fancy dress with a mask on his face. For one thing, when he rendered his Bengali poems himself he selected for translation all that was most general and least concrete in his writings and those in which the Bengali element was not so dominant as to offer an obstacle to Western appreciation. Furthermore, partly through intention and partly through the limitations of his writing of English, he presented his Bengali poems in a kind of English which in its self-conscious simplicity of diction and syntax were very near preciosity" (87-88). Chaudhuri remarks quite frankly that the translations of Tagore's poetry, novels and stories by others are crude and bad and did great injustice to him and that no publisher came forward to publish them at the time of his birth centenary. Chaudhuri points out further that after getting the Nobel Prize, Tagore had to endure the penalties of greatness as opined by Lord Hardinge, the Governor-General of India then.

Chaudhuri observes that Tagore was an educationist in a broad sense as the latter established Viswa-Bharati University and became a cultural icon by being named as Gurudev; that Tagore was a radical Hindu and also deeply influenced by neo-Hinduism; that a number of bereavements in his family—death of his wife, daughter, favourite disciple and father—induced a mood of renunciation in him.

Chaudhuri makes an insightful observation that the Nobel Prize put new and evil power behind this activity, but it also put activity on the reverse gear making it go from the track of nationalism into that of internationalism. Tagore believed in the idea of educating pleasantly as he hated the method of established schools, whether of the old Hindu or new English type. He commented on this type of education as 'parrot's education'. Chaudhuri shows how Tagore introduced a comprehensive kind of universal education in Viswa-Bharati—including dance, drama, music and painting and aimed at synthesizing the best in the East and the West by giving full play to his aestheticism and ritualism.

Chaudhuri points out the negative effect of Santiniketan on Bengali life when he says that archaizing and posing began to flow from Santiniketan and affected the Bengalis; that pose and pretense began to take the place of honest behavior. Even the British officers disliked the superficiality, shallow intellectual superiority, conceit, frivolity, skepticism and vanity of the young Bengalis. Chaudhuri shows how the Bengalis took greater recourse to pretence and neglected achievement.

Finally Chaudhuri deplores the falsity of Bengalis worshipping Tagore and hopes for the true worship of him by a Bengali in future, if at all such a one will be born in future.

12. MOHITLAL MAZUMDAR

In his essay, "Mohitlal Mazumdar" (unpublished, circa 1966-67), Nirad Chaudhuri pays tribute to a famous Bangla poet, Mohitlal Mazumdar by showing how he wrote poetry in Bengal when poetry was almost dead. He mentions Mohitlal's opinion in 1925 about the decline of Bangla literature and an all pervasive decline of taste and standards; insincerity, inefficiency and the trickery that results from both. Chaudhuri deplores the fact that Mohitlal wrote great poetry in Bangla but had no audience; that he was attacked by his contemporaries for his frank and bold critical analyses of Bangla literature. He, therefore, became a crusader and a literary martyr. "Literature has its martyrs no less than religion, and Mohitlal was in a very true sense one of them. He lived and died for literature. I think I can even say that he was driven to death by the passive persecution that his faith in literature and his militant expression of that faith drew on him" (97). Chaudhuri continues to appreciate him for his accomplishments. "He was by nature a poet and his severe literary apprenticeship gave him mastery over technique that brings to my mind the formal perfection of Baudelaire. In the content of his poetry he rose to a pitch of intensity and passion which is not paralleled in any other Bengali poet born after Tagore" (97).

Another reason why Nirad Chaudhuri remembers Mohitlal is that the latter happened to be his inspiring teacher in the High School. Chaudhuri gratefully acknowledges the guidance and encouragement that he received from Mohitlal, who introduced him to the literary society of Calcutta and inspired him to be a writer. That is why Chaudhuri has briefly described him and his literary inspiration and guidance in his *Autobiography of an Unknown Indian* and promised to write more elaborately about him in the second part of the autobiography in future, though he is sadly aware that at that time his teacher will not be alive to read it.

13. A BENGALI ON PONT DES ART

In his essay, "A Bengali on Pont des Art" (originally published in *The Statesman*, Delhi, May 13, 1956), Chaudhuri records his perceptive appreciation of Paris, especially its art expressed in a variety of things like statues, rivers, bridges, monuments and museums. He especially observes the beauty of Pont des Art, Place Dauphine, Palais de Justice, Notre Dame, Palais de Chaillot, the French Institute, Church of St. Germain, L'Auxerris and River Seine etc. He finds a conspicuous difference between the Oxford manner and the Sorbonne manner. Chaudhuri confesses his Bengali prejudice for French culture and literature. He feels that Anatole France is as readable as Rudyard Kipling is unreadable. His (as also other Bengalis') liking for France is sincere. He shows how the Indians' demonstrative liking for France has been recently transferred to Germany and to Soviet Union. A French man has certain typical traits of personality, which are observed by Chaudhuri. He says, "For one thing, a certain nimbleness of wit, quickness of perception, and logicality marked us out as these traits also marked out the Frenchman. Our humour too was somewhat French, with wit and irony as its main ingredients, and we had also a leaning towards persiflage, which made a very scholarly and didactic Bengali denounce Bengali writings of the first decades of this century as mere hors d'oeuvres" (101).

Chaudhuri opines that the beauty of French culture is deceptive in the sense that it escapes the notice of an insensitive foreign (especially Indian) observer. He comments on even Tagore's lack of deep response to French art and culture. "Even Tagore, whose sensibility to the Bengali scene was preternatural, failed to react to Paris. He visited it in 1890, when he was twenty-nine, and artistically perfectly mature. Yet all that he had to say was this, 'How can I describe Paris? It is a huge affair, with its streets, houses, carriages and horses, shops, gardens, palaces, statues, fountains etc.' *Voila tout*, and from a man who had already written stories as hard and brilliant as Mauppassant's, perhaps with full awareness of the fact" (101-02). Chaudhuri considers Eiffel Tower of Paris rather a grotesque symbol, which was noticed by Tagore. His remarks about the beauty and grandeur of Paris in particular and France in general are very perceptive holding mirror to his own refined artistic sensibility. "It is almost an insult to Paris to say that it is a city of obvious or assertive grandeur. On the contrary its splendor is of the most unobtrusive kind. My first mental note when I crossed the Tuileries Gardens just after my arrival was how reticent it was I suppose Paris makes the visitor overlook its magnificence by raising him to its own level, so that he does not notice the beauty, harmony, and graciousness which is there, and recalls them as soon as he has gone to a city which is less elegant and orderly, where everything appears mean, tasteless and shabby. New Delhi was a shock to me when I came back" (102). Similarly Chaudhuri observes the ubiquitous stillness and quietness of French life as contrasted with the cacophony and noise pollution of the modern metropolitan cities.

14. EIGHT WEEKS IN THREE THOUSAND

In his essay, "Eight Weeks in Three Thousand" (originally published in *The Statesman*, Delhi, August 14, 1955), Chaudhuri describes some of his artistic experiences that he had in England and Europe during the eight weeks of his Western tour. He clarifies that he loves his mother country, India and the West in different manners. "He points out how some Indians, who go abroad fail to notice certain artistic excellences there like statues, Nature, cathedrals, paintings and Museums etc. due to their lack of interest and insensitivity." A distinguished English writer gives his opinion to Chaudhuri, "But your people are not interested in the things of the senses" (104).

Because of Chaudhuri's refined artistic sensibility and sound historical and encyclopedic knowledge, he notices things in the West that are not noticed by the other Indians lacking in deep historical knowledge. For example, Chaudhuri has noticed that the uniform of Tantia Topi is preserved in London with a very derogatory inscription and is keeping the company of the skeleton of Napoleon's horse, Marengo.

Chaudhuri observes the beauty of nudes (portraits as well as statues) in the West and makes an insightful and contrastive observation about them and the Hindu ones. Whereas the Western nudes express the transcendental spiritual beauty shining through them, the Hindu nudes express pure sensuality. He also shows the cultural contrast between the Western behavior and the Indian one. Whereas the Westerner recognizes and owns his views about the physical beauty of the nudes, the Indian and the Hindu never has the courage to express it for reasons of decency. "Recently, a little boy, descended on one side from a Roman princely house, was showing the rooms of the Farnese Palace to a visitor. He duly identified the figures as this or that notability of a bygone age, for these were often portraits, and then pointing to an ample female, he said 'And that is my great great-grandmother.' Now, I do not think there is any Indian who, standing in one of the great national galleries of the nude in Hindu art, would care to point to a simpering lady and say: 'That is my great great-grandmother'" (105). Having thus shown the contrast between the eastern especially Indian and the Western behavior and attitude to art, Chaudhuri records his appreciation of the statues of Venus-da-Milo, Michaelangelo, the beauty of country houses and chateaux, the palaces like Penshurst Place, gardens like Borghese or Umberto gardens and Gothic Cathedrals.

15. THE DISCOVERY OF WOMAN IN BENGAL

In his essay, "The Discovery of Woman in Bengal" (originally published in *The Statesman,* Calcutta, April 18, 1965), Chaudhuri shows how different Bengali scholars viewed woman differently. For example, Bankim Chandra Chatterjee and Ishwar Gupta looked at women from opposite points of view. "The popular and flippant view, so far as it could be art, was voiced at its most artistic by the poet Ishwar Gupta. At times coarse, he was generally brilliant, though maliciously so. Bankim Chandra Chatterjee, his literary pupil in youth, summed up Gupta's attitude in the following words: 'All of you say that Bengali women are very pretty, very virtuous, very charming, that they are the embodiment of love, a solace for the heart, the source of morality. That may be true. But I (Ishwar Gupta) see that they are queer creatures. Men keep women as they keep monkeys. It is fun to make feast at both.' Bankim Chandra also pointed out that if connoisseurs in that line went to the *ghats* to see the beauty of bathing women, Ishwar Gupta enjoyed looking on their awkwardness with their wet clothes. Or again, if people admitted the self-sacrifice in their devotion to household duties, Gupta could not forget that they are up some of the raw rice before they began to cook it" (112). For Ishwar Gupta, women were only an object of satire. Chaudhuri offers a brief historical picture of the men's views of women in Bengal as elsewhere also. Others traditionally consider woman as a goddess in human shape, a view which is supported by our classical epics and Manu's *Dharma Sastra* etc. Later men began to consider woman as a beloved and an object of romantic love. Woman's love can mitigate a man's frustrations in other fields of his life. Chaudhuri offers the example of a clerk's life. "It was Tagore again who saw this role most clearly. He gave a very moving expression to it in the poem, *Premer Abhishek*, 'Crowning by Love'. A clerk, insulted in his office, found that his life had lost nothing of beauty or grandeur, because his wife's love could always draw him back into a world of intangible glory. This background of the piece was omitted at the instance of Loken Palit, but the poem would remain unintelligible without the background" (116).

16. CLOTHES AND THE PEOPLE

In his essay, "Clothes and the People" (originally published in *The Statesman*, February 14, 1954), Chaudhuri examines the Indians' attitude to the clothes that they have been wearing from time to time. He begins his essay by referring to the sartorial commotion in New Delhi. "The capital of the Republic is in for a revolution in dress" (118). The historical evolution of the sartorial habits in India may be constructed as follows. The essay easily testifies to Chaudhuri's keen observation, sound scholarship and historical perspective. For example, he begins from the beginning of the human habit of wearing clothes in human history. The aborigines, the descendants of the oldest hunters and food-gatherers wore 'decency clouts' or loin clothes. Earlier they used to wander about as naked as animals as testified to by anthropologists. Then the Aryans, who spoke the Indo-European languages, wore dhoti (men) and chadar (women) sometimes with the addition of third. "Thus a woman of the Vedic age wore the 'nivi', 'vasa', and 'adhivasa', as the Roman women did the tunica, stole and alla. Greek women put on at least two articles of clothing, the khiton and himation" (121).

Chaudhuri points out that the combination of salwar and kurta, together with the dopatta is generally regarded as Islamic. But Chaudhuri shows that it is a mistake and points out correctly that this costume was common in Middle Eastern countries, but was widely introduced into India only by the Muslims and that the Islamic attitude towards women came to absorb the Hindu idea of the same kind until it stood in opposition to the Brahmanic attitude. Chaudhuri remarks further that the sewn clothes were introduced into our country by Persians, Greeks,

Scythians, Persians and Huns for about a thousand years until it was permanently established by the Muslims.

But with the entry of the British into India, Chaudhuri points out; the coat became an important official dress for Indians, especially bureaucrats, though it is non-traditional. Though the drooping lapels are being transformed into erect lapels, the coat enjoys an important role in the official life of Indians. "But the coat with the new look is the expression of only one half of the revolution, there being a counterbalancing half. In fact, this revolution has neatly split itself into a political and ministerial movement on the one hand, and an official and administrative one on the other. The coat is the central feature of the official transformation, the sherwani with the churidar pajama of the political. More and more of our politicians and ministers, even those who formerly wore nothing but the dhoti and its adjuncts, are going into the sherwani. This dress is, however, no nouveau venu, nor a freak, but has a firm historical basis, although the affiliation is only to a single cycle of Indian history" (118).

Chaudhuri sees a connection between the people's clothes and their religious or official or political positions. "...I do believe that in India clothing is more interwoven with deep-seated ethical, political and cultural loyalties than anywhere else in the modern world" (120). For example, Chaudhuri mentions how dhoti became an important costume for the nationalists in the Gandhian era. "In the Gandhian epoch of the nationalist movement many political figures of northern India, who is ordinary circumstances would have been in sherwani and pajama, adopted the dhoti. So far as clothing is connected with politics, and I believe the connection is profound in India, there was a sound intuition and shrewd logic behind the adoption of the dhoti" (119).

Finally Chaudhuri summarizes the Hindu attitude to the feminine dress and says that the Hindu always like his women in sari, because sari has its own beauty, grace and respectability. Chaudhuri offers a more comprehensive picture of his sartorial philosophy in his famous book, *Culture in the Vanity Bag* (Jaico, Bombay, 1970).

17. A ROOTLESS FASHION

In his essay, "A Rootless Fashion" (originally published in *The Times of India*, May 7, 1965), Chaudhuri shows how the Indian women, especially the Westernized or modernistic women wear the new *choli* or blouse with the open waist, but he comments that it does not agree with the sari and that the Indian women indulge in mere imitation and pseudo-Indianization of their dress. "How can these women, seeking to be strikingly and prettily Indian, commit such a mistake? The explanation is simple. These women are not honest enough in their quest for Indianness, either intellectually or aesthetically, and what they are out to do is to put a pseudo-Indian veneer on their imitation of the West. Our fashionable women saw that their counterparts in the West bared a part of their body by way of adornment, wanted to do the same thing, but also felt that it would not do for them to bare the shoulders like their models. That would be too slavish, and rather stale for their Western admirers. So, they hit upon what they thought would be the Indian way of doing the same thing" (127). Obviously Chaudhuri shows the hollowness and even incompleteness in their imitation of the Western sartorial habits and their attempts to look Indian in a rather trivial way.

18. FROM BABOO ENGLISH TO INDIAN ENGLISH

In his essay, "From Baboo English to Indian English" (originally published in *The Illustrated Weekly of India*, June 15, 1950), Chaudhuri traces the dual approach of Indians to the use of English language colonially handed over to them by the British people. On the one hand, they wish to drive it out of India for political reasons, to decolonize their mind. On the other hand, they want to have proficiency in the use of it and dream of writing it like a native Englishman, but unfortunately end up in writing in Indian English. "On the other hand, those Indians who employ English as a medium of higher expression or read it for its cultural value, would not encourage or even tolerate, the idea of 'Indian English' in any circumstances. It was, and remains, the ambition of every Indian who writes English to write it like an Englishman; and this aspiration is independent of his ability or success in realizing it. In actual fact, he is deeply hurt if his Indicisms are pointed out to him" (129).

Chaudhuri points out that the Indian writer's habit to be modish and ultra-fashionable makes him un-English, though he wants to write like an Englishman. "Moreover, not only does an Indian want to write English as if he was to the manner born, he also wants to be fashionable, at times ultra-fashionable. On the whole, Indian writers who take the writing of English seriously also show an outstanding capacity to be modish, though by so doing, they have become un-English in a different way; for it is not the well-brought up Englishman's habit to be dressed in the very height of fashion. Most of those Indians who write the current 'smart' English would like to be members of the Athenaeum, but they think they can do so by dressing themselves, stylistically speaking, like a Pierrot" (129). Those writers, who write in Indian English, are not respected by the native Englishmen and that those who write in Indian English are not conscious of it and try to keep it on a low level. Chaudhuri points out that some Indians want to encourage Indian English in order to avoid Hindi. He detects some sort of 'un-historicity' in Indian English and says that it has not evolved like American English. He says that Indian English writers with literary ambition were not taught good English by the resident Englishmen. Similarly the Englishmen did not like the English of the Westernized Indians also. For example, Kipling caricatured Indian English of Huree Babus of Bengal. Quoting a piece of ornamental writing by an Indian, Chaudhuri shows why the Englishmen dislike Indian English, "This is typical Baboo English of one sort, the highly wrought and the self-consciously literary. But, at the other extreme, was the grotesquely illiterate Indian English. Englishmen often quoted the second kind as the normal one. That was wholly wrong. But literary or illiterate, Indian English was characterized by a common un-Englishness in everything connected with style-diction, sound and rhythm—though its degree varied from writer to writer" (132).

Another insightful observation made by Chaudhuri is that the compulsion to use English that was there in the colonial period is not there in the post-colonial period when the situation has changed a lot. No Englishmen are there in India now to communicate with and there is no necessity to seek employment under the British rule. But yet Indians want to use English for parading their snobbery and love of fashion.

Chaudhuri detects both the tendencies in India: (1) of Indianizing English (syntax etc.) and (2) Anglicizing the Indian languages. He points out that Indian English is generally flowery and Sanskritized. Chaudhuri comments that Nehru was the most Westernized Indian. He believes that the future of Indian English is very bleak.

19. MY WAY OF BEING PRO-BRITISH

In his essays, "My Way of Being Pro-British" (originally published in *The Illustrated Weekly of India*, June 25, 1978), Chaudhuri answers to the complaints by patriotic Indians as an Anglophile and justifies his pro-British stand. "In actual fact, instead of harming me the bad reputation has helped me in my profession of writer. White-skinned scribblers have two methods to make Anglicized Indians read their books: first by praising India and next by criticizing it. Both work, because the one feeds their megalomania and the other their persecution mania. In contrast, mere Natives like me have only one way if they want to secure a wide readership among these people. These Indians do not value praise of Indian life and civilization from the fellow countrymen, for that is only a shared feeling, devoid of extra authority. So the native must criticize and acquire the reputation of being anti-Indian" (135). He has been quite bold and frank in owning his pro-British point of view and confessed how it has helped him a lot in building a reputation for himself as a writer. Chaudhuri's views cannot be dismissed as blind he always gives proper reasons for his like and dislikes and hence his views cannot be ignored easily by any sensible critic.

Similarly, Chaudhuri attacks the British Indophiles as well as the Anglicized Indian chelas for their views on India. Although the British Indophiles talk about the love-hate relationship between the British and the Indians, Chaudhuri shows the discordance between the two. He says, "It has no relevance whatever be the Indo-British relationship because what Indians loved and what they hated were wholly unconnected. The love was for English life, civilization and values and the hatred for British rule in India. So it remains. At present the hatred is retrospective and the love very much of the moment" (136). Chaudhuri points out that this strange mixture of views by the Anglicized class is a grave threat to the social and cultural integrity of India.

Then Chaudhuri boldly justifies his stand as follows: "I am pro-British in my way and for my reasons, which do not need any apology. At the beginning of 1976 I heard that an Indian writer of some standing had said at a public meeting that Nirad Chaudhuri would bring back Queen Victoria to rule India if he could" (136). In his Taraknath and Mary Keatings Das Memorial Lecture before the University of Michigan at Ann Arbor on September 27, 1976, Chaudhuri defends himself by asking 'why not'? He argues quite rightly that the Indian Renaissance took place during the reign of Queen Victoria:

> Why not? It was during the reign of Queen Victoria that such Indians as Bankim Chandra Chatterjee, Keshub Chunder Sen, Bal Gangadhar Tilak, Rabindranath Tagore, Jagadish Chandra Bose, Mohandas Karamchand Gandhi, C.V. Raman, Jawaharlal Nehru or Subhas Chandra Bose were born. The year of the Diamond Jubilee of Queen Victoria, i.e. 1897, was the year of birth even of Nirad Chaudhuri. When the record has been matched by those born later I shall be glad to die and be reborn in the reign of Queen Indira. (136)

Being a product of that revolution he cannot disavow one side of his mental ancestry. "Of course mules do not like to recall their donkey fathers. But I am not a mule. I do not also like to be a child in a one-parent family, although to be that both fashionable and profitable in present-day Britain. An Indian always wants to be regarded as his *Bapka Beta*..." (137). Commenting on the anti-British view of the Anglicized Indians he clarifies further, "That is a family quarrel. Their anti-British attitude is like the grievances of an illegitimate son whose only claim to social status rests on the father but who, he feels, has not acknowledged and provided for him. It is also like the resentment of a legitimate son who has quarreled with his father over property" (137). Chaudhuri attributes it to the British rule and the lack of monetary opportunities created by it. This grievance is especially felt by the government servants in the British Rule in India. But the professionals like lawyers had no grievance on the score of money as they could earn as much and at times more than the District Magistrate. But Chaudhuri declares that he does not belong to this disgruntled class. Coming from a landed family, he took up a salaried post, but he mentions how he suffered in his job for various reasons. "...I was the first in my line to take up a salaried post. That never agreed with me, and I can say that I became fully myself only when I retired from the service of the Government of India in 1952 at the age of fifty-five. So at eighty I say I am only twenty-five years old.... Any hatred that I could feel against the British was on the score of our political subjection and the behavior of the local British. It had nothing personal. Thus, it appeared with the passing away of British rule, and I was then able to give expression to my historical view of it. And I was made to suffer for it. As it happened, I was a political suspect during the last decades of British rule. Even as late as 1944 the political police tried to get me dismissed from my post in AIR. And it was only an English Secretary to the Information Department who kept me in it. Thus, instead of making the best of both worlds as those who call me pro-British have done, I made the worst of both" (138).

After clarifying his hatred of the political rule of the British in India, he explains the reasons for his liking for the British culture and civilization. "What is denounced as my pro-British treachery to India is really my loyalty to English life and civilization by which I was formed. It had as its penumbra my adherence to the values created by European civilization. European cultural influences began to beat upon me from my childhood" (138). Then Chaudhuri mentions how the European knowledge came to him through English language and literature. That is why he became an admirer of British culture and language. But that does not blind him to the negative aspects of British life.

For example, he deplores decadence and permissiveness in contemporary Britain and their private interest overriding their public interest. On the whole, Chaudhuri claims to be a spiritual son of England (although he may not believe in spirituality proper in the traditional sense of the term).

20. BEWARE OF THE INDOPHILE ENGLISHMAN

In his essay, "Beware of the Indophile Englishman" (originally published in *The Statesman*, April 17, 1993), Chaudhuri exposes the opportunistic behavior of the British people, who come to India and begin to praise it for diplomatic, professional and private reasons. Chaudhuri contrasts this Indo-philism with the British people's racial arrogance and ill-treatment of Indians when they were ruling India and their description of Indians as 'Niggers'. Chaudhuri offers concrete examples of Sir Charles Trevelyan, brother in law of Macaulay and Lord Curzon calling the Indians d…d niggers. The British were notorious for their racial superiority, ill treatment of and contempt, malice, and cruelty towards Indians. "This was the stark truth. Englishmen assaulted not only ordinary Indians, but even the most eminent. Both Rammohun Roy and Bankim Chandra Chatterjee were dragged out of their palanquins by British officials for having had the insolence, as they thought of remaining in their palanquins in their presence. Indians of the highest ranks, including one of the famous Imam Brothers of Patna, were thrown out by force from first-class compartments of trains by the British passengers. An English colonel burst out in the hearing of Sir Walter Lawrence, later Private Secretary to Lord Curzon, that 'the country was going to the dogs and he would not submit to the indignity of a black man pushing into his carriage,' when a high-ranking Indian official entered it" (144-45). Chaudhuri shows the British contempt for Indians by narrating how the Englishmen complained that the Bengalis' legs were like those of slaves; that the English soldiers used to beat and kick Indians, who would be seriously injured because of their poor health.

Chaudhuri quotes the words of Archbishop Cosmos Lang and Lord Linlithgow to show their European prejudice against

Indians. "On 28 June, 1930, Archbishop Cosmos Lang of Canterbury, the highest spiritual authority in Britain wrote to Lord Irwin that 'Gandhi was a perverse and dangerous mixture of the mystic, the fanatic, and the anarchist'. On 17 February, 1943, Lord Linlithgow, Viceroy in India, wrote to Churchill: 'I have long known Gandhi as the world's most successful humbug'" (146). It is the harshness, malice, cruelty and ill-treatment etc. that are the details of true and natural English character. But it transformed itself into superficial Indo-philism after August 15, 1947. Chaudhuri continues to show the contradictions in the British character during the colonial and the post-colonial periods. "These men were speaking like true and natural Europeans, for it is impossible for anyone imbued with the European spirit to admire Gandhi without serious reservations. I prefer this plain-speaking to sycophancy about Gandhi shown today by Occidentals, which is partly the product of opportunism and partly of Western degeneracy. I cannot say what contempt I feel for the routine obeisance of Western dignitaries at the Gandhi memorial. The self-abasement of the British community from that time has been all-embracing. Just as all Indians from Bazaar porters to Rajahs were once 'Niggers', hence-forward all of them from the peasant to the political leader were to be angels. With the withdrawal of British rule the Yahoos of yesterday became the Houyhnhums of today" (146-47). Chaudhuri has shown how the British had lost their power and to deal with Indians in power and therefore adopted this Indo-philism as a practical way of getting on well with the Indians. He mentions how some English Indo-philes like Horace Alexander and Arthur Moore made stupid complaints against his *Autobiography of an Unknown Indian* (1951), which was well received in England.

Chaudhuri shows how the English Indo-philism is rather superficial and even opportunistic and how their basic opinion about India and Indians has not changed. He shows how they have a very low opinion about the Indian intellectuals. "The low opinion of Indians in all spheres of their mental activity is seen precisely among those Englishmen who are sincerely interested in India. More especially, these Englishmen hold a very low opinion of the intellectual ability and moral integrity of Indian intellectuals" (149).

Similarly, Chaudhuri comments on the Westernized Indian who provides an interesting parallel or counterpart to the English Indo-phile. "To give only a few significant particulars about their Anglicized life, their government is only embrowned British rule; their economic ideas are wholly Western; their education is in English and it is in this language that they reveal their mind; their clothes are Western, and even their girls are going into European clothes. There is nothing Hindu or Gandhian in them" (150). Then Chaudhuri mentions the rancor of Indians for the British rule and how as a consequence of this he had to suffer starvation for twelve long years as the Indians created a chain of problems for Chaudhuri in his professional career.

Chaudhuri thus insightfully detects a duality in Indians' attitude to the British—their hatred for the British rule but their love for English individuals. He remarks that even great Indians like Raja Rammohun Roy, Bankim Chandra Chatterjee and Swami Vivekananda had these dualistic views about British rule and culture.

Chaudhuri justifies the dedication of his *Autobiography of an Unknown Indian* to the memory of the British Empire in the light of his admiration for British culture and the positive influence of the British rule on Indian life, including his personal life. But he deplores the lack of intellectuals in India, which is true even now. Most of the Indian intellectuals are like parrots repeating the Western ideas in a blind fashion to show off their reading without looking around them for the harsh reality of India.

21. JOURNALISM WAS BORN IN SIN

In his essay, "Journalism was Born in Sin" (originally published in *The Statesman*, April 17, 1993), Chaudhuri attacks the modern sinfulness of man in almost all the cultures of the world, especially in Britain and America. He uses a beautiful theological image to describe it. "Journalism, like men in Christian theology, was born in sin, but journalists are always trying to cancel the original sin by professing to be made regenerate by means of their sort of baptism" (153). The journalists are comparable to lawyers and prostitutes in so far as they are born to fulfil the public demand without bothering about the moral rightness or wrongness of it. He says further that the sexual morality or better immorality is to be judged according to the climate of opinion prevalent in a society. For example, kissing and hugging are supposed to be atrocious in Indian society, but even sexual intercourse in public places including gardens may not be atrocious at all, but a very natural event of biological satisfaction in countries like England and America. Chaudhuri gives an example from his own observation in England. When he took his seventy-two-year-old wife, suffering from arthritis to an English country town he is told by his wife what she saw there from sitting inside the car. "We had gone to see a pretty English country town with some English friends in their car. As my wife cannot walk owning to her arthritis, she had to be left in the car in the public car-park of the town. While waiting for our return she first saw a young man driving in and stationing his car before ours. Soon after, clearly by previous appointment, a young woman of about the same age arrived in another car. She was brought to the young man's car. Though she was wearing a wedding ring they could not be husband and wife, obviously. Then to her astonishment my wife saw them having sexual intercourse before her eyes in broad daylight. She was so near that she would have been in serious danger had the mating couple been wild animals like tigers, which do not like to be watched at such times. But the couple were only a commonplace English adulterer and adulteress who, far from feeling a tiger's resentment, did not even have the human bashfulness in such matters, probably because what Thomas Gray has called 'the blushes of ingenuous shame' had been quenched in them by large doses of aphrodisiac provided by the Press, the theatre and the films, in obedience to the existing climate of opinion. It was a very purposive although hurried mission, for the operation began without any delay, and the two persons drove off in separate cars as soon as it was finished. My wife was outraged, and in the existing climate of opinion she would certainly be accused of trying to 'put the clock back'" (154). Chaudhuri deplores the disappearance of the elegant feeling of love between young men and women in England now and the wide practice of shameless exhibitionism and promiscuity these days. That is because the climate of opinion has changed in England in the past few years. Chaudhuri can forgive the lawyers and prostitutes but not the journalists, who have a ring of hypocrisy in their professional duties. "But while I give the credit for being honest to the lawyers and prostitutes as professionals, I cannot think of the journalists in the same way. Those of them who are in the B.B.C. have indeed frankly given up their pretence to be something other than providers of the kind of entertainment their listeners or viewers want. They have thrown Sir John Roth's policies overboard. But newspapermen still like to say that they are not purveyors of the merchandise their readers want, but are upholders of the public good, etc. This has a very unpleasant ring of hypocrisy. Yet they have no awareness that they are hypocritical" (154).

Note

1. Nirad C. Chaudhuri. *From the Archives of a Centenarian*, Kolkata: Mitra & Ghosh Publishers Pvt Ltd, First Published, 1997. Second Reprint, 1999. (All the page references are to this edition.)

Chapter 14

Why I Mourn for England[1]

1. APOLOGIA PRO SCRIPTA SUA

In his essay, "Apologia Pro Scripta Sua" (originally published in Granta, Special Indian Number, May 1997), Chaudhuri writes about the literary writers and their careers. He opines that a man becomes a writer out of his inner compulsion, like a tiger becoming a hunter. Then he classifies the writers broadly into vocational and professional ones and remarks that the professional writers far outnumber the vocational.

Then he offers an interesting suggestion that writers should be described according to zoological taxonomy. "Members of each one of them can be regarded as an animal of a distinct species—say, a lion, a horse, a dog, or cat. There is, however, a fundamental difference between the zoological correlatives or writers and those of other professions. Members of all professions are one animal, differing among themselves only by their standing as that particular animal. For instance, a successful barrister in a High Court may be an Arab horse, while lawyers of lowly rank in a court of the lowest jurisdiction will be a hackney" (9-10). Then he subdivides them further as follows: "But writers, zoologically classified, are not one animal; they are different animals. That is to say, if one writer can be regarded as a lion or horse, another will be a bullock, or donkey or a monkey, or even a skunk. Therefore no one can form a correct idea of what a particular writer is or does by simply considering him as a writer" (10).

Chaudhuri describes himself as a vocational writer and compares himself to a camera and implies that his views are dependent upon his observation of the external world around him. He rightly opines that there is no such thing as one standard rhythm of English prose and that English prose rhythms are bewilderingly diverse. Then he reveals certain secrets of his writing career and its success. He confesses that he has learnt his English not from the Englishmen, but from his Bengali teachers. He reads out loudly what he writes and the rhythm of the language helps and guides him to improve and chisel it. "The habit of writing by sounding has led me to another basic discovery in regard to diction. I have found that the mood and temper created in me by anything I see or feel control the rhythm and tempo of what I write. For instance, if my mood is excited and dramatic my diction at once becomes staccato in rhythm and allegro or even presto in tempo; whereas when I am contemplative these become legato and adagio or even lento" (11). Chaudhuri comments that the style is decided by the subject itself.

Proceeding further Chaudhuri calls himself more a journalist than a man of letters. This may be regarded as his tongue-in-cheek humility because a mere journalist would not have written the stiflingly serious stuff that he has written. It is not for nothing that Chaudhuri has been awarded the honorary D.Litt. degree by the Oxford University. He is regarded by serious scholars as one of the most brilliant scholars of the world hailing from India. Then Chaudhuri mentions how the Indians' reaction to his Autobiography was ferocious on account of his pro-British views. He states frankly that his English style is not accessible to the general run of educated Indians. Apart from being a journalist, Chaudhuri claims to be a preacher also.

Chaudhuri's views definitely help the readers to understand and interpret his own works in the light of his views.

2. WHY I MOURN FOR ENGLAND

In his essay, "Why I Mourn for England" (originally published in *The Daily Telegraph*, London, February 20, 1968), Chaudhuri traces the decline and decadence of English culture and English mind, as evidenced in the shrinkage of English vocabulary, absence of colour in diction and monotony of rhythm. He deplores that the English mind; English clothes and

English diction have lost their grandeur. "Moral insensitivity and cultural insularity are now the marks of the English mind" (16). Commenting on the popularization of the diction of the English Bible and Prayer Book, Chaudhuri suggests that it is also a part of the decadence of English culture, "In this the Anglican Church is showing a strange inconsistency. It is not making its princes give up their archaic vestments to go into jeans, but putting its scriptures into a linguistic equivalent of that popular garment. It is, however easy to explain this: the populace have eyes to cringe at the spectacle of grand clothes, however out of date; but they do not have the minds to understand traditional religious diction" (17). Chaudhuri points out how this so-called modernity (or post-modernity) symbolizes the laxity of faith. "Respect for this incapacity will not save English Christianity. In all ages and among all peoples religion has created its special diction and its hold has depended on it. Therefore, all religions have been staunchly conservative in regard to language. The Hindus have not permitted any change in the Vedas, nor the Muslim in the Koran. As long as a particular faith remains living, its special diction also remains intelligible" (17).

Chaudhuri deciphers a sort of contraction of the British mind in its outward expression of emptiness. "Yet the contraction of the mind is not the worst part of the decadence in England. What is more ominous is that as the mind is contracting the sense of emptiness within it is increasing. The emptiness is made visible to me by the number of young people I see roaming the city of Oxford, where I now live, with headphones over their ears. These young things, who are not afraid of their parents, of their teachers or even of policemen, are afraid of their own minds" (18).

Chaudhuri's observation of the decadence of England in particular and of the world in general is confirmed and consolidated in his later writings like *Thy Hand, Great Anarch!* and *Three Horsemen of the New Apocalypse*.

3. BRITAIN THROUGH AN INDIAN'S EYES

In his essay, "Britain through an Indian's Eyes" (originally published in *The Daily Telegraph*), Nirad Chaudhuri observes and records his views on the recent changes in Britain and British life. For example, he observes that the mingling of male and female sexes has increased. "This life beats on me even at Oxford, once a city of dreaming spires, the home of lost causes, and unisexual. The spires dream no more, lost causes have no place in it, and no man is without a woman. The intrusive women are no longer only the wives of the fellows released from celibacy, nor the *virginculae* of Somerville and Lady Margaret Hall of whom Max Beerbohm spoke" (19). He comments on the laxity of sexual morals and tells us about how the girl-friends or mistresses of the undergraduate boys are allowed in the hostel during the day time. He remarks that sexual behavior has undergone a major revolution in the British way of life.

Next to sex, the pursuit of money has become the most important obsession of the British people. There has been a sort of nationalization of commercial philosophy going under the name of national economy. Even education and authorship and collection of books have become part of investment. Thus economics has become the new religion. Acquisition of wealth has become a way of self-assertion. "In a sense this is natural. Acquisition of wealth is the simplest outlet for man's innate urge for self-assertion. So when a people lose their political ambitions, they turn to money-making.... So it cannot be wrong if the British people, who have lost a great empire and not merely failed to acquire one, should also be doing the same thing. The only question is whether they are having success in their new enterprise" (20). Chaudhuri offers his typical and interesting simile to describe the dilemma of the British men and their economy. "Here the British monetary obsession is like the worries of a great nobleman who can neither become poor nor remain wealthy.... The British national economy is like a sick old gentleman kept going by the doctors and a strict regimen" (20).

In spite of the low profile of the British economy, Chaudhuri points out that there is a great contrast between the British and the Indian economic levels of life. He says that even the working class men of Britain are equal to the high official in the Government of India. Referring to the British working class he says, "The working class, too, are rich by our standards, for their style of living would compare favourably with that of a high-official in the Government of India" (20). Every Briton (like every man elsewhere in the world) is hankering for more and more money. Chaudhuri describes this competition for the acquisition of wealth through an animal imagery. "Everybody is wanting more and more money, and each class has its style of hunting. The top people roar like lions, the salaried men are steady on the scent like drag-hounds; the working classes form a gigantic pack of foxhounds in full cry. They are the noisiest, but with better reason than the others" (21). As a consequence of this competition for wealth, Chaudhuri notices a class war going on in England.

4. DECADENCE OF ENGLISH LIFE AND CIVILIZATION

In his essay, "Decadence of English Life and Civilization" (originally delivered as a speech at the British Housewives' League, Spring Meeting on the Dissolution of the Nation, April 27, 1988), Nirad Chaudhuri makes his observation of British life and civilization clearer with relevant examples from life. His earliest observation made in 1946 holds true as late as 1988 and even after that. Some of his seminal ideas expressed in this article are later worked out in great detail in his later books like *The Apocalypse of the Three Horsemen*. The main observation of Chaudhuri about the English life is that it has reached the stage of decadence in many ways. He says quite clearly and boldly that in England, which is aged now, national maturity did not go with a political philosophy.

Nirad Chaudhuri states quite interestingly that he noticed decadence in Bengal (during 1920-41) and therefore went to live in Delhi. Then noticing decadence in Delhi also, he went to England. Ironically enough, after going to and living in Oxford he began to notice decadence there also. Thus decadence has become almost a universal phenomenon of human life now. "I found that the Bengali life and culture in which I was brought up was disintegrating. So I fled from Bengal to Delhi, and finding fossilization in northern India thought of coming away to England. But even before the war was over the general election of 1945 made me feel that England too had been struck by decadence. Since then the spectre has been treading at my heels wherever I have gone—to the shores of the Pacific in Canada and to Texas in the United States. I found that the New World was more decadent as a human community than the Old World, not only in Europe but even in Asia" (42).

According to Chaudhuri the British decadence expresses itself in different forms. For example, mere word-mongering and use of jargon is feature of decadence. "I might say that if some people among you are trendy it is because English life is decadent. The intellectual trend in decadence is to impose a pattern of mere words on all reality. Discussion of all human affairs loses touch with reality and becomes word-mongering. I found that when I studied the decadence of the ancient Hindu civilization. At that stage all Hindu writing became an interminable and even absurd rigmarole. So, it is quite natural that in your decadence you should establish professorships in your universities to teach this Hindu rigmarole and also establish popular centres to propagate its charlatanry" (43).

Chaudhuri proceeds further to show that female adornment is another expression of decadence and that it adds to the falsification of appearance and leads to adultery. He remarks rightly that decadence loosens the marriage tie. He gives the example of India, especially Bengal by saying that economic independence of a married woman is something unheard of in India and Bengal. On the contrary the British way of giving house-keeping allowance and pocket money to married women is something very strange.

Commenting on women's liberation movement Chaudhuri opines frankly and insightfully, "Yet, the feminist movement has not succeeded in freeing women from men for women today is only freedom from half the man: from that that part of him only which exists above the belt. Submission to the part below the belt is now more whole-hearted than it ever was in the past" (48).

Thus, Nirad Chaudhuri has shown important examples from life in general, but that of the West in particular to show how decadence expresses itself in different forms and ways.

5. THE ENGLISH LANGUAGE AND INDIAN LIFE

In his essay, "The English Language and Indian Life" (originally delivered as a speech in Weekly Literature Festival, 5 July, 1986), Nirad Chaudhuri stakes that the reading of English literature brought about a mental revolution thereby removing the state of stagnancy and stupor in the Indian context. Chaudhuri mentions the characteristic features of cultural decadence by pointing out that during such a period of decadence it is the readers who dictate to literature and literature has to obey in order to survive; that this produces the best-seller thereby converting the literary activity into a branch of commerce.

Chaudhuri shows the paradox that the hold of English on Indians has become stronger after the end of British rule, which logically should have weakened it; that the official language of India remains English even after 1965.

Another paradox shown by Chaudhuri is that the Indians are so enthusiastic about and affectionate towards the English language though they hated the British rulers of the past.

Addressing the British audience, Chaudhuri shows how the British are not willing to Hindu-ize themselves by practicing yoga, whereas the Indians are more than willing to Anglicize themselves and ready to write in English even to their wives. "It is certainly curious that the end of British rule should have produced both among you and us effects which are the opposite of what would have been natural. You are not Hindu-izing yourselves not only by taking to yoga, but also by becoming vegetarian. We, in contrast, are Anglicizing ourselves further and have begun to write in English even to our wives" (50).

Chaudhuri gives the examples of his parents, who had made him read Shakespeare at the age of ten. His mother had told him the stories of *King Lear*, *Merchant of Venice* and even of *Iliad* through the Bangla translations.

Chaudhuri speaks about the universal principle of linguistic evolution and attributes this (change in the usage) to the change in the mind of the speakers of that language. He offers several examples of how certain words have changed their meanings and connotations. For example words like 'fair sex', 'make love', etc. One may remember how T.S. Eliot has shown that the word 'boyfriend' has now become a euphemistic alternative for lover. Chaudhuri suggests that the change in the language shows the change in our mindset and the cheapening of language is an example of British decadence.

Commenting on the role and importance of English language during the colonial period in India, Chaudhuri offers insightful remarks. He says that during the British rule in India Britons enjoyed political power and privileges, which were connected with their (English) language. But when they left India, they left only the English language to the Indians. Therefore the Indian ruling order considers English as their regal appendage.

Chaudhuri connects this to the secondary education of two kinds: Timocratic (English medium) and Democratic (Indian language medium). In the British Raj, English was the medium of instruction and Bengali (or Indian language) was called the second language in the syllabus. Chaudhuri tells how he was thoroughly gilled in grammar and idioms. So the Bengali boys defiantly declared that "The English people do not know the grammar of their language, as we do."

During the British rule there was no class snobbery attached to the knowledge of English language. But the British rulers, who created a class of Indians knowing English, treated them as untouchables.

Chaudhuri confesses that he did not learn English language from any Englishman in his school or college and had some difficulty in following the English pronunciation of Englishmen in his later life.

But Chaudhuri comments upon the positive and negative influences of the English language on Indian people. He says that it brought in a comprehensive mental revolution and even became a means of Westernization. He offers examples of how the English language made the Hindu concubinage as sanctified as the Hindu connubium.

He traces the positive influence of the English language on Indian life and culture: one, moral consciousness and two, a new life of passion (a new love for God, country, Nature, man and woman). He is quite right in his insightful observations. He mentions how the English language changed the behavior and occupations also of Indians. For example, needlework of all kinds was an accomplishment for marriageable girls; that the reading of English literature incited a revolt against arranged marriage. As an influence of reading English literature, the Indians (Bengalis in this case) fell in love with love-marriages (and felt the lure of adultery also), but most of these love-marriages were failures and ended up in divorces. Chaudhuri offers two examples of two kinds of marriage. He shows how Jawaharlal Nehru's arranged marriage with Kamala Nehru and Mrs. Indira Gandhi's love-marriage with Firoz Gandhi turned out to be failures for different reasons. Chaudhuri mentions how the Bengalis were influenced by Shakespeare's Romeo and Juliet and the European Romantic Movement and that the writers began to write frankly and openly about love, kissing and hugging etc.

Chaudhuri's remarks about the positive and negative influence of English on Indian life, literature and culture are insightful and valuable for all the students and teachers of English language and literature.

6. THE FUTURE OF IMPERIALISM

In his essay, "The Future of Imperialism" (originally published in *The New English Review,* November, 1946), Chaudhuri records his views on the nature and future of imperialism. He begins his essay with an important observation that imperialism is in disgrace today. His definition of Empire is very clear. He says, "There is no empire without a conglomeration of linguistically, racially, and culturally different nationalities and the hegemony of one of these over the rest. The heterogeneity and the domination are of the very essence of imperial relations. An empire is hierarchical. There may be in it, and has been full or partial freedom for individuals or groups to rise from one level to another; but this has not modified the stepped and stratified structure of the organization. An empire is not, inter-racially or internationally, egalitarian. A true empire may confer citizenship on its subjects, but does not set them up in independent states" (68-69).

Chaudhuri opines that the present-day British people are in an anti-imperialist mood, because of their fear of being unfashionable. They change their allegiance from the old order to the new quickly. Chaudhuri offers a beautiful feudal image for the change of loyalty from the old master to the new; or from the UNO to the British Commonwealth. "When Louis XVI as Dauphin and Marie-Antoinette were waiting in their apartments for news of the dying Louis XV, they suddenly heard a noise like thunder. It was the crowd of courtiers rushing out of the antechamber of the dead monarch to greet the new. Our ideological courtiers are turning out in the same manner to greet the ideological heir-apparent. But while the old courtiers waited till Louis XV was actually dead, the new do not care to ascertain whether their old man is really so" (70).

Chaudhuri makes an interesting observation that Empires have died only to give place to new Empires. He offers the examples of Samaria, Egypt, Greece, Rome and Islam and points out that "An internal consolidation and external extension of imperialism is going on simultaneously" (71).

He remarks that although the Spaniards, the Portuguese and the French have extended their empires, the British people have been its supreme architects.

Chaudhuri makes an important observation that the historical process is a continuation of the biological process. "There is the testimony of history. Again, the historical process is only a continuation of the biological process, through which from age to age new classes and orders of animals have emerged, each manifesting a higher value in life and domination the earth in succession. Instead of an egalitarian molluscaean democracy we see saurian imperialism succeeding Piscean imperialism, mammalian imperialism succeeding reptilian imperialism, human imperialism succeeding general mammalian imperialism. In short, neither biological evolution nor human history reveals anything like equal status for all. They do not bear witness to the achievement of anything good, great wise, abiding or new by the exercise of the equal vote. The cosmic process is revealed as a living and ever-growing pyramid, whose apex is rising higher and higher, leaving more and more strata underneath" (72). Chaudhuri has expressed his views through a chain of scientific, especially biological images.

Chaudhuri remarks that nowadays imperialism is connected with immorality, but he advises us to exercise our moral sense. He opines that both imperialism (and its opposite) nationalism are the products of biological order, but not wholly, because they are a product of mental and moral order also. He repeatedly reminds us that human history is only the continuation of biological evolution. He makes an important observation that imperialism can save people from relapsing into barbarism. "But there is also a more positive and humane *role*. Imperialism has also taken over the keepership of civilizations whose creators had become incapable of maintaining and defending them. Imperialism has received as equals those who come forward to join the civilized order. It is only the active influence of imperialism which has saved this portion of mankind from the atavistic drag. When not rescued by it, they inevitably fall a prey to the enemies of civilization or to their own inertia" (76). Chaudhuri points out that the real antonym to imperialism is nationalism.

7. PERMANENT CONSERVATISM

In his essay on "Permanent Conservatism" (originally published in *The New English Review*, December 1946), Nirad Chaudhuri offers his insightful remarks about the inherent disposition of the English people towards conservatism. "At the present stage of their national evolution and in the existing state of their relationship to the rest of the world, conservatism will be for them both a virtue and a necessity" (78).

He then comments that the British Leftism is a reactionary movement and that it originates from the fear generated by Nazism and Fascism, just as the Fascism originated in the fear of the Communist revolution. "As a reaction to Fascism and Nazism, Leftism is fulfilling its historical function of cancelling the legacy of these two aberrations" (79).

Chaudhuri states that India also may be influenced by Leftism temporarily before being disillusioned by it. He employs a literary simile by comparing Indian situation to that of Thomas Hardy's novel. "I may perhaps add that our unfortunate country —India—might figure as Fanny of the piece, destined to be seduced and abandoned by the meretricious English Leftist as fickle in his lovers as in its coldness and sloppily egoistic in everything" (79).

Chaudhuri shows how man's utilization of power outside of his body began with that of animals (nearest to him) and ends with that of mechanical power (most alien to him). Thus everything is fluid. Then he mentions how there are two conceivable ways of dealing with this fluidity: one, adoption of a dogma; second, the European domination of the world.

Chaudhuri points out that the factors of internal maturity and external possessions are accompanied by a philosophy of frustration, which cancels the exercise of intuition and the collective impulse. Chaudhuri mentions that the British people are no longer fit for adopting a politics of adventure.

Chaudhuri shows the final antitheses in a nutshell, "...in the present state of the English people certain mental qualities present themselves in pairs, one in the pair being indicated and the other contra-indicated. They are the following: Empiricism against Dogmatism; Freedom against Regimentation; Augustinism against Catilinism; Reason against Intuition; Aristocracy against Demagogy. There is no reason to identify this antithesis with the existing party division..." (86).

8. 'STASIS' IN ENGLAND

In his essay, "'Stasis' in England" (originally published in *The New English Review*, January 1947), Nirad Chaudhuri points out how the party politics has been working in England and the political power was held by the Conservatives and the Liberals at different times. He points out further that the Labour's policy falls inside the limits of English party politics. Then he shows how the British portion of the Empire has been transformed into an association of free nations called the British Commonwealth. He enumerates seven important points about the formation of the British Commonwealth: (1) For example, it was formed not by shame-faced defeatists, but by avowed imperialists. (2) The Commonwealth relationship was not created at one stroke by an executive act, but matured over long periods. (3) It was ever the dissolution of a pre-existing relationship, but the creation of a positive bond. (4) The Commonwealth relationship was never extended to any non-British community without attaching it to a numerically larger British element which could counterbalance the separatist inclinations of the foreigners. (5) Self-government was not conceded to any part of the Commonwealth under the threat of succession or revolt. (6) A Dominion was never made free in geographical or historical circumstances which allowed it to treat Great Britain and other Powers on equal terms. (7) The right of self-government was never conferred where self governing aptitudes, habits and institutions were not present, so that there was no voice or anarchy after the discontinuance of the authoritarian regime. But none of these features of the Commonwealth relationship is present in the case of India. The Indians insisted on independence and got their claim recognized.

"The British people," as shown by Chaudhuri, "with their humanistic system of values have sought to accomplish the work of God through the Man, and they have been remarkably successful in making both ends meet" (92). Their capitalist economy has been able to sustain immense national enterprises, including two colossal wars along with maintaining the high standard of living. But Chaudhuri asks the important question: whether the socialist economy can do the same?

Chaudhuri mentions that in the Labour party, the 'stasis' is the very breath of their nostrils. But nowadays the party politics is at the cross-roads. "The presence of an element with a definite frustration bias within the governing party of the day is a very significant development in English politics. This is without precedent. English politics have generally been very tolerant of newcomers and have not had any inhibitory class consciousness. But so far, they have always managed to pass all newcomers through a filter, so to say, and consequently, when these found themselves within the ruling set, in office or in opposition, they came to share the outlook, ideas, and the language of the old members. Even if they brought new ideas, no fundamental cleavages developed. Somehow or other the old battle and the new wine went well together. There were indeed party red rags. But the Free Trade question and Irish Home Rule, which created such bad blood within the English ruling class in their time, seem trivialities today. The superficial brutalities of the old party politics have disappeared only to be replaced by a cold, untamed rancor in the heart" (94).

9. THE GLORIOUS REVOLUTION THAT NEVER WAS

In his essay, "The Glorious Revolution That Never Was" (originally published in *The Spectator*, July 16, 1988), Nirad Chaudhuri records his views on the English Revolution of 1688. He says, "The so-called revolution of 1688 was really the prevention of an attempted revolution by James II and the reassertion of the status quo in a clearer form. Therefore it had no revolutionaries, but only plotters, who were opportunists without principles" (98). He explains it further that the gang of seven who brought about the revolution of 1688 were not only no crusaders, but were a band of ad hoc conspirators and that the only heroine of the revolution was his consort, Mary of Modena. Chaudhuri states clearly that the hatred of both Pope and Popery made this revolution possible.

10. REMEMBERING A THIRTY YEARS WAR

In his essay, "Remembering a Thirty Years War" (originally published in *The Spectator,* November 12, 1988), Nirad Chaudhuri makes an important observation that "the two world wars (1914-18 and 1939-45) were really not two but one continuum with a small break". Of course, all historians today see the two wars as one, only divided into two phases by a long armistice. They are quite disposed to see the combination of the two wars as a new Thirty Years War of Europe. To me as well, they constitute a thirty years war, but are less like the European war of 1618-48 than the Greek thirty years war of 431-404 BC, or in familiar terms the Peloponnesian War" (104)

Chaudhuri makes his observation about the necessity of war in human life. "In actual fact, all wars arise out of a fundamental human urge, which is not seen in animals. It is the urge for self-assertion, both individual and collective, which soon becomes the urge for self-aggrandizement and which cannot tolerate the self-assertion of any other human group" (105).

Then Chaudhuri talks elaborately about the German military strength and strategy which helped it to achieve success in war. Then he proceeds to observe that the real war has been between America and Russia and Britain has been forced into it only accidentally and that Britain had to fight not for its hegemony but for mere survival. "For the British people the war became purposeful only when they had to fight for survival. They fought it then as they would have fought it from the beginning, had they realized that it was a resumption of the war of 1914-18, which had only been broken off by a truce. And even the survival was achieved by the attack of Germany on Russia and the attack on the United States by Japan, none of which could be foreseen in 1940 and were basically irrational" (108).

11. DIARY

-I-

In his essay, "Diary" (originally published in *The Spectator*, issues of September 17, 24 and October 1 of 1988), Nirad Chaudhuri shows how the English journalists use their own language wrongly. For example, he shows that their use of the word, 'fusillade' is wrong and suggests that it should have been 'salvo'.

Chaudhuri uses his wit and says that he is not an immigrant in England, because he has not grown rich like the other immigrants but has become almost a pauper. But the reason why he has been living in England is that he wants to show the Englishmen how their fathers wrote (correct) English, dressed and drank their wine of high standard. He gives his own example of writing correct English, dressing in top-class apparels and drinking the expensive and old wine.

-II-

Chaudhuri comments on the paradoxical approach of Indians to the English people. Although they hated the British rulers and burnt the British manufactured cloths, they had extraordinary love for the British game, cricket and its material adjuncts (of British make).

Then he comments on the postal strike in Britain and says how the letters from Delhi take a minimum of thirteen days to reach him in London.

-III-

Chaudhuri comments on the changes in British life, especially moral degeneration and sexual immorality or promiscuity and lack of faith in man's integrity and trustworthiness. All these changes have taken place simply because 'Times have changed' (116).

Note

1. Nirad C. Chaudhuri, *Why I Mourn for England*, Compiled & Edited by Dhruva N. Chaudhuri Kolkata: Mitra & Ghosh Publishers Pvt. Ltd., First Published, 1998. Second Reprint, 1999. (All the page references are to this edition.)

Chapter 15

The East is East and the West is West[1]

1. CIVILIZATIONS IN INDIA

In his essay, "Civilizations in India" (originally published in *The Statesman*, January 3, 1926), Nirad Chaudhuri mentions that Lord Ronaldshay's discovery that the heart of Aryavarta still belongs to Vedanta philosophy. He opines that the revolt against the British and European civilization is the result of the clash of these philosophies.

Chaudhuri sees a paradox in the Indian attitude to European civilization. On the one hand, the Indians dislike and even hate the Europeans on political and racial grounds, but on the other hand, they want to imitate and assimilate the European culture slowly. He expresses this process of acculturation through a cosmic image. The ambition of the Bengalis is quite modest. "It is to assimilate, by slow degrees, the ways of Europe, till at last civilization in India becomes the provincial edition of the civilization of Europe, palely reflecting like the moon, its borrowed light from the great sun beyond" (2).

Indian nationalism, according to Chaudhuri, has a soft corner for socialism, Pacifism, Bertrand Russell, Romain Rolland, Karl Marx and Tolstoy.

He points out that the process of Europeanization of India is as remarkable as it is imperceptible. The revival or Oriental art is also part of the revival of nationalism. But paradoxically this revival was done by a European, Dr. Anand Coomarswamy.

The European influence on literary circles is more powerful than on anything else. The intellectual centre is transferred from Calcutta to London. A favourable review of a Bengali novel in *Times Literary Supplement* gives the most undignified joy to the novelist and a great heartburn to that writer whose book does not receive any review at all in the same paper. Recognition in London by a British critic was considered as the highest achievement for an Indian writer.

2. LIFE AND WORK OF RABINDRANATH TAGORE: A QUEST FOR SELFHOOD

In his essay, "Life and Work of Rabindranath Tagore: A Quest for Selfhood" (originally published in *Calcutta Municipal Gazette*, 1941), Nirad Chaudhuri shows how Tagore was a multi-faceted genius; that he was not a jack of all trades, but a unified and integrated whole soul. Chaudhuri points out that the great driving and unifying power of Rabindranath's life is the quest for personal enrichment or self-realization and that he did not wish to run away from the worldly life but wanted to dwell in it and enjoy its beauty and meaning. That is why he said, "I want to live among men."

Rabindranath, according to Chaudhuri is both a mystic and a humanist at the same time; that in spite of his faith in an eternal existence transcending death, he believed in the beauty and joy of this worldly life; and that Rabindranath is a mystic and a worshipper of Mother-Earth at the same time.

The entire body of his artistic, intellectual and even social activities is part of his quest for selfhood. His versatility and eclecticism are amazing. Chaudhuri compliments Rabindranath for combining his asceticism and sensuous or artistic enjoyment of life. "He has felt alternatively drawn towards asceticism and sensuous enjoyment of life, towards nationalism and internationalism, towards extreme sophistication as well as folk cultures and beliefs" (12-13).

Chaudhuri points out that Rabindranath was a rebel all through his life and admires his serenity, courage and magnanimity. "Rabindranath's struggle against his environment started with his school days and has continued. Any other man would certainly have been left morally scarred by it. It is not that there is not in Rabindranath, too, a strain of disillusioned bitterness. Certain sentences in his prose writings rasp out a lack of charity about his fellow-countrymen, which hurts and rankles. But these rare and passing moods do not mar the permanent serenity, courage and magnanimity of his nature.... No one can say that Rabindranath has not suffered, it is all too evident in his life and works, but for all that he has gone through he has not succumbed to bitterness or frivolity, the two refuges of weak characters" (14).

One may easily see how Chaudhuri has given the right analysis of Rabindranath's personality without any prejudice or ill-will. His observations help the reader to understand Tagore's personality better.

3. THE CONGRESS IN CHAINS

In his essay, "The Congress in Chains" (unpublished, circa 1940-41), Nirad Chaudhuri records his observations about the Congress Party of India. He shows how the Congress Party was opposed to the Indian participation in the war. He, then, shows how the Congress Party is made up of hard-headed businessmen, and how they are influenced by the middle class intelligentsia of India. "This part of intelligentsia—which, by the way, is its most substantial part—is composed of people in all walks of life, lawyers, doctors, teachers, professors, engineers and similar professional men, clerks and other employees of mercantile offices, businessmen and shop-keepers, public servants in the employ of the Government and local bodies, ranging from those of high degree in the provincial capital to the lowly ones in the sub-divisional headquarters, in short almost the entire body of middle-class people, who have received English education. It is they who back the Congress with their moral support, it is they who send the Congress to power in local bodies and legislatures, and thus their hold on the Congress is perfectly intelligible" (21).

4. NANDALAL BOSE

In his essay, "Nandalal Bose" (originally published in *The Statesman*, 1943), Nirad Chaudhuri traces the painting career of Nandalal Bose, who has done his work over a long period.

Chaudhuri rightly opines that the Indian painters of our age have no living tradition to fall back on and work independently according to their self-formulated doctrines.

Chaudhuri laments the absence of a living tradition of painting and shows how it developed eclecticism in imitation which reduced it to pastiche and to patchwork.

Chaudhuri comments on the absence of a strong social and aesthetic motivation of art in India, especially in painting, which compelled it to become literary and illustrative; that the modern Indian school of painting in the first decade of its existence was intolerably cloying in its sentimentality.

Nandalal Bose was a restless experimenter in the field of technique as well as of conception and achieved true style and a personal style, for which Chaudhuri compliments him.

"Perhaps the addition to recipes is the greatest vice of modern Indian art" (24). But Chaudhuri compliments Nandalal Bose for his integrated work which is 'a personal expression'. He admires Nandalal Bose for properly welding the subject and the form thereby achieving the element of illustration and remarks that he is the greatest modern Indian exponent of the linear style of our art,—of the entire Orient art in general. "European art critics are prone to underrate painting which does not show plasticity and three dimensional qualities. Its overriding importance is stressed as much by Berenson as by Roger Fry. But Nandalal Bose has worked in a very different manner; he has retained the linearity and flatness of Indian painting, or, for that matter, of the Persian, Chinese and Japanese, without degenerating into the merely decorative. He has respected the un-crossable border between painting and the decorative arts. He is always reminiscent of the great fresco style of India, although he never really got a chance to show what he could do as a fresco painter. Tagore did much for him, but he could not be what Julius II was to Michelangelo" (24). Chaudhuri admires Nandalal Bose not only for being a great painter, but also for being a great man.

5. THE LOST RIVERS AND LOST HAPPINESS

In his essay, "The Lost Rivers and Lost Happiness" (originally published in *The Statesman*, 1965), Nirad Chaudhuri laments the Bengalis' unawareness of the loss of their rivers following partition. "It seems strange to me that the Bengali people should be so unconscious of their greatest loss from the partition of the province, when they are so obsessed with its political and economic consequences. This unawareness can be taken in itself as the sign of a mummification of the Bengali mind, which seems to have set in. I say so because the loss is of the great rivers which made Bengal what it was. Herodotus said that Egypt was the gift of the Nile. Bengal was equally the gift of three rivers with their ancillary waters. They were the Meghna, the Brahmaputra and the Ganges in her two branches—the Bhagirathi and the Padma" (26).

Having shown the loss of rivers by the Bengalis, Chaudhuri makes an important literary-critical observation that "all Vaishnava poetry is interwoven with the waters and offers many examples in support of his argument. Similarly the water in its different aspects or moods becomes a metaphor for the different aspects of love between man and woman.

Chaudhuri laments that the waters have now been lost to the Hindu Bengalis and hence they have lost their happiness also connected with those rivers.

6. STANDARD OF LIVING: WRONG SORT-RIGHT SORT

In his essay, "Standard of Living: Wrong Sort-Right Sort" (originally published in the *Illustrated Weekly of India*, 1969), Nirad has shown himself as a microscopic critic of Indian culture, like in most of his earlier works. In the present essay he comments on the Indians' standard of living which is of the wrong sort rather than of the right sort.

He points out that the underdevelopment of the Asiatics is proportionate to the philanthropic imperialism of the West. Then he shows how the traditional Hindus equate the quality and style of living with luxury, which involves expense and hence becomes a sin. For Chaudhuri was called a reprobate for buying a few books and pictures.

Chaudhuri satirizes the Indians' style of living not for their comfort and aesthetic enjoyment, but more for ostentation, and jealous competition with relatives and friends. He offers many examples from daily life.

He comments on how the visitors in India develop and exhibit their respect and admiration to the host in proportion to the grandeur and variety of his furnishings. Hence the items like wardrobes, sofa-set, tape-recorders, kitchen gadgets, even cardigans, dressing gowns and cars have become the symbols of prestige for them.

Chaudhuri satirizes the failure of Indians to see the material things as symbols of their inner spiritual life, and are content with having a mere patchwork of things. "The second shortcoming in the style of living of the class, I am now dealing with, is lack of artistic integrity. In this country, in modern times, we have not inherited any tradition. So we pursue what is fashionable for the time being and flounder into a pastiche of archaisms, modernism, and exoticisms, and have any or all without discrimination" (37).

Finally, Chaudhuri laments the monotony and triviality of the Indians' lives.

7. SEX ON THE MIND, FEAR IN THE HEART

In his essay, "Sex on the Mind, Fear in the Heart" (originally published in the *Illustrated Weekly of India*, 1969), Nirad Chaudhuri begins his essay by showing the popularity of the *Kama Sutra* in the West and among the Anglicized Hindus. When Indians go abroad, they notice the widespread promiscuity there and write about it in their letters to their relatives in India. Similarly when the Westerners come to India, they are disappointed to see the sexual union only in the cave stones at Khajuraho.

Chaudhuri shows how the modern Indians are highly inhibited about sex, although they are naturally obsessed with it. But in ancient India, love ranged from the sexual to the romantic and chivalrous. "The gamut of man-woman relationship in ancient India extended from the physical, through romantic love and conjugal devotion, to the disinterested but chivalrous social meeting. It is a delight to read the conversation between men and women in such association in Sanskrit books" (42).

Chaudhuri mentions how Indian men in their offices are attracted to their lady colleagues, especially the younger ones, in an unusual way. He offers some examples from his experience with his colleagues.

Contrasting the present India and the ancient India Chaudhuri says that the modern Indians are inhibited whereas the ancient Indians were uninhibited. "The Hindus, who were probably the most uninhibited people in regard to matters of sex, are today the most inhibited and taboo-ridden" (45).

Chaudhuri points out that the promiscuity of ancient India has shifted from family to society in modern India. "But in India there is no expansion even of the penumbra. A certain amount of promiscuity has always been present in Hindus society, despite its rigorous sexual taboos. What has really happened is that the area of the irregularity has shifted. Thus, instead of being confined to family relationships, it has spilled out into social relationships, so that the liaisons are now with the friend's wife, instead of being with the sister-in-law. In other words, it is a change in the veneer" (45).

Chaudhuri laments the absence of friendly admiration, appreciation and correspondence between men and women in India due to the rigid social norms and restrictions. Finally, he concludes that the Indians are crushed by obsessions and inhibitions.

8. THE PALACE OF HUNGRY STONES

In his essay, "The Palace of Hungry Stones" (originally published in *The New Delhi*, 1971), Nirad Chaudhuri points out the changes that took place after the capital of British India was transferred from Calcutta to New Delhi in 1911 by Lord Hardinge.

Delhi, as shown by Chaudhuri, was an immense cemetery before it was built as the capital city of India. Lord Hardinge transferred the capital from Calcutta to Delhi to avoid the undue influence of the Bengalis on the Viceroy's Council and the Legislative Assembly. After the transfer of the capital, Bengal ceased to be an all-India force and came under some sort of political eclipse.

Chaudhuri borrows a metaphor from Rabindranath Tagore to describe the new city of New Delhi as the Palace of Hungry Stones, suffering from the nurse of the old witch, and growing barren except producing a Brown Colonialism. "By entering

New Delhi with independence, the Indians who succeeded the British as rulers of India, entered Tagore's *Kshudhita Pashan*, the Palace of Hungry stones. The spirit which haunted Tagore's deserted palace was that of young and beautiful slaves, whose youth and beauty had been immolated on the altar of lust.... But the spirit which dominated New Delhi was that of an old and wizened witch who in revenge for her expulsion laid her withered and withering hand on the new Indian government. She saw to it that all incipient life in the new regime would be frozen and stillborn, and the only thing which would flourish in India would be her illegitimate child, a Brown Colonialism" (52).

Chaudhuri points out how the Indian National Congress was not revolutionary in spirit, but wanted only freedom from the British Rule. Instead of removing the old bureaucracy and appointing new staff, they continued the old bureaucracy, simply because they did not wish to build a new India.

Similarly the Congress Party yielded to the partition of India because they were not willing to fight with the British as they were physically and mentally tired.

Chaudhuri attacks the sudden change of British opinion about the Indian members of the ICS from contempt to enthusiastic patronage on the morning of 15 August 1947. "As a result, British opinion of the Indian members of the ICS changed overnight. I know a good deal of the contempt which was shown towards them by their British colleagues and superiors since Satyendranath Tagore entered the Service as its first Indian member. This contempt changed to enthusiastic patronage as soon as the cock crew at dawn on 15 August, 1947. I have been provoked by the opportunism of the Indians in that Service after that day, but their somersault was nothing compared with the grotesque revision of the British attitude. It scandalized me" (55). Chaudhuri vents out his righteous anger when he says, "In the years after independence, I felt more and more strongly that the Indian bureaucracy which had served the British and in which the dominant element was constituted by the Indian members of the ICS, was the most formidable obstacle in the way of progress, and in my usual exuberant way I used to say that all the Indians in the ICS instead of being confirmed in their position in the administration, should have been hanged from the nearest lamp-post on the 15th of August. I repeated the bad-tempered joke once to my social discomfiture" (55).

Chaudhuri rightly points out that the Congress leaders' extraordinary respect for the ICS was due half to their own inferiority complex and half to a fear of revolution.

Then he offers a systematic classification of the human group in New Delhi. He says that there are three groups which dominate in the capital city: (1) politicians representing their constituencies and not rally attached to Delhi; (2) capitalist entrepreneurs (especially Punjabis) who consider New Delhi as only an operating camp for them; (3) the diplomatic corps (including foreigners) are also a floating population in New Delhi. Chaudhuri points out that the machinery of the Central Government is really controlled by the bureaucrats, who are rooted in New Delhi and yet not attached to the general public. Their main motto is the advancement of their class interest. "The New Delhi personality is, of course, the Indian bureaucratic personality, and New Delhi, as a living organism, is constituted by the men who have this personality. Theirs is a solid egocentric, and rootless order, which by its very nature, is not only uncreative, but even unproductive. Its only purpose is to perpetuate itself by inbreeding, and ensure its prosperity. It has no closer ties with India than the British bureaucracy had" (58). That is why Chaudhuri developed revulsion for the bureaucratic class.

These bureaucrats tried to push their own children into the Indian military also. Chaudhuri opposed this tendency on the ground that it would create the ideal of an imitation Englishman having no attachment to our land. "What is more, the ideal of an imitation Englishman will never attract the best manhood of India. There will be plenty of people, of course, who will join the army for the sake of the money or the prestige. But from the military point of view, they will hardly be candidates who are most desirable" (59).

Chaudhuri laments the lack of emotional attachment or loyalty to society in the bureaucrats and their sole loyalty to themselves and their vested interests. They increased their remunerations and salaries immensely.

In spite of some politicians' (from the lower middle-class) effort the control to control the Indian bureaucracy they have not succeeded. Therefore both of them have been exploiting India. "The only people who could have put an end to or at least curbed the power of the bureaucracy were the nationalist politicians from the lower middle-class. But even immediately after independence, I saw that they had admitted defeat. I referred to that in a chapter of my autobiography which was written immediately after independence. In it I employed a Miltonic image and called the politicians, sons of Moloch, aggressive, rough, uneducated, but on the whole, authentic. To the members of the bureaucracy, I gave the name of Sons of Belial, intelligent, educated, polished, plausible, with an unlimited gift of the gab, but to the core corrupted by self-interest, and therefore, insidiously dangerous. I said that it was the Sons of Belial who had won in the last round, and not the Sons of Moloch. At that time I could not perceive an alternative—that the Sons of Moloch and the Sons of Belial would conclude an alliance and exploit India in combination. That however, is what was happened. New Delhi is the capital of that combination, which so far as any rational forecast can be made is unshakeable. Old men like me might cry like the old Roman Cato—*Delenda est Nova Delhia*, but that would not destroy New Delhi" (61).

9. THEIR WAY OF BEING ANTI-BRITISH

In his essay, "Their Way of Being Anti-British" (originally published in *The Illustrated Weekly of India*, 1972), Nirad Chaudhuri highlights certain characteristics features of the Anglicized upper middle class of India. Although he likes them as individuals, they are totally evil as a class. One of the conspicuous qualities of these people is their servility to British things. "For the present, however, I shall consider only one trait of the collective personality, which is its degrading servility to things British in every aspect of their thinking and behaviour. This they have inherited from their fathers who served the British. Political independence has not liberated them from their psychological servitude" (63).

These Anglicized Indians have a mania for foreign degrees especially from the British Universities like Oxford and Cambridge (and not from Berlin or Paris). "This worship of Oxford and Cambridge, which like the Quran was imposed on India by the sword, has become a native religion like Islam among Anglicized Indians. It persists as an exercise of faith in the era of independence. Otherwise, it is difficult to explain why even now high-placed Indian officials come to these universities for refresher courses and that too with British Council or Commonwealth scholarships" (64).

The Anglicized Indians, who are so servile to things British, are very arrogant otherwise in their general behavior and deplorably lack any originality. "Their intellectual efforts, when they undertake any, are extraordinarily barren, and at best secondhand. Even when they were born with a high intellectual capacity and have received a rigorous intellectual training, they remain incapable of putting forward any true or original idea about their country or its civilization and only repeat what they have learnt from Western Indologists, economists or sociologists. It is in respect of Hinduism more particularly that they are incapable of taking any true view" (64-65).

Chaudhuri accuses that the Anglicized Indian imitate the Western views and opinions in a very servile fashion. He offers a very beautiful example of the Indian scholars imitating the Western scholars on Hinduism by quoting a story of the *Taittariya Upanishad*. He describes it as lapping up the Western vomit. "In regard to their writings on India, which are not large in volume and often are turned out merely as grist to the mill, I say these are all *Taittariya Upanishads*. Perhaps that calls for an explanation. This peculiar name, derived from the Sanskrit word *tittirai* (partridge or quail), has a story behind it. One day, a young Rishi went to an old Rishi to be instructed by him. For some reason, the latter did not want to impart his knowledge. So, in order to make it unacceptable to the young

Rishi, he vomitted it out. But the disciple was not to be balked in this fashion. He at once turned into a quail, licked up the vomit, and became wise. All the Anglicized Hindu exponents of Hindu life and culture are like this young Rishi. They lap up the vomit of their Western masters and regurgitate it for the benefit of their readers and students" (65). Chaudhuri comments on Indians who admire books on India by British and American authors as they lack self-respect and confidence. Yet they read them avidly. "Yet it is these books which are devoured by Anglicized Indians as sweets and ice-cream are by children. The British and American pot boiling authors have discovered this weakness and have begun to publish in India. Stranger still, Anglicized Indians, who wish to become authors imitate these writers. This mental servitude has left India without any valid ideology to renovate the life and culture of the Indian people" (66). This weakness has aggravated into an epidemic called Westernization and become a threat to India's integrity. "This debased Westernization is not remaining confined to a small minority, but spreading to the masses. It is on account of this extension that the present form of Westernization of India has become a threat to the cultural integrity of the Indian people as a whole" (66). Chaudhuri points out further that the power of this kind of Westernization seems to be irresistible.

Again Chaudhuri points out how the Indians' unusual attraction for and imitation of D.H. Lawrence in writing, and the fashion of wearing jeans both by men and by women is simply ridiculous and symptomatic of our cultural decadence. For example, Indian girls in jeans pants look like scarecrows and men in jeans look like gorillas. Originally jeans pants and shirts were meant for factory workers and cowboys in America, but in India our young men and women think of them as part of great fashion, especially of Westernization. Chaudhuri says quite patriotically that he would have his Kalidasa and Bharatachandra and the Arabic or European classics rather than D.H. Lawrence for literary enjoyment and appreciation. "I shall refer next to fashions in dress. It is a well-known fact of cultural history that whenever society shows indifference to dress, or any inclination to be shabby or merely piquant in a gross form, it is on the road to decline. But that is what is most obvious among young people of the West today. Their worship of ugliness is assertive, the blue denim jeans being the most typical symbol of decadence" (68). Pointing out the difference between the Western people and the Indians in the wearing of jeans garments Chaudhuri says very frankly as follows: "I tell the young Indians who adopt these that the English Beau Brummels of today have their complexion to redeem the uncouthness in respect of clothes and hair, and they keep their hair combed, they even approach the grace of the Afghan hound. But my young countrymen going in for the same kinds of hirsuteness appear like gorillas" (68). Referring to the Indian girls wearing jeans Chaudhuri says, "The creatures in jeans are all scarecrows. Yet, our girls imitate them, and go into jeans, although they are either too big or too small for them" (69).

Similarly he shows the decadence in the world of music and dance. "The addiction to 'Pop' music and dancing on the part of young Indians is another feature of the debased Westernization, which is sweeping over India" (69). The Indians are forgetting their own beautiful folk music and dance and blindly imitating the pop and jazz music and break dance shows their servile imitativeness and lack of knowledge of their own rich tradition.

Chaudhuri sees a contradiction in the behavior of Indians. For example Indians admire the Communist countries like Russia but do not like the art-works from those countries. "Their vogue in India would seem surprising, for Indians are pro-Soviet in their political and social attitudes. Yet, with all that, they would not touch the products of art from the Communist countries, preferring those from the democratic West. Really the contradiction only perpetuates an established dichotomy of Hindu behavior. The Hindus have gone to their Guru for religious inspiration, but to the Muslim whore for their pleasure" (69).

Then Chaudhuri deplores the widespread influence of Western sensuality, promiscuity, homosexuality, rape and murder on Indian life. "All these features of Westernization of Indian life today are only collateral expressions of a central impact, that of the contemporary Western sensuality. All over the West it is pervasive, and it has reduced the man-woman relationship to a level of crudity unintelligible in the light of the past in Europe. There is no respite therefrom a superficial and yet irresistible lust. Yet, strangely enough, its theory is fanatical, in the same sense as dipsomania or satyriasis or nymphomania can be described as fanatical. But it has a Rightist or heterosexual version as well as a Leftist or homosexual version" (69)

Commenting on the laxity of sexual morals in the West Chaudhuri offers many shocking examples. "Promiscuous sexual intercourse at all times is a birthright, and should not be denied to anybody. So wives are allowed to visit prisoners and the latest proposal is to allow families to come over in a caravan and park in the grounds of the prison, so that prisoners may have family life. Bachelor prisoners are allowed to have prostitutes. Outside prisons, the choice is unlimited" (70). The abnormal practices of sexuality like homosexuality and lesbianism have become very common in the West. For example a woman MP (sitting) of Britain around 1972 proclaimed that she was a confirmed Lesbian. Chaudhuri is sad to observe that the "contemporary Western sensuality is spreading over India like an oil sick. A good deal is also being manufactured or recycled locally under license, so to speak. And there is obvious catering of vicarious sensuality. The replacement of the old Hindu sensuality, which had something demoniac about it, by this low Western product, is the most bizarre outcome of the moral and cultural meeting between India and the West today" (71).

10. A STERILE INTELLIGENTSIA

In his essay, "A Sterile Intelligentsia" (originally published in *The Times of India*, May 25, 1980), Nirad Chaudhuri records his views about Indian intelligentsia which he has observed before and after going to England in 1970. He is sad to notice that the entire world has become a battle front and the worldwide disintegration of civilized life. When he looks at India from his Oxford house, he is very sad to observe the failure of Indians in building a great nation because of the vested interests, sterility, defeatism and money-making. It has degenerated beyond repair. Chaudhuri quotes a Bengali proverb which says: When the snake has bitten on the head where is one to tie the tourniquet? He rightly accuses that the Indian intelligentsia has been imitative, passive and rather superficial and therefore lacking in self-confidence. Chaudhuri's remarks are at once insightful, candid and scathing. "The failure in India is due to the shortcomings of its dominant minority, the whole of the intelligentsia. To me, it seems that the mind and character of the class have succumbed to the circumstances. The whole class is blind to its failure and inadequacies. It is throwing the blame on the leaders, on the politicians, on the parties, even on the one-time British rulers. The reluctance to shoulder the blame is, in itself, significant. Stubborn reluctance to accept responsibility is always seen in weak characters, who have lost self-confidence. In British days, the Indian intelligentsia was both assertive and creative. It has become almost wholly sterile today, and wholly defeatist. The members of the class are retiring more and more into private life, turning their back on public affairs, so that even public affairs have become a money-making racket for just adventurers" (74). Chaudhuri's views on the intellectual degeneration of Indians are repeated in many of his books because it has been a conspicuous phenomenon of Indian academic life.

11. IN BRITAIN, FATHERS DON'T MATTER

In his essay, "In Britain, Fathers Don't Matter" (originally published in *The Times of India*, June 8, 1980), Chaudhuri shows the social change that has been taking place in England during the twentieth century. He opines that there is no sanity in the collective English opinions and behavior, because its mind has ceased to function. The institution of marriage is seriously damaged or even destroyed by the extreme freedom of women, degeneration of moral values and increase of adultery in general. Consequently, the number of the single-mother families has been increasing in England. Says Chaudhuri, "To begin with, I take only one of these ideas. It is that, among human beings, fathers do not matter, and the mother should be enough. More precisely put, this means that human children need not have a determinable father, and a perfectly natural family may be made up of a woman and her children born out of causal sexual associations with many male persons. The advocates of this doctrine could not be more dogmatic if bi-sexual reproduction had altogether disappeared among men" (77).

But the irony is that the single mothers enjoy not only respectability, but also substantial monetary concessions and help from the British government. On the contrary the married women have no end of worries in England. "Another incident was not less significant. An unmarried mother was living comfortably on the allowance granted to young women in her situation, but for some reason, it was reduced. So she went to the social worker in charge of the matter, who was a conventional wife. She committed an indiscretion when the young mother began to quarrel, and said that unmarried mothers were having a good time while, she, a married woman, had no end of worries about money" (78).

By contrast the situation in India is quite different. Chaudhuri points out how the name of the fathers is a very important factor in the family records and matters in India. "This would sound incredible in India, for whether Hindu or Muslim, we have always sworn by a determinable even though putative father, and taken pride in being *bapka beta*. Governments in India, too, have always insisted on a legally constituted father for all individuals with whom they have made to deal" (77).

Then Chaudhuri displays his sense of humour when a British lady tells him proudly of the 'father' of her big sized bitch and when questioned by Chaudhuri she clarifies further that the bitch is not from a 'one-parent family,' 'Oh, no, no,' observed the lady, 'that cannot be,' and laughed at my surprise. "But by being traditional and therefore reactionary the British people are making their animals better and better, while progressive thinking is making human beings worse and worse" (78).

12. POLITICAL *SANYASIS* WITH THEIR HORDES OF *CHELAS*

In his essay, "Political *Sanyasis* with Their Hordes of *Chelas*" (originally published in *The Times of India*, June 22, 1980), Nirad Chaudhuri talks about the selfishness, greed for money, lack of intelligence and will of the politicians, which have paved the way for the ordinariness and sordidness of life in general in India.

He comments on the combination of politics and spirituality in the Gandhian politics. "Actually I think that the creation of an order of political *sanyasis* with their hordes of *chelas* by the Gandhian national movement is at the bottom of our political failures since independence" (79). Sometimes the Indian politicians are present absences due to their ineffectuality.

Commenting on the parasitism of the Indian politicians, Chaudhuri says, "At best, the political monasticism brought into existence a Vinoba Bhave, at worst a Morarji Desai, both dispensable in any kind of rational politics. The emergence of the Naga politicians has no more benefited Indian politics than the existence of Naga *sanyasis* has benefited Hinduism. The relationship between both the kinds of Nagas and the cults they have embraced is different. The Naga *sanyasis* have been parasites supported by Hinduism, while the Naga politicians have been parasites on Indian nationalism" (79).

In addition to their parasitism the Indian politicians are also known for their shameless greed for money. The main motto—sole and whole—of Indian politicians is to make money without sacrificing their security. "In contemporary India, however, the career politicians are not men who have brought their talents as evinced in worldly success to bear on politics, but are those who have made demagogic politics a stepping stone to worldly success. It is pointless to say that besides the spirit of service, personal ambition, too, makes men turn to a political career. Personal ambition is not to be blamed in a politician if it has made him sacrifice the product of greater wealth in his profession or business for the sake of devoting himself to public affairs. I rather regret the absence of this kind of enlightened personal ambition in India today, for that has handed over Indian politics to those who want money, but have no capacity to make it except through politics" (80). But Chaudhuri is sad about the fact that those who have sacrificed their lives for politics like Satyendra Prasanna Sinha are not remembered today by the general public.

Chaudhuri points out that Jawaharlal Nehru came to politics from the elite class, whereas Gandhi became a proletarian in politics. He remarks quite frankly that the politics is abandoned by the highest section of the Indian intelligentsia because of their disillusionment with a world which is marked by the absence of ideals and values. Chaudhuri rightly opines that the present politicians are known for their weakness of will and character and sheer opportunism.

13. THEY ARE OBSESSED WITH SEX

In his essay, "They are Obsessed with Sex" (originally published in *The Times of India*, July 6, 1980), Nirad Chaudhuri comments on the British people's obsession with sex and revolt against motherhood. He offers an example of the right to abortion introduced in the British parliament and how the bill was rejected and could not become law. Some people offered economic argument for abortion with a pretence of rationality. Chaudhuri's sense of humour about pro and against the case arguments is noteworthy. "The economic argument for abortion is put forward with a pretence of rationality. But not so the emotional resistance. Its ferocity can be seen at the demonstrations. There was one when the bill was being discussed, and the crowd was behaving like mujahidin. Of course, there was also a procession against abortion. But its appearance was like a pack of spotted hyenas of the African Veldt. They were all so ugly, unkempt and dirty that I, for one, would recommend abortion for all of them, lest they bring things like themselves into the world" (83).

Chaudhuri states clearly that the true motive behind the support for abortion is "to safeguard unrestricted and promiscuous sexual intercourse" (83), which is claimed as a fundamental birth-right.

Then Chaudhuri points out how the decadence in the realm of sexual morality is accompanied by linguistic decadence also. Referring to the car crash of a woman of 54, namely Mrs. Beatrice Bovington, Chaudhuri says that this accident made sexual intercourse very painful for her and that she sued the woman who had caused the crash and got damages to the extent of £ 22,733 or about four lakhs of rupees and that the *Daily Telegraph* described her as a 'Stoic Lady'. Chaudhuri shows how the modern language also has lost its original dignity and sanctity and degenerated into a means of communication of sordidness of life. "This Beatrice is certainly not Dante's Beatrice, and even more certainly not a Stoic of the order of the Roman Emperor Marcus Aurelius, whose *Meditations* I read as a very young student. Please also note the language. Words which once stood for the beauty of the man-woman relationship, now only express the tactile sensation of the contact of genital organs. To make love means having sexual intercourse, and if anyone employs the term 'fair sex', he would be understood to speak about a hearty bout of coitus. It should be kept in mind that all decadence has its linguistic accompaniment" (83-84).

14. THE ANGLICIZED INDIAN IS ARROGANT

In his essay, "The Anglicized Indian is Arrogant" (originally published in *The Times of India*, July 20, 1980), Nirad Chaudhuri deplores the intellectual bankruptcy of Indian intellectuals and their blind following of earlier mind. Most of the Indians have become imitators of Western ideas and slogans, but their arrogance seems to be unlimited. "But the decline of intellectual capacity has not brought about a decline of intellectual arrogance. This, however, is shown only towards those who threaten their class interest. The whole class has an uncanny sense of what ideas are dangerous for them, and even then they do not attack unless they are sure that the critic of their order is weak and isolated. Thus their arrogance is based on the strength of their worldly position" (86).

Chaudhuri highlights the insolent coxcombry of the young Indians who combine the Hindu chauvinism and the snobbery of Oxbridge education. "This arrogance, too, appeared long ago. I give an example. In the late summer of 1939, I was speaking about the intellectual poverty of the nationalist movement to a young Bengali who had come home from Cambridge for the long vacation. I said incidentally that among the nationalist leaders, only Jawaharlal Nehru could be regarded as an intellectual. The young man looked at me quizzically, and remarked in English although I was speaking in Bengali, 'You call him an intellectual, do you? We were travelling in the same compartment from Bombay, but I did not feel like talking to him.' Apart from all else, Nehru was exactly the age of his father. This arrogance or rather insolent coxcombry has become more common now, and brought in its wake a blackout of intelligence. Its basis is the obsolete Hindu chauvinism, but to it have been added two reinforcing struts: superstition without religious feeling, which is seen in the adherence to a wholly new and commercialized form of the Hindu Guruvada: and snobbery derived from a foreign and more especially, Oxbridge education" (86).

15. THERE ARE TWO ENGLANDS TODAY

In his essay, "There are Two Englands Today" (originally published in *The Times of India,* August 3, 1980), Nirad Chaudhuri clarifies the point that he has given up the false idea of loyalty, as taught by his parents. In India, Chaudhuri is described by the fanatics as an Anglophile as a dog wagging its tail in a widely circulated Indian journal. It is true that Chaudhuri is an admirer of the positive aspects of English culture and civilization. That is why he is accused by Indians as an Anglophile.

But now Chaudhuri is disconcerted to know the negative side of the English civilization that he admired. "To have written about England as I have done and will do can never be any kind of recantation, for what I am denouncing is a barbarism which is threatening the very life and civilization I have admired. No believer in civilization is allowed to forget that there are two Englands today, one of civilized men and women and another of unspeakable savages" (90). He enumerates two kinds of barbarism preached by the un-clean English barbarians. This kind of barbarism is part of the general decadence of life all over the world, which he has expatiated in his epical autobiography, *Thy Hand, Great Anarch!*. The ten examples of barbarism are simply horrible. For example, (1) Going about in London has become insecure. Lord Home, the former Prime Minister was beaten up by a young thug. (2) A barmaid stabbed another barmaid, her colleague under the premenstrual stress. (3) A youth deliberately derailed the Aberdeen-London express by placing a rail across the line. (4) Two brothers bored by the luxurious life they led, shot an old official for fun. (5) A public schoolboy with a grievance against his house-master set fire to his house and caused £158,000 worth of damage. (6) A 14-year boy threw a stone at a girl of 6 and then killed her. (7) Compelled by superstition two men kicked a woman to death in order to exorcise her of the evil spirit with which they thought she was possessed. (8) A pregnant woman killed her husband with a carving knife because he forced her to have sexual intercourse by branding her with lighted cigarettes. (9) Wife-swapping has become quite common in British society. (10) Raping women and killing them (and their lovers, in some cases) has become very common.

Through all these abundant illustrations Chaudhuri shows that there are two Englands today: one is a civilized England and two, the other is the barbaric England. What puzzles Chaudhuri is the passivity of the public even after hearing about such happenings.

16. IN SEARCH OF A LEADER

In his essay, "In Search of a Leader" (originally published in *The Times of India*, August 17, 1980), Nirad Chaudhuri points out how the Indians have always needed a leader in their political life and how the three persons like Nehru, Gandhi and Subhas Chandra Bose were the leaders during the nationalist struggle.

Chaudhuri shows how the Indians want to have a leader or some leaders, because they want to be free from the cares and responsibility of a leader and be blissfully ignorant about the challenges of life. He shows further that the Indian intelligentsia lacks the qualities of leadership.

Then he offers examples of leaders from other countries of the world and shows the range of his international reading and scholarship. For example, Napoleon became the dictator of France at the age of 30; the Emperor of Japan (Mutsuhito) was only 16; in China, San Yat-sen emerged as a leader at the age of 30; and Mustafa Kemal of Turkey was only 41. Compared to these examples, Indian leaders were all above 50. Nehru was 58 when he became the Prime Minister. "It might also be added that all the Indians, who attained to the position of leaders in the nationalist movement, had emerged as such between the ages of twenty-five and thirty, talent being precocious in India. But no upsurge of young men was seen in 1947, when it should have occurred. So, Nehru himself nearly 58, had to form his government with men who were even older than he. The only man who was below 50 was Sardar Baldev Singh, and everybody knows why he was included. About the men with whom he had to run the government of independent India from 1947, Nehru had already written in 1939, when many of them were at the head of the Congress governments formed in the provinces under the Act of 1935: 'They are worn out in mind and body and their troubles from all directions tend to increase. I would hate to have their job.' I myself have the original of this letter. In addition, many of his senior colleagues suffered from incurable cardiac trouble. In the 30 years (and more) which have followed, not one man of exceptional political ability has appeared in India" (95). Nobody can deny the veracity of Chaudhuri's observation.

17. INEQUITIES IN BRITISH EQUALITY

In his essay, "Inequities in British Equality" (originally published in *The Times of India*, August 31, 1980), Nirad Chaudhuri discusses the history and practice of the doctrine of equality in the world. He says, "The moral doctrine of equality of man was unknown to all ancient civilizations, e.g. the Greeks, Romans, Hindus or Chinese. It was the creation of Christianity. But its social and political extension came long afterward with the American and the French Revolution" (96).

Chaudhuri points out the irony of the actual situation to be seen in different countries. He gives an example from his personal experience. He found in a great American University a club was reserved only for Full Professors to which even the Assistant Professors were not admitted. Similarly in many universities he saw three rooms of different status. In hostels also he saw this gradation. In other words, he points out the irony of equality in a country like America wherein equality is professed loudly. Similarly he refers to the practice of inequality between the White and the Black Americans.

Chaudhuri then points out the class-hatred practiced in England in spite of their profession of equality and he attributes it to the political rancor. The class-hatred is regarded as an accompaniment as well as instrument of British decadence. He illustrates the practice of inequality in the Sporty Cult of England. "The true character of the contemporary British egalitarianism is seen in the cult of sport. No one ever says all football and cricket players, all boxers, all runners, or all swimmers are equal. A prized football player is sold from club to club like a race horse. On the contrary, in Britain today, no religious teacher, statesman, soldier, scientist, writer, musician except the Pop exponent, or artist can aspire to the position a football player has. Even film-stars have fallen to the third rank before these stars of non-purposive, specialized and mindless physical prowess" (98).

A similar contradiction is seen by Chaudhuri in women egalitarians also, who hate men on the basis of gender-inequality but practice inequality among themselves i.e. between beautiful woman and plain women and by encouraging beauty contests for the position and prestige of Miss Universe, Miss Englands and Miss Indias.

18. ARE ALL MEN EQUAL IN MENTAL POWER?

In his essay, "Are All Men Equal in Mental Power?" (originally published in *The Times of India*, September 14, 1980), Nirad Chaudhuri comments upon the modern man's intolerance of inequality. For example, in Britain the people cannot accept the superiority of mental accomplishment and the inferiority of physical strength and power. They, therefore, want to prove their worth by opposing mental achievement by engaging themselves in sports. In fact, they give extraordinary importance to sports.

Then Chaudhuri points out how the British people are no longer one united nation, but constitute two, divided by irreconcilable antagonisms.

Chaudhuri shows the philosophical truth that all creation is the creation of various kinds of inequality and so democratic egalitarianism is uncreative. He points out further that decadence creates its corrective of intolerance of mental power; and that all human progress is accomplished by a minority of talented people.

He offers a fine literary simile from Shakespeare's *The Tempest* to show the negative aspect of democracy. "But since Western civilization, as created after the Graeco-Roman, is in decline, it will never provide the strength to resist the egalitarian malevolence. We, who belong to the Davidsbundler, would not march to victory to this glorious tune: because our enemy is no longer Goliath with his Philistines. The new enemy is Caliban, who has come into the inheritance of his mother Sycorax, the Mother-Goddess of democracy. He has killed Prospero, raped Miranda, imprisoned Ariel again in the withered tree, and is guffawing in obscene triumph all over the world" (102-03).

In spite of all this evil in modern life and democracy, Chaudhuri has not become a pessimist unlike Bertrand Russell who had become desperately pessimistic about modern life and its decadence. "I tried to reassure Bertrand Russell with this hope when I met him 25 years ago. He was in a mood of unrelieved pessimism regarding the future of civilization. I told him that civilization has always been cyclical, and if it goes down it also comes up. He replied: 'You are saying that on the analogy of what happened after the collapse of the classical world. But that took 500 years. I shall not live 500 years to see it.' I was too obscure a man to retort: 'What does it matter if a Russell lives or not, so long as humanity and civilization survive?' Voltaire said that we must go on cultivating our garden. I say, we must go on fighting as long as we live" (103). Chaudhuri has reiterated that human civilization has been cyclical and one need not grow desperate at the sight of the present decadence all over the world.

19. ARE WE GOING BACK TO THE LAST DAYS OF THE MOGULS?

In his essay, "Are We Going Back to the Last Days of the Moguls?" (originally published in *The Times of India*, September 28, 1980), Nirad Chaudhuri articulates his political insight and wisdom and says that all the governments of modern independent India have been weak and ineffective—including Nehru's government. "The truth of the matter is that all governments in India since 1947, including Nehru's have been weak. The power that was given to Nehru by the people of India was virtually unlimited. He did not exercise it from his weakness of will. Very few people realize how weak he was both positively and negatively. He was always denouncing what he called 'linguism', which really was provincial nationalism based on language, and his government at first used military force to suppress the demands for and Andhra State and Greater Maharashtra. But he yielded in respect of both. Again, his economic policies were dictated by his fear of the inertia of the Indian people, and so to he took the line of least resistance by building costly infrastructures, which I always called the Pyramids of Nehru. I think it can be said today that the dams, Chandigarh, and other structures are his funerary Stupas" (104).

Chaudhuri sees a similarity between the modern Indian government and the Last Days of the Moguls. He enumerates them as follows: (1) Complete ineffectiveness of the State; (2) Concessions were made and accepted as a matter of expediency and not as a matter of principle; (3) The ineffectiveness was primarily due to the exhaustion of Muslim power (both inside and outside India) and secondarily to Indianization; (4) Political life and State service came to be regarded as the means of promoting private interests alone; (5) The Marathas and the Congress have similar characteristics. The Marathas were impelled by two motives—Muslimophobia and mercenary motive of plunder and exaction. The Congress resembles the Marathas in the sterility, lack of originality and imitativeness of its political ideas; (6) The effect of the decline of power of the states on the masses was twofold: one, it made one par predatory and two, the other panicky; (7) There grew up a habit of tolerance of anarchy and corruption, or at all events, resignation to them.

This essay holds mirror to Chaudhuri's historical sense, political analysis and a sharp sense of observation of the contemporary India.

20. THEY ARE AFRAID OF THEIR PAST

In his essay, "They are Afraid of Their Past", Nirad Chaudhuri gives us the idea that the Leftists display their animus against the greatness and achievements of Britain in the past. This is illustrated by their behavior at the Russian intervention of Afghanistan.

Then he comments that the Amir of Afghanistan did not show his firm loyalty either to the British or to the Russians.

21. COMMUNISM IS THE OPIUM OF FAILURES

In his essay, "Communism is the Opium of Failures" (originally published in *The Times of India*, October 12, 1980), Nirad Chaudhuri shows that communism has not been successful in India and that the Communists have admitted their defeat in politics. "Communism has become the drug of those who have admitted defeat in politics" (111). Chaudhuri rightly opines that although the Communist doctrine is universal, there are sectarian differences among its various regional practitioners in the application of the doctrine. "Communism taken in its universal aspects is not one thing everywhere in the world. In fact, in its practical effects and implications, it can be amazingly contradictory, whatever it might be in its doctrinal and dogmatic aspect. But in that too, there are ferocious sectarian differences. This, however, is nothing special to Communism. All dogmatic systems generate internal differences. For instance, Christianity is, by basic definition is one. Yet Christians have burnt more Christians than those whom they regard as heathens. In the same manner, Communists have killed more Communists than Capitalists. The internecine feud among the Communists is continuing, and its most striking international exhibition is being given by the Soviet Union and China. When one considers all this, one becomes incapable of accepting Communism as one political doctrine. It may have united the workers of the world up to a certain point, but it has not united the nations" (111). Nobody can fail to notice the insightful observations of Chaudhuri about Communism. He proceeds to say further that "The European Communists are everywhere wreckers" (113). He is quite right in highlighting the opportunism of the Congress party people. He says that the Congress politicians have profited from whatever Communism there has been in India.

22. WHY INDIA CAN NEVER GO COMMUNIST

In his essay, "Why India can never Go Communist" (originally published in *The Times of India,* November 23, 1980), Nirad Chaudhuri states categorically that the Hindu (in India) being obsessed with money cannot be an active Communist. "This paradoxical, but for them, natural schizophrenia, will, in itself make it impossible for the Hindus to be Communists in action" (114).

Chaudhuri classifies the Indian Communists in two categories: one, active politicians and two, salaried employees. Chaudhuri very insightfully states how the intelligent and competent Communists of India are finally exploited by the Congress Party. He articulates his satire through a beautiful plant- image, "The Communist politicians do not realize that solely by coming forward to work within the constitutional framework of present-day India, they have opted for self-immolation. Perhaps I may describe their political role by comparing them to the marrows and courgettes I grow in my little kitchen garden. All the plants (vegetal or human) put forth gorgeous yellow flowers. But some of them are sterile. They blaze in the garden or the legislature and shrivel into black stumps. The others go beyond the floral stage; in fact shed the flowers; and become fat courgettes or marrows in offices, although only to be plucked for the Congress kitchen" (114-15).

Chaudhuri deplores the futility, failure and frustration of the Communists in India and offers a beautiful ritualistic metaphor to describe them. He narrates a brief legend popular in Bengal and then relates it to the Communists' voluntary exploitation by the Congress-wallas. "This always reminds me of a legend we have in our part of Bengal. In my mother's district of Comilla, there used to be a famous temple of Kali in a village called Mahar. She was supposed to be a 'very awake Kali,' and strange stories were told of her power. People told me, and they assured me that this was seen by all who went to Mahar, that when the goats were brought to be sacrificed before this Kali, they behaved in a strange manner. They were stood in a row at the far end of the yard and when the door of the temple was opened, the goat which saw the image first rushed forward and put its neck in the sacrificial frame before the temple at the other end, so that its head could be cut off. One by one, all the goats did that. When I think of the Bengalis who as my contemporaries and near contemporaries turned Communist, and most of them were men of outstanding intellect, I recall that legend. They have behaved like the goats at Mahar and put their necks in the sacrificial frame of their Kali Communism" (116-17). There cannot be a more powerful satire on Communism than this comparison.

23. HISTORY MARCHES ON WHILE WE TALK

In his essay, "History Marches on while We Talk," (originally published in *The Times of India,* January 4, 1981), Nirad Chaudhuri comments on the Indian habit of endless and meaningless talking. For example, a debate like whether the Presidential system of government like that of USA would not be more suitable for India than the present parliamentary system would be pointless and futile. But Indians have the habit of talking and talking, while being blissfully ignorant of the harsh realities of life. "They not only exhibit the familiar incapacity of academics to deal realistically with reality, but do something worse—impose a pattern of empty words on all reality, so that they might be protected from contacts with the realities with which they have no capacity or inclination to deal. From 1920 to the date on which they accepted the partition of India, they showed this proclivity in facing or rather in refusing to face, the terrible reality of Hindu-Muslim relations. They let loose a flood of *inane* words until what was bound to happen, happened. In India, history marches while Indians talk" (118).

Then Chaudhuri shows the courage of his conviction when he comments on Nehru's plebiscitary dictatorship as well as his incapacity to use his great power. "Since 1947, and as long as Jawaharlal Nehru lived, India was governed by a plebiscitary dictatorship, in spite of the silly and opportunistic talk of British journalists about India being the greatest democracy in the world. I can say that I was never under that kind of illusion. I knew that for all practical purpose, India was under a dictatorship and I expressed that opinion categorically in an article published in the *Illustrated Weekly of India* of May 10, 1953. The only person who did not recognize that position was Nehru himself, and his reluctance or incapacity to use his great power to the full has been a disaster for India" (119).

Chaudhuri deplores the absence of outstanding personalities in the Indian politics. Commenting on Mrs. Indira Gandhi's possession of political position, he says that it is not equal to power. "Certainly, as far as possible, Mrs. Gandhi holds the position which was Nehru's. But in reality does not, and need not, depend on the occupation of a formal office or status. In fact, in politics, reality of power has no necessary connection with a formal constitutional position.... Effective political authority is a combination of self-assertion by an exceptional individual with willing submission by a people. When there is no real self-assertion, there is no real submission either. Status is not power" (120).

24. VERY SOON THE MANTRAS OF DURGA PUJA WILL ALSO BE RECITED IN ENGLISH

In his essay, "Very soon the Mantras of Durga Puja will also be Recited in English" (originally published in *The Times of India*, January 18, 1981), Nirad Chaudhuri satirizes the abnormal Anglo-mania of Indians. During the British days the power of the English language was at its highest, like the power of the Empire, but after the departure of the British from India, the power of English seems to have increased to a great extent. Even Bankim Chandra Chatterjee had noticed it as easily as 1872 in his famous literary magazine, *Vanga Darshan*. "He wrote: 'Leaving aside scholarly and literary discussion, nothing is carried on among the new generation of Bengalis nowadays in Bengali, Public business, meetings, lectures, addresses, proceedings are all in English. If both sides know English, conversation too takes place in it, at times 100 percent, at others 75 percent. However that may be, letter-writing is never in Bengali. We have never seen that when the correspondents knew even a little English, any letter has been written in Bengali. We have the expectation that very soon the *mantras* of Durga Puja will also be recited in English'" (121-22).

Writing letters by fathers to sons and from husbands to wives in English had been a fashion and matter of prestige for many Bengalis (as also for Indians of other linguistic States). Talking in English is associated with upper class/caste and high intelligence in India. Like talking, writing in English has also become a great ambition for Indian writers, starting from M.M. Dutt and Bankim Chandra Chatterjee onwards.

25. SHAKESPEARE FOR THE BABU'S DOWRY

In his essay, "Shakespeare for the Babu's Dowry" (originally published in *The Times of India*, February 3, 1981), Nirad Chaudhuri puts forth his views on the use of English by Indians. He rightly opines that Indians are very self-conscious in their use of English language and their desire (or rather weakness) to write fine English amounts to foppery.

Chaudhuri points out the irony of the situation in the colonial India. For example, the British officers did not like or tolerate Indians writing good English. But the British Council wants to popularize the use of English in the post-colonial India. The British officers did not want to appoint the Indians as clerks, if they knew good literary English. On the contrary they preferred to appoint ordinary Indians, who knew only Babu English (i.e. bad English) as clerks in their offices. Chaudhuri offers an example of Bankim Chatterjee's short story to prove this fact.

Mr. G.W. Stevens laughed at the Bengali students who told him that they studied English literature, especially Shakespeare and passed their MAs (rather than merely BAs) to raise their price in the marriage-market and get a higher dowry than otherwise.

Finally, Chaudhuri suggests that Indians can write good prose if they mind it and should not imitate the British or the American journalese.

26. WHY APE THE LECHERY OF THE WEST?

In his essay, "Why Ape the Lechery of the West?" (originally published in *The Times of India,* February 22, 1981), Nirad Chaudhuri records his views about Indians trying to imitate the British writers and their trendy style. He confesses that he was also a victim of this fashion. But he realizes and also advises other Indian writers with literary ambition not to imitate the British or American writers, but to follow their own natural, individual method. He observes that even the British people appreciated the good English written by Indians in the colonial period. He is quite optimistic that the number of Indians writing in English will decrease, but that they will write better English. "If, however, I see the trendiness of our English writing making more progress, I shall go up to two hundred rupees to illustrate an article on it with a photograph. And I shall do it all the more because I am informed that in India, the Hijrine journalese is now showing itself, not only *singar-karke, balki kapde bhi utarke.* I am seeing too much of lechery in print in the contemporary West, and am not likely to have much respect for its third-rate aping in India. What I cannot understand is that any Hindu or Muslim, with his exalted tradition of licentiousness, would stoop to learn from Americans. That is like a lion of the African veldt with his harem of seven lionesses becoming one of seven mongrels running after one mongrel bitch in season" (132). Finally Chaudhuri's advice to Indians is that they should not try to imitate the writing fashions of the Western journalists, but follow their impulses and intuition to write their own brand of English language.

27. A PAN-INDIAN OR 'NATIONAL' LANGUAGE FOR INDIA

In his essay, "A Pan-Indian or 'National' Language for India" (originally published in *The Statesman Festival Number,*

1992), Nirad quotes Lord Irwin's observation about the contrast between what Indians say and think. This gulf between word and thought may be seen in regard to a national language for India. Chaudhuri points out the paradox that although India happens to have a rich tradition of several regional languages (sufficiently developed), yet Indians have been using English language more and more. Such an Anglo-mania of Indians is not justified. Nirad Chaudhuri has his contingencies of life which account for his use of English as a medium of communication. As he has been living in Oxford with no prospect of returning to India, he cannot help using English for his writings.

Chaudhuri points out the absurdity of thinking about a common language for India, while ignoring the linguistic, religious and cultural diversity. Searching for a single national language is the work of Indian leaders. India had a geographical unity, which could be brought under one political sovereignty. But without realizing this, they yielded to the two-nation theory (of Hindus and Muslims) and to the partition. The division of the country was expedited by the British rulers. It was geography which created Indian imperialism. The Hindus called this imperialism *Sarvabhaumatva* or 'omni-territoriality', but neither the Hindus, nor the Muslims could realize this ideal fully. "It was only the British who were able to do so, and when they ruled India they boasted about it as one of their two great political achievements in India, the other being the establishment of *Pax Britannica*. But when abandoning India, they behaved like a vindictive father who disinherits his ungrateful sons, and decided to break up India, so that their political heirs might not enjoy the benefit of their great achievement. They succeeded in imposing this disintegration on the Indian nationalists. For the conduct of the latter, too, I have a simile from family life. They behaved like brothers in a joint family who quarrel after the death of the father, and divide their ancestral home by erecting flimsy bamboo fences" (135-36).

Chaudhuri attacks the Indian leaders for being indifferent to the linguistic situations in India. Nehru with his foreign education in English felt that the regional languages of Indian were not so important and thought them to be crude also. "Of all Congress leaders, it was Jawaharlal Nehru who was most obstinately opposed to the idea of provinces based on linguistic unity. He was denouncing the demands for them as the product of 'linguism', to him an irrational sentiment. In this, he was both shortsighted and unwise, but certainly not insincere. He had no affiliation with any naturally spoken Indian language. For him, the only language in India was that in which alone he was at home, namely, English. Since it was an all-India language he saw no need for another language.... I developed a feeling that Nehru looked down upon the Indian languages as crude" (136-37).

Chaudhuri attacks the Indian leaders for their indifference to the linguistic problem of East Bengali Muslims, who revolted against the imposition of Urdu on them, as part of their subjection to foreign rule (by Pakistan).

He points out correctly that the Indian nationalism was initially negative, i.e. on their intention of driving out the British rulers. It was dependent on chauvinism and historical myth. The negative nationalism was acquired by the educated Indians through their readings (in English language) about the rebellions of certain European countries against other European countries like the American War of Independence, Irish Nationalist Movement and the Italian Nationalist Movement.

As observed by Chaudhuri, the nationalists of India neglected the linguistic situation because their conception of nationalism was almost wholly negative. The main agenda of their nationalism was to get rid of the British rule. The Indian nationalism was not positive in its approach as it lacked the awareness of a national identity and pursuit of progress in the nation's economic, social and cultural activities. The English education was combined with the Hindu xenophobia in their negative nationalism. Their historical hatred against the Muslims was turned against the British when they established their rule. The hatred of the British rule was intensified by Mahatma Gandhi's socio-political action.

Then Chaudhuri shows the positive side of Bengali nationalism which expressed itself in the love of the country and pride in the cultural achievement of ancient India. But at the same time he points out the weakness of the Bengalis like their megalomania, hoping Bengali language to be the national link language and identifying India with Bengal rather than identifying Bengal with India. He approves of Mahatma Gandhi's pleading for Hindi as a national language.

He offers a brief historical survey of Pan-Indian languages. The first is Sanskrit. Though not spoken by the ancient Indians, it was accepted as the artificial, literary and official language. But it was Prakrit which was spoken by the masses. Classical Sanskrit reached its height during the Gupta period.

The second Pan-Indian language was Persian. Although it was not spoken even by Muslims, it was accepted as an official (and literary) language for Pan-Indian intercourse.

The third Pan-Indian language happens to be English. Chaudhuri clarifies a misconception about the English by saying that it was not thrust upon Indians by the British rulers, but was chosen by Indians voluntarily for social prestige and snobbish purposes. English was chosen by the Congress Party as a medium of official communication and Jawaharlal Nehru used to be its drafting secretary. English was accepted as the official and administrative language of India. But in spite of all this, English cannot be the national language of India. Chaudhuri is very clear about it.

Chaudhuri rightly attributes the popularity of English language in India to the wider force and current of Westernization. The speakers of English belong to a new elite class and have a sense of superiority. Chaudhuri remarks correctly how the English language involves its sartorial adjunct. Just as the Indians who spoke Persian, wore Persian clothes, the modern Indians, who speak English, necessarily wear the English clothes like pant, shirt, suit (for men) and skirt or gown (for women). Speaking about a Bengali woman Chaudhuri offers a beautiful animal image: "A Bengali woman who is ignorant of English but it in jeans will be as impossible to come upon as a carnivorous cow" (153).

Chaudhuri shows how in India, there is a great gulf between those who go to the English medium schools and those who go to the regional language medium schools. The cultural foreignness (a result of the use of English) remains permanent in India. The masses of India are a Neolithic pastoral and agricultural population. Obviously Chaudhuri has pointed the wide gulf between the English educated Indians and the uneducated Indians.

28. THE HINDU-MUSLIM CONFRONTATION IN INDIA

In his essay, "The Hindu-Muslim Confrontation in India" (originally published in *The Statesman Festival Number,* 1993), Nirad Chaudhuri has written seriously about the Hindu-Muslim confrontation in India. He has touched upon this problem in his other books also. After quoting the ideas of Alexis de Tocqueville about democracy in America, Chaudhuri shows that the Hindu-Muslim conflict in India is more complex and complicated than that of Black and White people in America. That is because the difference between the Whites and the Blacks in America is mainly genetic, whereas the difference between Hindus and Muslims is not mainly genetic (though it so partially), but cultural and philosophical. "From what then comes this irreconcilable opposition between the Hindu and the Muslim? Not from religious tenets, so far as the Hindus are concerned, and only partly from religion strictly so-called on the Muslim side. The opposition is between two comprehensive and totalitarian ways of life, neither of which can admit the validity and legitimacy of the other. But there is a basic difference between the Hindu and the Muslim in this respect. The Hindu intolerance is for the human being, who is born non-Hindu, the Muslim intolerance is for the unbeliever. The Hindu attitude is static, passive and defensive; the Muslim in stark contrast is dynamic, active and offensive" (156).

Chaudhuri summarizes the fundamental and non-flexible philosophy of Muslim separatism, very clearly. "When fully developed, the Muslim view was that their way of life was the only right one for mankind, and it was their duty not only to be loyal to it, but to bring the non-Muslim part of mankind under it. Starting with this assumption, they created a theory of permanent revolution, and dividing the world into two distinct halves called them Dar-ul-Islam (Land of Peace) and Dar-ul-Harb (Land of Strife). It was the mission of those who had created the Land of Peace to make the entire world that by putting an end to the existence of the Land of strife" (157).

Then Chaudhuri shows some major differences between Hindus and Muslims: (1) Whereas the Hindus were genetic, the Muslims went by conviction and free choice. (2) A Muslim is a revolutionary, as he rejected all his pre-Islamic past to begin with and called that the Jahaliya period, the age of ignorance. But the Hindus have great reverence for the ancient ways. (3) A Muslim belongs to an open society, into which any man can enter, whereas a Hindu has a closed society, determined by his birth. (4) A Muslim is a cosmopolitan, whereas a Hindu considers India as his homeland and forgets his European origin. (5) The Hindus in their historic existence acquired an absurd megalomania. A Hindu is passive, whereas a Muslim is active and even aggressive.

Chaudhuri confesses that the Hindu decadence, unadaptability and petrification were caused by the emergence of Islam, though he cannot ascertain the exact period when it happened in the Indian history. Whereas a Muslim is offensive, a Hindu becomes defensive and makes Kalki, the tenth incarnation of Vishnu, an extirpator of Muslims.

The contrast between Hindus and Muslims is pointed out by Chaudhuri authentically. "The view of life, weltanschauung, which the Hindus held when the Muslims began to make serious inroads into India (c.1000 A.D.), was radically opposed to that of the Muslims in every aspect of human life. To give an idea of the popular view of the antithesis I shall relate what I as a boy used to hear from the ladies of my family: 'How can we get on with the Mussalmans when we worship looking towards the East and they towards the West; when we wear the dhoti with the kachha and they without it; when we eat from the right side of the banana leaf and they eat from the wrong side; when we worship the cow and they eat her; when we read from the left side and they from the right; when we eat with five fingers and they with three?' But this was the expression of a historical animosity, and in actual life I never saw any of their ladies treating their Muslim servants with less friendliness than their Hindu servants" (158). Chaudhuri enumerates a few differences between Hindus and Muslims as seen in history: (1) Whereas the Hindus are genetic, the Muslims go by conviction and free choice, (2) a Muslims is a revolutionary and (3) belongs to an open society, (4) is a cosmopolitan, but (5) the Hindus have developed an absurd megalomania.

Chaudhuri points out the intractability of Hindu and Muslim relations and shows the usual contrast between the Muslim ferocity and fundamentalism and the Hindu hatred of Muslims. The Hindu-Muslim hatred has been historically generated. He shows how it started in the eighth century with the Arab invasion of India, Muhammad of Ghazni's invasion in 1000 A.D. and the Battle of Terrain in 1221 A.D. Although this hatred is temporarily toned down, it smoulders like lava. Chaudhuri offers a beautiful geological image for this hatred: "After the establishment of Muslim rule in India it could not be voiced openly. But it remained alive and went underground. During the entire period of Muslim rule from 1200 A.D. to 1707 A.D. the date of the death of Aurangzeb, the Hindu hatred was like the glowing lava visible down the funnel of a quiescent volcano. In spite of the vegetation on the outer slopes and even vines there, the lava below lay in wait" (164).

Chaudhuri comments on the positive achievements of Muslims in India before highlighting the negative features o the Muslim rule in India in order to offer a balanced picture. He does not want to be mistaken as an anti-Muslim scholar. He points out briefly the political and cultural achievements of Muslims in India. The political achievements were (1) the partial restoration of the political unity of India lost after Asoka; and (2) the creation of an administrative system, including provincial organization and land revenue assessment. The cultural achievement of Muslims was equally great, says Chaudhuri. The quality of painting, architecture and literature produced by Muslims is very high. In literature, Amir Khusrau, Sauda, Mir and Mir Hasan are great writers and testify to the cosmopolitan character of everything Islamic.

Then he highlights the negative aspects of Muslim rule in India. He rightly opines that the Islamic presence in India was an extension of the universal Islamic imperium into India. Then he shows how the Hindus throughout the length and breadth of Aryavarta were persecuted by the Muslims. The negative activities indulged in by Muslim rulers were as follows: (1) the destruction of Hindu temples; (2) seizure of Hindu women and (3) penal taxation. For example, they destroyed all the Hindu temples of Aryavarta, right from Kathiawar to Bihar and from Kashmir to the Vindhya Mountain. Aurangzeb had a mosque built on a shrine of Siva in Varanasi. Similarly the Muslim practice was to seize the Hindu women (wives and daughters) of the kings after defeating the latter. The worst example of this practice was Sirajuddaula, who cleverly and cunningly abducted the Hindu women bathing in the River Ganga. The Muslims practiced this habit in the case of their own Muslim kings also defeated by them. Likewise the Hindus were made to pay the penal tax called *Jiziya* to the Muslim rulers in order to be alive. Otherwise they had to embrace Islam or die. They had no other choice. These are the horrible practices of Muslim rulers in India. The historical memories of such events and phenomenon have added to the Hindu-Muslim hatred ever since.

Chaudhuri highlights how the Muslim rule brought about a demographic revolution in northern India; how consequently the entire Hindu ruling order and the aristocracy disappeared; how the two upper castes of Brahmin and Kshatriya underwent a social and economic degrading for want of patronage and became peasants.

Similarly he shows how the lower Hindu castes like Kayastha and Banias, who were essential for Muslim administration, survived. Though they remained Hindus in their religion, the rest of their life was Islamized. As a result of the Muslim rule the classical language of Sanskrit was replaced by Urdu for all communication. That is why even the famous writer, Premchand wrote in Urdu until 1914, before switching over to Hindi.

Chaudhuri is quite frank in saying that Jawaharlal Nehru himself was an Islamized Hindu and most of the government institutions were headed by Muslims in his regime. For example the central Sahitya Academy is spelt as 'Akademi', which is an Arab word for the Greek word Academy. It shows Nehru's pro-Muslim attitude.

With the emergence of British rule in India, both the Hindus and Muslims experienced some minor changes in their life. When the Arab king, Mohammad bin Qasim conquered Sind in eighth century, he and the subsequent Muslim rulers wanted to follow in principle the tenets of the *Quran* strictly by demolishing Hindu culture and converting the entire land into a Muslim one, but could not practice it strictly until Aurangzeb came on the scene when the Islamic doctrine and practice were combined.

When the British rule started in India, the Hindus were happy to be liberated from the Muslim oppression. On the whole, the British maintained high level of impartiality in the treatment of Hindus and Muslims. Though there happened the Hindu-Muslim riots in 1729, (Wahabi fanaticism in) 1820 and 1947 the British Government maintained its neutrality between Hindus and Muslims till the end of 19th century. But they started their party politics with the break of Nationalist Movement in India. In the Nationalist movement both Hindus and Muslims developed their revivalist attitudes.

Chaudhuri observes that the English education in Bengal brought about the Westernizaton of their life, expedited by the establishment of Calcutta University in 1857. Chaudhuri's observation is very insightful when he says that this Westernization gave a new, historical consciousness and a revivalist Hinduization. The Hinduization was expedited with certain academic events like Mr. Carey, a Baptist Missionary compiling a Bengali Dictionary by removing the Urdu words from it and making the Bengalis conscious of their Hindu identity. Consequently there was a recovery of ancient names like *Arya* for Hindus and *Yavana* for Muslims. The Hindus began to consider themselves proudly as Aryans and later began to glorify the Rajput, Maratha and Sikh resistance to Muslim rule.

Whereas the Muslims were antagonistic to Sikhs and Marathas, the Hindus wanted to revive the memories of

Sikhs and Marathas. Muslims were antagonistic to nationalist Movement of India because they considered Swaraj as Hindu Raj simply because of their Muslim separatism.

As pointed by Chaudhuri, the Muslim resistance expressed itself in three ways: (1) popular; (2) in Westernization; and (3) in its international aspect. First: in popular way means the Hindu converts to Islam still practice Hindu rites at least partially. For example, in Bengal they still worship Krishna and Chinnamasta. Second: the Muslims modernized themselves through English education. The Aligarh Muslim University was established in 1873 by Sayyed Ahmad Khan and this University paved the way for the spread of English education among the Muslims and helped them to modernize themselves. The Indian Government has given some concessions to Muslim personal law, Sharia etc. hence they consider India as Land of Peace (Dar-ul-Islam) and not a Land of Strife (Dar-ul-Harb). The result of the English education was the increasing group-consciousness of both Hindus and Muslims. For example, when the Indian National Congress was founded in 1885 and the Muslims were invited to join it, they refused to do so. Although at that time the Congress had a liberal, non-communal character, the Muslims assumed, that it would become a mouthpiece of Hindus. A Muslim leader said that "his community tied to the wheels of the Juggernaut of majority, would be in the end crushed out of all semblance of nationality. This will show that the so-called two-nation theory denounced by the Hindu nationalists was not a creation of Jinnah or even of the Muslim league. It was not a theory, but a fact of history brought out into the open by the growth of group-consciousness of both Muslims and Hindus alike by their English education" (178-79).

Third: Islamizing the Bengali language came from the third feature of the Islamic resistance i.e. international aspect. As a result of this emerged a new self-consciousness and separatism of Muslims from Hindus and European Power in Western Asia. Sir Sayyed Ameer Ali was the champion of Pan-Islamism.

★★★

In North Africa and Western Asia, the Muslims conquered and Islamized the local cultures and imposed their languages like Arabic and Persian. But in India the duality continued because of the presence of Hindus as antagonistic to Muslims. Chaudhuri rightly attributes all the trouble to the incompleteness of Muslim conquest of India.

Lord Curzon's partition of Bengal was a decisive event in the history of Hindu-Muslim relations. This partition had only an administrative motive behind it. The Bengali Muslims did not have the feeling of solidarity of all Bengalis because their Pan-Islamic sentiment came in the way.

Lord Curzon was dogmatic and one-sided on the issue of partition of Bengal. But he was free from racial and colour prejudice. He was tough, impatient and satirical towards those who opposed him. He was also known for his boyishness and mischievous nature. The portrait of Lord Curzon cutting the Mother (Bengal) above the heart was quite popular in those days.

Chaudhuri rightly points out that the Gandhian movement would not have emerged without the Bengali Movement; and that the Bengali Muslims wanted to get free from Hindus' rule and the British yielded to their demand. He remarks that the Muslims had developed aggressive group consciousness, fanaticism and were influenced by the Pan-Islamic Movement. Because of the group consciousness, the Hindus' hatred of Muslims was renewed and the consequent rivalry between the two led to the partition of India in 1947. Chaudhuri mentions how the Muslim leaders met Lord Minto and demanded a separate electorate and succeeded in getting one. "The cat was let out of the bag by lady Minto herself. Referring to her husband's favourable reply to the delegation of Muslims which asked for a separate electorate, she said that he had done 'nothing less than pulling back of sixty-two millions of people from joining the ranks of the seditious people'" (200). Chaudhuri shows very insightfully the ulterior motives of Muslims in separating themselves from Hindus: "The same blind hatred made them incapable of seeing through the game the Muslims were playing. They were not actuated by any naïve love for the British. As a matter of fact, the Muslims of India cherished a more venomous hatred for the British than the Hindus, because it was they who had been deprived of political power by the British, and more recently. Thus, they were as eager to see the end of British rule as were the Hindu nationalists. But the Muslim leaders knew that their fight against the British was being quite effectively carried on by the Hindus, and there was no necessity for them to sacrifice immediate advantages they could gain by showing apparent friendliness to the British. There was also a strong practical motive for doing this. They felt sure that British rule would come to an end sooner or later, and they would be left to the mercies of the Hindus. So, they must side with the British to ensure that their own position will be safeguarded before they left India" (200).

Chaudhuri mentions how Rabindranath Tagore (who was on his tour to America) wanted Shantiniketan to be free from the turmoil of politics, from Non-Cooperation and Khilafat Movement.

Another insightful observation made by Chaudhuri is that the Muslims turned their attention from Pan-Islamism to Pakistanism, because in 1923 the Indian Muslims were like Trishankus, as they had no territory of their own. They, therefore, fought the creation of Pakistan. Iqbal and Jinnah took the lead for this task. This transition of Muslims from Pan-Islamism to Pakistanism is articulated by Chaudhuri in an astronomical image. "The form it took can be given an astronomical symbol. A big planet disintegrated violently with a big bang, and threw out a satellite. That satellite, too, broke up to create a second but smaller satellite. The two satellites are now revolving round the planet causing tides and ebbs. But the smaller satellite has not yet become wholly inert. It is thus pouring showers or meteorites on the planet" (206).

Chaudhuri has offered an excellent survey of Hindu-Muslim relationship in India with all the relevant historical information. It shows his deep historical sense and incisive intelligence.

29. BRITISH RULE IS DEAD, LONG LIVE BRITISH RULE

In his essay, "British Rule is Dead, Long Live British Rule" (originally published in *The Statesman Festival Number*, 1994),

Nirad Chaudhuri records his insightful remarks about the British Rule in India and its aftermath. He rightly points out that though the British rules have left India, their institution, especially the bureaucracy made of ICS members, has continued even now, rather mechanically. To show the change of power from the British to the Indians Chaudhuri gives an excellent example of Louis XIV from the French history. When Louis XIV was about to die, all his courtiers were eager to shift their loyalty to the new five-year-old king, Dauphin. "The crowds in every big Indian city did the same thing. The mafficking was as wild as it was exultant. They assumed that an Indian Louis XV was to succeed the British Louis XIV; a Louis XV *minus* the mistresses did succeed (or am I to believe the recent slanderers and say *plus* the mistresses?), and he ruled India for seventeen years. The comparison with Louis XV is more valid than it would appear to be at first sight. In 1715, the French crowd did not realize what Louis XV was to lead to, no more did the Indian crowds think about the result of Nehru's rule. In 1947, Nehru was fifty-eight in actual years, but in respect of ability to govern, like Louis XV, a child of five. Louis reigned for sixty-four years; it is forty-seven years since India got her independence. So, there are still left seventeen years for the parallelism I have drawn to be fully revealed" (210).

Chaudhuri states that the Indian bureaucracy is inherited from the British rule; that this bureaucracy is mainly made up of the ICS officers and their clerks. The ICS officers, who were generally efficient and smart had grown opportunistic and forgotten the nationalist feeling and pride. "In natural course of events, the nationalist leaders, when they became *de jure* rulers of the country, should have got rid of the Indians in the higher ranks of the Indian bureaucracy, who as 'loyal' agents of the British rulers had put into execution the policy of repression of the nationalist movement. This is what happens after every political revolution, as was seen after the French, Russian and Meiji revolutions. At the outset the Indian bureaucrats averted this by their opportunism. I perceived this at once and wrote at the end of 1947: 'I was able to enjoy with the most malicious delight the spectacle of the Sons of Belial, including the arch-

Belialids of the former Imperial Secretariat of the Government of India, cringing to the Sons of Moloch whom they had despised and jeered at till yesterday'" (211). Chaudhuri points out how there has been a divorce between character and intelligence in the ICS officers, who have grown opportunistic and career oriented and put their children also in the same profession to amass as much money as possible.

Chaudhuri goes further to point out the difference between the ICS officers and the nationalist political leaders of India. Whereas the ICS members are known for their sophistication, cowardice and incompetence, the political leaders are notorious for their crudity of behavior, bankruptcy of ideas, feebleness, inertia, absence of any spirit of adventure and senility; and are not capable of doing anything positive and not ready for the exertion of mind or body. They are known for mere administration, which is rather mechanical. The only exception to this rule was Jawaharlal Nehru who was Anglicized by his education and known for his class-consciousness.

The dramatic change in the behavior of the (British) ICS members at the time of partition and transfer of power from the British to the Indians is beautifully conveyed by Chaudhuri through a literary-satirical image. "But overnight, after August 15, 1947, the same British personages began to cringe to the same Indians. This disgusted me so much that I wrote in my autobiography: 'When I remember how until even ten years ago all those Englishmen who had anything to do with us or our country, as a rule, denied every capability and every quality in us, and when I set the interested superciliousness of yesterday against the interested complaisance of today, I blush for the English character.' For them the Yahoos of yesterday became the Houyhnhnms of today" (217).

Chaudhuri rightly remarks how the Indian ICS officers went on aping the arrogance of the British ICS officers, though they did not have the same efficiency and adventurous spirit in them. But India is caught in the net of Babuism and in the uncreative grip of the policy of clerks. Both the ICS officers (nowadays the IAS officers) and the clerks are the essential features of Indian bureaucracy. Chaudhuri offers a motor-vehicular image to describe this bureaucracy. Whereas the ICS officers are the chassis of a motor vehicle the clerks are its wheels and the clerks have the ability to stop the vehicle anytime they like.

The anglicized order of the Indian government is strongly opposed by the BJP. Chaudhuri opines correctly that the Congress Government has been bribing the masses with several privileges just to remain in power and continue the British form of bureaucracy minus their efficiency and adventurous spirit.

Note

1. Nirad C. Chaudhuri. *The East is East and The West is West,* Compiled and Edited by Dhruva N. Chaudhuri, Kolkata: Mitra & Ghosh Publishers Pvt. Ltd. First Published, 1996. Third Edition, 1999. (All the page references are to this edition.)

Chapter 16

Chaudhuri's Prose Style

Indian English Literature has a rich harvest of prose written by a wide range of professional scholars like historians, philosophers, jurists, biographers, autobiographers, religious thinkers, letter-writers, travelogue-writers, essayists, educationists, sociologists, anthropologists and journalists. All the Indian English prose may be described as the prose of thought. Great writers like Raja Ram Mohun Roy, Bal Gangadhar Tilak, Swami Vivekananda, Sri Aurobindo, Rabindranath Tagore, Mahatma Gandhi, Jawaharlal Nehru, B.R. Ambedkar, Radhakrishnan, Srinivasa Sastri, J. Krishnamurthy, Frank Moraes, Khushwant Singh, Kuldeep Nayar are prolific prose writers of India. Nirad Chaudhuri belongs to the galaxy of these prose writers. He has enriched the realm of Indian English prose by writing two autobiographies, a biography, essays of cultural criticism, a history (of Hinduism) and other speculative works including his thoughtful columns in the famous British and Indian weekly journals. He is comparable to Carlyle, Aldous Huxley and Jonathan Swift in different aspects. His contribution to the prose-style is remarkable as it is known for its clarity, pedantry, ironical and a satirical tone, caustic humour, encyclopedic range and force of argumentation and persuasion. His prose is neither exhortative like that of Swami Vivekananda, nor romantic like that of Jawaharlal Nehru, not incantatory like that of Radhakrishnan, but is realistic, analytical, satirical and scholarly at the same time. Although Nirad Chaudhuri worked as a military commentator and a journalist for some time, he cannot be equated with other journalists, who look at the contemporary life and write about it independently and sleekly without supplying the historical background and perspective.

But what contradistinguishes Nirad Chaudhuri from them is that his analysis of contemporary Indian society and life is backed up by his vast and deep historical scholarship and historical sense. Even when he seems to be commenting on micro-historical events, habits and aspects, he has a remarkable scholarship of relating them to those of macro-history. That is exactly why his argumentation acquires such force and depth. One may not agree with him fully, but one cannot help admiring him for his hard won insights.

Of all the Indian-English non-fiction writers Mr. Nirad C. Chaudhuri is perhaps the best because of his robust thinking and clarity of style. His popularity both in India and abroad depends as much upon his controversial views as upon his uninhibited and fearless style. In spite of having started his writing career rather late in his life he has written extensively by now and achieved an international reputation. Like all men of originality and strong conviction he has expressed his views boldly and incurred the wrath of many and earned the admiration of a few. In spite of the contradictory responses of the readers towards his writing Mr. Chaudhuri simply cannot be neglected.

The present article is intended to highlight the striking features of his prose style, which is of course coloured and conditioned by his satiric vision of life. Chaudhuri's prose-style can be easily contradistinguished from Sri Aurobindo's, Tagore's, Radhakrishnan's, or Khushwant Singh's. His style can be defined negatively also. His prose style has neither the epic grandeur of Sri Aurobindo's, nor the lyrical delicacy of Tagore's nor the idealistic elevation of Radhakrishnan's, nor the passionate fervour of Raja Ram Mohun Roy's, nor the ebullience of Vivekananda's, nor the penchant brevity of Khushwant Singh's. What then is the distinctiveness of Mr. Chaudhuri's prose style?

Since Chaudhuri is a man of keen perception and thinking his language is marked by concreteness of diction. The words that he employs for the communication of his thought are always concrete, precise or pinpointed and never vague, ambivalent or obscure. His keen and almost photographically microscopic observation of life is expressed in his vivid and graphic description of things and beings of life. His keen observation of life is ideally combined with the forcefulness of expression and radiance of style. Describing his house at Kishorgunj, Mr. Chaudhuri says, "The land on which the house stood was about two acres, with a frontage of about sixty yards. The plot was thus deep one and it was divided up into three portions: the front or outer house, the inner house and back, which was orchard, bamboo- plantation and waste land, mostly overgrown with weed. The real nucleus of the house was the inner courtyard, kept, as I have already related, religiously clean of grass. But there was a coconut tree in one corner of it. The coconut is a rather rare palm in our district and so the tree in our inner yard was not cut down at the time of building the house as I saw guavas being."[1] In this regard his perception of the phenomenal world attains almost photographic minuteness and vividness and testifies to his precise use of abundant vocabulary. He never lacks the nomenclature that is required for the expression of the big and the small; the clear and the hazy; the near and the distant. This quality of Mr. Chaudhuri cannot be found in any other Indian English prose-writer. His style is as realistic as elaborate.

In spite of the similarity between the prose-styles of Mr. Chaudhuri and Mr. Khushwant Singh as far as realism is concerned, there is a subtle difference between the two. Whereas Mr. Chaudhuri's style is characterized by elaboration, Mr. Khushwant Singh's is marked by relative brevity. That explains the reason why Chaudhuri makes slow reading and Singh, fast reading. A good contrast to Chaudhuri's style could be seen in Vivekananda and Radhakrishnan, whose styles are marked by emotional and imaginative outpouring. Reading Chaudhuri's works is like entering a mountainous area of arid climate whereas reading Vivekananda and Radhakrishnan is like entering a hill-station in an area of humid climate. The same difference might be shown in a different manner. For example, reading Chaudhuri is like witnessing the Indian newsreel, which shows reality in its stark nakedness, whereas reading Vivekananda or Radhakrishnan is like watching a commercial

Hindi film (a romantic Hindi film will be a tautology), which shows reality richly covered in gorgeous clothes of idealism.

Since Chaudhuri is a solid and comprehensive thinker backed up by his vast historical knowledge, he cannot help thinking about large issues of life in an elaborate fashion. Thus because of his serious temperament used to sustained thinking and the gravity of the issues selected for treatment, he uses large periods or paragraphs. His is not a hurried and therefore short thinking but a steady and therefore continuous thinking. The paragraphs of his books tend to be quite elaborate sometimes running into pages. In this regard he is easily comparable to Edmund Burke, Bertrand Russell, Vivekananda, Sri Aurobindo and Radhakrishnan. Chaudhuri has an epic mind, which thinks of large entities and their interrelation.

As K.R. Srinivasa Iyengar rightly opines about him, "Nirad Chaudhuri...is a master of prose style, an intellectual who has the courage to stand aside and be different from the crowd, a critic of Indian society with almost a Swiftian capacity for making surgical probes. Each in his own way has tried to interpret Indian history and thought, and although their approaches are different, there can be no question about their integrity. Radhakrishnan is, perhaps, more of an eclectic, Raghunathan more of a conservative, and Nirad Chaudhuri more of an irritant gadfly—but these are really deceptive terms. Scholars and thinkers at once, they are all equally fascinated by Indian —Hindu—thought, they are equally critical of the latter-day obscurations and perversions, and equally sensitive to the glassy undying essence, the true inwardness of Indian culture. They differ only in their sense of measure, the degree of objectivity they bring to their studies, and the extent of inclusiveness in their views."[2]

Since Chaudhuri is basically a student of history he exhibits his sound knowledge of the great historical movements and patterns of the world. Besides, he has his own theory of man based upon his knowledge of history. In this sense he is easily comparable to Carlyle. Whereas Carlyle believed in the theory that the entire history of the world is nothing but the history of great lives. Chaudhuri believes in the view that man is nothing but a product of historical and environmental forces. Whereas Carlyle is a romantic, Chaudhuri is an anti-romantic and hence the difference of emphasis in their theories. It is this kind of historical perspective that enables Chaudhuri to place the events or persons in their proper context and show their relation with the wider world. The historical substratum of Chaudhuri's arguments prevents him from mythifying and glorifying the persons or events under discussion. His vision of life is, therefore essentially earth-bound. For example, he endeavours to connect the present Indian life with the three great movements that swept the world: the Indo-Aryan movement, the Indo-Turkish and the Indo-British. Nobody can deny the validity of Chaudhuri's theory.

Although Chaudhuri is primarily a student of history he cannot be labelled as a historian. The anti-Chaudhuri critics of India make a lot of ado about this aspect of his personality. Their view is obviously a prejudiced one. What distinguishes Chaudhuri from the historians proper is the personal note that he brings into his writing. All his articles and books have the Chaudhurian climate only on account of the personal anecdotes of his life. His books are the honest records of his response to the world around him. His childhood in the native village Kishorgunj; his graduate days at Calcutta, his service in the AIR of Delhi; his trip to England etc., have enabled him to gather extra-ordinary and rich experience which are made all the more meaningful by his sharp perception and wide reading. These personal experiences of Chaudhuri naturally enable him to see them in the light of his encyclopaedic knowledge. It is these personal anecdotes that give him the status of a creative writer and make him comparable to the great essayists of the world like Addison, Steele, J.S. Mill and Bertrand Russell.

Chaudhuri's encyclopedic range of interests and reading is simply marvelous. In fact, being a bibliophile he had the habit of wide reading. He had the habit of reading the encyclopaedias and absorbing the material. He had the knowledge of many areas of human knowledge like history, archeology, sociology and anthropology, geography, zoology, military science, Indology, classical languages, literature in

Bengali, English, French, Sanskrit, some of the sciences, a few philosophers like Bergson, Western music, and art-criticism. In later years he mastered Arab history and Islamic studies and social psychology—which are a formidable array. He is thus known for his monumental scholarship. His knowledge of such multifarious branches of human knowledge has enriched his vocabulary, which has become rich and abundant. Because of his wide range of knowledge he is described by some critics like R.K. Kaul and Paul Verghese as the Renaissance man who has a comprehensive knowledge of life including many areas in it. Chaudhuri's "unacknowledged ambition," says R.K. Kaul, "is to attain the versatility of a Renaissance master. He appears like Bacon or Scaliger to have taken all knowledge as his province."[3]

Khushwant Singh rightly opines that as a stylist and craftsman, Nirad Chaudhuri is an "artist par excellence". He is a man in whom "at long last, India had produced a writer who did not cash in on naïve Indianisms but could write the English language as it should be written—and as few, if any, living English men could write."[4]

Being a conscious writer practicing his art of writing in the second language, he takes extra care to make his style impressive, forceful and radiant. He chooses the words carefully with the full knowledge of their usage. He has a sensitive ear for the music of sounds of words hence the use of onomatopoeic words.

He is bold and creative at the same time in borrowing many words from many fields of knowledge and coining new attractive words like Vedantizing, Kamasutrizing and feranghizing etc. His encyclopaedic knowledge contributes to his rich and abundant vocabulary. His allusive phrases testify to the fact that he is deeply steeped in English Literature, art, painting, architecture and many areas of human knowledge.

Another allied qualification of Chaudhuri is his awareness of art-criticism. He knows how to describe and analyze the artistic achievements like paintings, statues, and architecture of India and other countries. This awareness of art-criticism is part of his encyclopaedic range of interests.

His powers of observation with the eye of a painter are remarkable. He was sensitive to the varied colours of Nature because he had studied and been influenced by the painters of landscape. Many times he looks like a poet-painter. He was deeply influenced by the poetry of Wordsworth. That is why sometimes his descriptions of Nature come nearest to a mystic vision. That is why he is capable of depicting vivid images and descriptions of things around him. His memory is photographic and microscopic and therefore his descriptions are colourful.

He has a facility for composing character sketches of men and women. He had the makings of a Joseph Addison or perhaps P.G. Wodehouse. Not only that, he had a capacity for creating fiction unintentionally.

The concreteness of Chaudhuri's style is naturally ascribable to his use of concrete words i.e. nouns, adjectives, verbs and adverbs. Another striking feature of his prose is his scholarly style. The use of non-English (not necessarily always foreign) words, phrases, and sentences is a conspicuous aspect of his writing. Being a polymath he delights in using a large number of keywords from different languages of the world thereby lending an exotic beauty to his style. Tara Sinha, therefore, says, "Mr. Chaudhuri's style derives much of its force and strength from his scholarship and vast knowledge. His writings are replete with Latin tags, French quotations, German titles and Sanskrit citations—a stylistic characteristic that reminds one of Miltonic allusions."[5] For example he uses the Sanskrit words like *angarika, pitri-bhakti, tamasik, dharma, snataka, sagnika, pritunitambini pina-payodhara, purusayita* etc.; the Hindi words and phrases like *Ek-rupiya chauda ane, kilo, dada, didi, bhai, bon, mahal* etc.; the Bengali words like *kartago, kothey gele* etc.; the Urdu words like *sherwani, pajama, shagird* etc.; the Greek words and phrases like *Megale polis, megale cremia*, etc.; the Latin words like *magna civitas, magna solitude, vanitas, vanitafum, gartia, salus, pudenda muliebra* etc.; the French words and phrases like *Les absents ont tojours tort, coeur, fau pas, pere de famille; rez-de-chaussee* etc.; the German words like *Sturm und Drang, weltanschauung* etc.; the Italian words like *via dolorosa, alfresco* etc.; the Scottish words like *auld lang syne* etc. Chaudhuri's use of such a wide range of words from many languages other than English is really an evidence of his extraordinarily wide reading. Far from using these words merely to show off his knowledge he resorts to this method only in order to achieve brevity, exactitude and sometimes-local colour. In this context Chaudhuri is easily comparable to Khushwant Singh though the latter uses them less frequently than the former. Readers, who are not familiar with the non-English words are likely to be dismayed and therefore to dislike him. Many times the readers are not qualified to read Chaudhuri on account of their unlimited ignorance.

Another feature allied to the use of non-English words is the use of quotations at relevant spots. These quotations are so many in number that they cannot be reproduced here for lack of space. Quotations in Chaudhuri unlike in many lesser Indian English writers are used not as decorations but as integral parts of the main argument. He uses them at the beginning, in the middle or at the end of the essay and weaves them so closely with the web of his thought that they cannot be removed without damaging the overall pattern of the essay. He uses these quotations either to support his own argument or to refute an idea or ideology that runs counter to his. One of the specialties of Chaudhuri is the habit of changing a word or two in the quotation and giving it a Chaudhurian slant. This kind of intellectual grafting gives a fresh meaning to the sentences and holds mirror to Chaudhuri's creativity. A couple of examples will suffice to prove this. "There is a saying that to scratch the Russian is to find the Tarter, it could also be said that to scratch an elderly Indian intellectual was to discover the Hindu."[6] "Of course, there is the Greek proverb, 'Call no man happy until he is dead', which may be represented into 'Don't say that anyone has survived until he is dead.'"[7]

Likewise, Chaudhuri has the creative habit of coining new words, especially verbs from the Indian words, especially nouns—like Vedantizing, Kamasutrizing and feranghizing etc. All this wordplay testifies to his rich and abundant vocabulary, which is part of his conscious craftsmanship as a prose writer. Far from being a native speaker of English, who is generally satisfied with his limited vocabulary, Chaudhuri has enriched his vocabulary from different fields of life and knowledge systems and given it a rich texture and exotic beauty. His wide reading and conscious craftsmanship makes him employ allusive phrases referring to literature, art, painting, architecture, geography, the Bible, Vedas, Upanishads and what not. He seems to be greatly fascinated by big and high sounding words, which contribute to the onomatopoeic melody and beauty. Because of his wide scholarship and abundant vocabulary, he uses high sounding and impressive words, rare words and technical words from different branches of knowledge. Tara Sinha has given a long list of such stylistic peculiarities of Chaudhuri. The Indian students and teachers of stylistics have a rich gold mine in Chaudhuri's writing for profitable analysis and appreciation.

The wide use of non-English words, phrases and quotations points to the extra-ordinary scholarship underlying them. Chaudhuri's vision is panoramic and is supported by his encyclopaedic knowledge. Whenever he discusses a topic he will be aware of and making reference to a number of aspects of the same almost simultaneously. He is never given to thinking in terms of isolated entities. On the contrary, he will be thinking about it as part of a universal phenomenon and with the help of his encyclopaedic knowledge, will be able to connect the particular to the general. For example when he discusses the problem of Indian marriage, he refers to the social, economic, psychological and other aspects and suggests or demonstrates similarities and contrasts with the Western counterparts.

One of the most important methods of Chaudhuri is the analysis and not mere description of his personal experience. He never describes the experience and leaves it at that. On the contrary he describes it only to analyze it in terms of psychology, ethnology, sociology, anthropology and history. Chaudhuri's prose, therefore, can be labelled as analytical or expository prose. He uses the analytical method of these sciences without using the jargon indigenous to them. For example, when he discusses the Bengali customs, fairs and festivals that he had seen in his childhood, he tries to describe them analytically and ethnologically. When he sees the Hindu-Muslim riot in

Calcutta, he analyses it in the light of his historical knowledge. When he observes the lethargy of the Indians, he analyzes it in geographical-historical-sociological terms. When he notices the Indian rituals and purity mania etc., he analyzes them in terms of the psychology of religion. Thus Chaudhuri's personal experiences come to be presented through the prism of his scholarship.

One of the happy things about Chaudhuri is that the native charm of his mind outshines the rich garment of his scholarship. In spite of his wide reading, he never ceases to make fresh observations and original comments about the things, persons and situations that come his way. He likes life very seriously and thinks seriously. That is the reason why many statements that he makes come to have the stature of epigrams. His books and articles are studded with innumerable epigrams. A few examples will suffice: "In Hindu society, so long as appearances are saved, nothing is wrong."[8] "We Hindus only tolerate or endure changes, but never sanction them."[9] "There is a style and genius in prostitution as there is in all other human activities."[10]

Though Chaudhuri is a serious scholar always making serious observations about life, he is also capable of laughing at people sardonically and ironically. Therefore there is quite a bit of frolicsome humour, black humour and morbid mirth. His serious style, peppered with such humour provides some comic relief to the reader. His satire in the *Continent of Circe* shows his acquaintance with Jonathan Swift and shows him to be an embittered and angry man.

Although Chaudhuri is a vigorous intellectual and an incisive analyst he cannot help using the similes and metaphors whenever he wants to convince the readers about a particular aspect of his topic. These similes and metaphors or images borrowed from a wide range of scholarship contribute a lot to the poetic beauty of his prose. They add grace and charm to his otherwise exhausting style and show that there is a poet hidden behind a prose writer. It may be said that the similes and metaphors are like pretty shrubs and plants, which lessen the pain of walking on rocky mountain under the hot sun. Thus a poetic current runs through his vast and bewildering geography of intellectual abundance.

What kind of similes, metaphors and images does he employ in his writings? He uses a bewildering variety of metaphors and similes from various branches of knowledge, which is eloquent of his wide experience as well as his voracious reading. The list of the different fields of knowledge from which he has borrowed his images is so large that it cannot be discussed here in detail for lack of space. He uses the athletic and the military images, the scientific, the technological, the medical, the agricultural, the horticultural and entomological images; the geographical, the navigational, the zoological, the aquatic and the chemical images; the historical, the architectural and the archeological images; the sanitary, the cosmetic, the sexual, the matrimonial images; the economic, the numismatic and governmental images; the religious, the magical, the mythical and the supernatural images; the scholastic and the commercial images and so on. Obviously, a detailed analysis of all these images requires to be covered by a separate article. But here only four examples can be seen from branches, which are not commonly cited by the critics of Chaudhuri. Here is an athletic image: "The English politics gave me the feeling that I was watching a swimming pool."[11] A scholastic image may be seen in Chaudhuri's description of Robert Clive: "The poor boy and the son of a pretty attorney wanted to show in England the prizes he had won in India, as any school boy does."[12] An architectural image may be seen in his description of the Indian journalists: "Most Indian editors are as monumental as temple-idols and their monumentality is accentuated by the high salaries they are getting in these days."[13] A sanitary image may be seen in his description of the Indian wife: "So, one might say that for most Hindu husbands the wife is a beautiful bath of gleaming porcelain, with both cold and hot water taps, with this difference, however, that the taps are not under control but flow as they list and by turns the husband is bathed in a cool spray of love or scalded in a geyser of anger."[14]

He describes the Indian sadhus through an ophidian metaphor when he says, "The Hindu Sadhus were pythons of the psychic world, whose slumberous coils contained, and at the same time hid, the force of a battering ram in the head."[15]

He describes the unexpected birth of the British Raj through a biological-sexual image, "The Indian Empire was born like the child of an inexperienced unmarried girl, that is to say, without any design to found it, or even awareness that it could come into existence, or any admission of its legitimacy."[16]

Chaudhuri describes the difficulty and problem of Max Muller's cosmopolitan life that he had to lead at Oxford for the sake of pursuing his career through a musical image, which is epical in its elaborative description, "This is true cosmopolitanism, which in spite of its diverse elements is a stable, though compound, product. The unity of such lives is that of harmonic and contrapuntal music. The basic strand in it is always the deep bass of the early environment, punctuating the other melodic lines and sometimes surging above them. Then comes the middle register of work and workaday life, and, above all, there is the treble line of creative moods and moments of revelation, all accompanied by the trills and other decorative figures of sense experience. Such a life is no more ill-organized than a symphony. But it is not easily put together."[17]

For example, referring to his late marriage, Chaudhuri offers the metaphor of a river. He says, "Marriage made the river cut through rock and push through shoals to reach the sea."[18] Describing his experience of poverty and insecurity, he says, "It was like being on a raft after being picked up by a ship."[19]

Chaudhuri offers a musical metaphor to describe the dictatorship of the Nehru family when he says, "The dictatorship of the Nehru family continued with short interruptions, which were like the 'accidentals' in a musical composition. The normal key was quickly restored."[20]

He describes Mrs. Indira Gandhi's sudden change through a literary metaphor when he says, "The position brought about a transformation in Mrs. Gandhi's character paralleled by the promising Ivan Ramonov becoming Ivan the Terrible."[21]

Another striking feature of Chaudhuri's prose style is the freedom from fear and inhibition of any sort, which is determined partly by the topic that he selects for discussion and partly by his own temperament, which is satirical. He can criticize or admire anything and everything without being afraid of any race, community, institution, region or government. He can criticize the Hindus, the Indian Christians, the Eurasians and the Muslims without any fear of these groups. He can point out the mistakes in the personal as well as governmental behaviour of Mr. Nehru, who was in power as the Prime Minister of India. He can show negative aspects of the English culture and people when he is right inside the English country. He can describe the drabness of Indian life as meticulously as Bernard Shaw did of English life in his plays. He can discuss sexual matters like coitus and venereal disease with the same ease with which he discusses religion and history. He shocks the smug and the complacent, irritates the hypocrites, hurts the idealists and whips the slothful and slumberous sentimentalists. Because of his courage to see the problems in the face, he does not shy away from the ugly, the indecent and the discordant. The kind of uninhibited boldness shown by Chaudhuri can never be expected in other Indian English authors like Vivekananda, Sri Aurobindo or Radhakrishnan. The only writer comparable to Chaudhuri in this regard is Mr. Khushwant Singh.

These are the components of Chaudhuri's prose style. There are many Indian critics who deliberately exaggerate the negative side of his style. Whereas one group of them accuses him of using the pedantic style, the other group dubs his style as merely journalistic. But these views are equally unsympathetic and testify to the critics' inability and unwillingness to understand and enjoy Chaudhuri's style. Most often the Indian critics at least are not well equipped to understand him because of their own temperamental or educational limitations. There is another set of critics who complain that Chaudhuri uses not English but Graeco-Roman style. Robert de Souza says, "...the style of the book smacks of a mixture of the Graeco-Latin and the Indian—a result of outgrown dump of a book worm. And surely the Goans know not such a language, which its author calls

English."[22] But whatever style is used by Chaudhuri, it is the natural style of an Indian, who has learnt his English through dictionaries and Indian teachers and who has not de-Indianized and Anglicized himself to use the snobbish style. Most of the Indian haters of Chaudhuri belong to the Anglicized class whose superficiality and hollowness are ruthlessly exposed by him. Chaudhuri offers a real test to the critic to see whether he can achieve a psychic distance in understanding Chaudhuri in spite of being hurt by his views.

So far I have enlisted the positive qualities of his prose style. But there are many detractors of Nirad Chaudhuri who have found fault with his style either because of their lack of sympathy for him or because of professional jealousy or because of ideological differences with him. They contemptuously describe him as a scholar gypsy notorious for his pomposity, exaggerated style, or stilted and labored style. Some critics delight in describing his style as 'crusty, musty, fusty'. Some unsympathetic critics accuse him of using an aggressive language and dislike his self-aggrandizement, aggressiveness, arrogance, self-opinionatedness and exhibitionism and call him a polemical writer.

Notes

1. Nirad C. Chaudhuri, *The Autobiography of an Unknown Indian*, Bombay: Jaico Publishing House, 1973, 20.
2. K.R. Srinivasa Iyengar, *Indian Writing in English*, Bombay: Asia Publishing House, 1973, 572.
3. R.K. Kaul, *Nirad C. Chaudhuri: The Renaissance Man*, Jaipur: Rawat Publications, 1998.
4. Khushwant Singh, *Khushwant Singh's India*. Ed. Rahul Singh. Bombay: IBH Publishing Company, 1970, 190.
5. Tara Sinha, Nirad C. Chaudhuri, *A Sociological and Stylistic Study*, Patna: Janaki Prakashan, 1981, 18.
6. Nirad C. Chaudhuri, *The Intellectual in India*, New Delhi: Associated Publishing House, 1967, 33.
7. *Ibid.*, 55.
8. Nirad C. Chaudhuri, To *Live or Not to Live*, Delhi: Hind Pocket Books, 1970, 177.
9. *Ibid.*, 137.

10. Nirad C. Chaudhuri, *The Continent of Circe*, Bombay: Jaico Publishing House, 1974, 315.
11. Nirad C. Chaudhuri, *A Passage to England*, Delhi: Orient Paperback, 1972, 200.
12. Nirad C. Chaudhuri, *Clive of India*, Bombay: Jaico Publishing House, 1976, 323.
13. Nirad C. Chaudhuri, *The Intellectual in India*, 65.
14. Nirad C. Chaudhuri, *The Continent of Circe*, 277.
15. Nirad C. Chaudhuri, *Hinduism*, Oxford: Oxford University Press, 1979, 5.
16. Nirad C. Chaudhuri, *Clive of India*, Bombay: Jaico Publishing House, 1977, 17.
17. Nirad C. Chaudhuri, *Scholar Extraordinary*, New Delhi: Orient Paperbacks, 1974, 48.
18. Nirad C. Chaudhuri, *Thy Hand, Great Anarch!* London: Chatto & Windus, 1987, 343.
19. *Ibid.*, 364.
20. Nirad C. Chaudhuri, *Three Horsemen of the New Apocalypse*, New Delhi: Oxford University Press, 1997, 115.
21. *Ibid.*
22. Robert De Souza, *Goa and the Continent of Circe,* Bombay: Jaico Publishing House, 1973.

Conclusion

In conclusion it may be said that Nirad Chaudhuri is an expatriate or diasporic writer from India who is known for his anglophilia. He is known for his encyclopaedic scholarship of many areas of human experience. Because of his personality cult and highly individualistic opinions and insights, he has been a provocative writer who whips up the latent feelings, especially anger of the lethargic and smug readers and scholars and makes them rethink the problems of life. Due to his vast knowledge of world history his views made against that background gain the weight of scholarship and insight. Being a historian he has the habit of making sweeping generalizations and observations about the large rhythms of historical movements and cyclicities. Being an encyclopaedic scholar he could claim that he could teach the British history to the British scholars themselves. He could correct a mistake made by Bonamy Dobree who met him on his birthday sometime.

Like a philosopher he has the habit of using abstract ideas and notions. His phenomenal and photographic memory helps him depict the life around him very graphically and microscopically and colourfully. Being an anglophile he defended the British rule in India. Because of his satirical talent, he can make scathing remarks about the follies and foibles and vices and weaknesses of human beings—both eastern and western. His mastery over the history of mankind has enabled him to make prophetic remarks and observations about the decadence of life all over the world. He plays the role of Cassandra and becomes the prophet of doom.

It is a remarkable achievement for a dark/brown Indian to be honoured with D.Litt. degrees from the Universities of